Egyptian Hieroglyphic

Charles E. Nichols

Preface

This dictionary divides the Egyptian Hieroglyphic "alphabet" into the traditional "A to Z" section created by the late British Egyptologist Sir Alan Gardiner around seventy years ago. The alphabet is reprinted at the beginning of this dictionary. The rest of the dictionary consists solely of Egyptian hieroglyphic words translated into English.

Using this dictionary is very straightforward and far less complicated than any other hieroglyphic dictionary you may have come across. I have sorted the words into hieroglyphic order instead of using some arbitrary arrangement as is usually the case in so many other dictionaries of this language. For example, if one is translating a line of hieroglyphic text and comes upon an unknown word, such as:

We know this word begins with the hieroglyph. We can then look through the alphabet printed at the front of the book and find that the hieroglyph is the 36th in section "D" labeled "Parts of Human Body" and that the hieroglyph is a picture of an arm:

D36
Arm

Next we turn to the page for words beginning with and scroll down until we find the word we are looking for. In this example, it is the third entry down - a bee (or honey bee).

encampment

sweet clover?

bee, honey bee

buzz (of insect)

This dictionary is intended for the first year student, tourist and arm-chair Egyptologist. It is not intended, nor does it pretend to be an exhaustive work. The most complete dictionary published to date is the famous "Worterbuch" which, unfortunately, is in German, has hand-drawn hieroglyphs and is out of print. I am aware that many people would have liked an English to Egyptian index. Unfortunately, there simply wasn't room for one. As it stands, this book reached the publisher's page limit for a paperback book of this size. That said, I hope you find this first edition to be useful.

Charles Nichols

A. Human Beings, Male

A1
Seated Man

A2
Putting Hand to
Mouth

A3
With One Knee
on Ground

A4
Arms Raised

A5
Hiding behind
Wall

A6
Pouring Water
on Hands

A7
Collapsed

A8
Jubilant

A9
Holding a Basket

A10
Holding an Oar

A11
Holding a
Scepter and
Crook

A12
Archer with One
Knee on Ground

A13
Kneeling with
Arms Tied

A14
Falling with
Head Wound
and Blood

A14a
Variation of A14

A15
Falling

A16
Bowing

A17
Seated Child
with Hand to
Mouth

A18
Child Wearing
the Red Crown

A19
Old Man Leaning
on Stick

A20
Leaning on Stick
(less so than
A19)

A21
Stick in One
Hand,
Handkerchief in
Other

A22
Statue with Stick
and Scepter

A23
King Holding
Stick and Club

A24
Using both
Hands to Strike
with Stick

A25
Using One Hand
to Strike with
Stick

A26
Standing with
One Arm Raised

A27
Running with
One Arm Raised

A28
Both Arms
Raised Towards
Sky

A29
Upside Down

A30
With Arms
Outstretched

A31
With Arms
Outstretched
Behind

A32
Dancing

A33
Holding Stick
with Bundle

A34
Pounding in
Mortar

A35
Building a Wall

A36
Brewing

A37
Brewing in Vat

A38
Holding Neck of
Two Animals

A39
Variation on A38

A40
Seated God
Wearing Wig
and Beard

A41
Seated King with
Uraeus on Brow

A42
Seated King with
Uraeus on Brow
Holding a
Flagellum

A43
Seated King
Wearing the
White Crown of
Upper Egypt

A44
Seated King
Wearing the
White Crown of
Upper Egypt and
Holding
Flagellum

A45
Seated King
Wearing the Red
Crown of Lower
Egypt

A46
Seated King
Wearing the Red
Crown of Lower
Egypt and
Holding
Flagellum

A47
Seated
Shepherd
Holding a Stick
and Rolled Up
Mat

A48
Seated, Holding
Some Tool
Knife?

A49
Syrian, Holding a
Stick

A50
An Official,
Sitting on a
Chair

A51
An Official,
Sitting on a
Chair and
Holding a
Flagellum

A52
An Official,
Squatting and
Holding a
Flagellum

A53
An Erect
Mummy

A54
A Recumbent
Mummy

A
Mummy on Bed

A17a
Seated Child
with Hand
Outstretched

B. Human Beings, Female

B1
Sitting

B2
Pregnant

B3
Giving Birth

B4
Giving Birth

B5
Nursing

B6
Holding Child

B7
Queen

 # C. Anthropomorphic Gods

C1
God with a
Human Head
Wearing the
Uraeus Sun-Disk

C2
God with a
Falcon Head,
Wearing the
Uraeus Sun-
Disk, Holding a
Sandal Strap

C3
Thoth, God with
the Head of an
Ibis

C4
Khnum, God
with the Head of
a Ram

C5
Khnum, God
with the Head of
a Ram, Holding
a Sandal Strap

C6
Anubis, Jackal-
Headed God of the
Dead

C7
God with the
head of Seth

C8
Ithyphallic God,
wearing feathers
and holding the
flagellum

C9
Goddess
wearing the sun-
disk and horns
(Hathor)

C10
Maat, Goddess
wearing a
feather

C11
Seated God,
arms raised,
wearing the sign
M4 on his head

C12
God wearing two
large feathers
and holding the
scepter S40

C17
God with falcon's
head, wearing
the sun-disk and
two large
feathers; holding
the sign S34.

C18
God wearing the
Atef Crown

C19
Mummy shaped
God holding the
scepter S40

C20
Variation of C19,
God placed in a
shrine

 D. Parts of Human Body

D1
Head in profile

D2
Face

D3
Lock of hair

D4
Eye

D5
Eye with two
lines of paint

D6
Painted eye

D7
Eye underlined
with a line of
paint

D8
Eye surrounded
by an ellipse

D9
Eye shedding
tears

D10
Eye of Horus

D11
Left side of the
cornea of the
wedjat-eye

D12
Pupil of the
human eye

D13
Human eyebrow

D14
Right side of the
cornea of the
wedjat-eye

D15
Lower part of the
cornea of the
wedjat-eye

D16
Bottom part of
the wedjat-eye

D17
Features of
falcon cheek

D18
Ear

D19
Upper part of the
face, in profile

D20
Variation of D19

D21
Mouth

D22
Mouth
surmounting two
lines

D23
Mouth
surmounting
three lines

D24
Upper lip
revealing the
teeth

D25
Lips

D26
Liquid coming
from the lips

D27
Breast

D27a
Breast

D28
Arms
outstretched

D29
D28 on R12

D30
D28 with
appendage

D31
Arms
surrounding the
sign U36

D32
Arms embracing

D33
Arms holding an oar

D34
Arm holding a shield and a battle-axe

D34a
Arm holding a shield and a battle-axe

D35
Arms in a gesture of negation

D36
Arm

D37
Forearm with hand holding bread X8

D38
Forearm with hand holding a rounded bread

D39
Forearm with hand holding the vase W24

D40
Forearm with hand holding a stick

D41
Forearm with the palm of the hand downwards

D42
Var. of D41, the upper part of the arm being in a vertical position

D43
Forearm holding the flagellum S45

D44
Forearm holding the scepter S42

D45
Arm holding the scepter

D46
Hand

D47
Hand with curved palm

D48
Hand without a thumb

D49
Fist

D50
Raised finger

D51
Finger in a horizontal position

D52
Phallus

D53
Phallus with liquid

D54
Legs walking

D55
Legs walking backwards

D56
Bended leg

D57
Leg with knife

D58
Foot

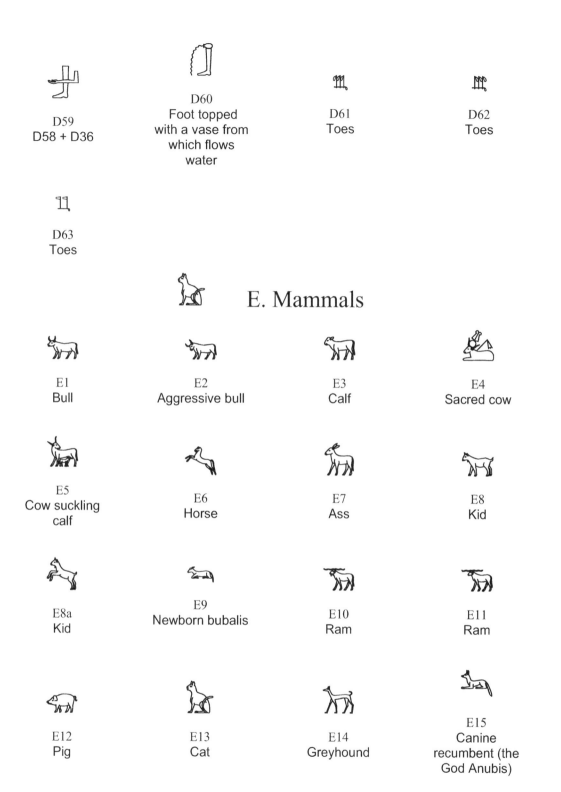

D59
D58 + D36

D60
Foot topped
with a vase from
which flows
water

D61
Toes

D62
Toes

D63
Toes

E. Mammals

E1
Bull

E2
Aggressive bull

E3
Calf

E4
Sacred cow

E5
Cow suckling
calf

E6
Horse

E7
Ass

E8
Kid

E8a
Kid

E9
Newborn bubalis

E10
Ram

E11
Ram

E12
Pig

E13
Cat

E14
Greyhound

E15
Canine
recumbent (the
God Anubis)

E16
Canine recumbent on a shrine.

E17
Jackal

E18
Canine on R12

E19
Archaic form of E19, with a club across the sign R12

E20
Animal of the God Seth

E21
Animal of the God Seth recumbent

E22
Lion

E23
Lion recumbent

E24
Panther

E25
Hippopotamus

E26
Elephant

E27
Giraffe

E28
Oryx

E29
Gazelle

E30
Ibex

E31
Goat wearing a collar with a cylinder seal

E33
Monkey

E34
Hare

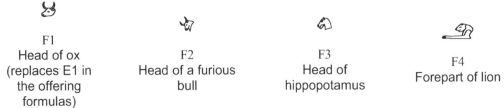

F. Parts of Mammals

F1
Head of ox (replaces E1 in the offering formulas)

F2
Head of a furious bull

F3
Head of hippopotamus

F4
Forepart of lion

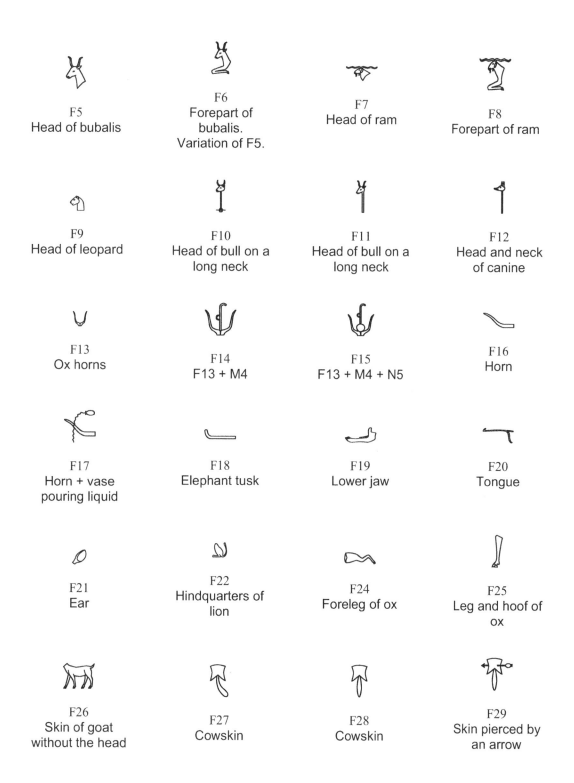

F5
Head of bubalis

F6
Forepart of
bubalis.
Variation of F5.

F7
Head of ram

F8
Forepart of ram

F9
Head of leopard

F10
Head of bull on a
long neck

F11
Head of bull on a
long neck

F12
Head and neck
of canine

F13
Ox horns

F14
F13 + M4

F15
F13 + M4 + N5

F16
Horn

F17
Horn + vase
pouring liquid

F18
Elephant tusk

F19
Lower jaw

F20
Tongue

F21
Ear

F22
Hindquarters of
lion

F24
Foreleg of ox

F25
Leg and hoof of
ox

F26
Skin of goat
without the head

F27
Cowskin

F28
Cowskin

F29
Skin pierced by
an arrow

F30
Water-skin

F31
Three skins tied
together

F32
Belly of a
mammal

F33
Tail

F34
Heart

F35
Heart and
windpipe

F36
Lung and
windpipe

F37
Backbone, with
marrow and ribs

F38
Backbone and
ribs on one side
only

F39
Var. of F38, with
flow of marrow

F40
Var. of F39, flow
of marrow at
both ends

F41
Vertebrae

F42
Rib

F43
Ribs (of beef)

F44
Femur or tibia

F45
Uterus of heifer

F46
Intestine

F47
Intestine

F48
Intestine

F49
Intestine

F50
F46 + S29

F51
Piece of flesh

F52
Excrement

G. Birds

G1
Vulture
percnopterus

G3
G1 + U1

G4
Buzzard

G6
Falcon holding
the scepter S45

G7
Falcon G5 on
R12

G7
Falcon G5 on
R12

G7a
Falcon G5 in
boat

G7b
on a pedestal

G8
G5 + S12

G9
G5 + N5

G10
Falcon in Sokar
bark

G11
Falcon statue

G12
G11 with
flagellum

G13
G11 with double
plumes (S9) and
sun-disk

G14
Vulture

G15
G14 + S45

G16
G14 and I12 on
V30

G17
Owl

G18
G17 twice

G19
G17 + D37

G20
G17 + D36

G21
Guinea-fowl

G22
Hoopoe

G23
Lapwing

G24
Lapwing with
twisted wings

G25
Crested Ibis

G26
Sacred ibis on
standard

G26a
Ibis. Var. rarely
used of G26

G27
Flamingo

G28
Black Ibis

G29
Jabiru

G30
Three jabirus

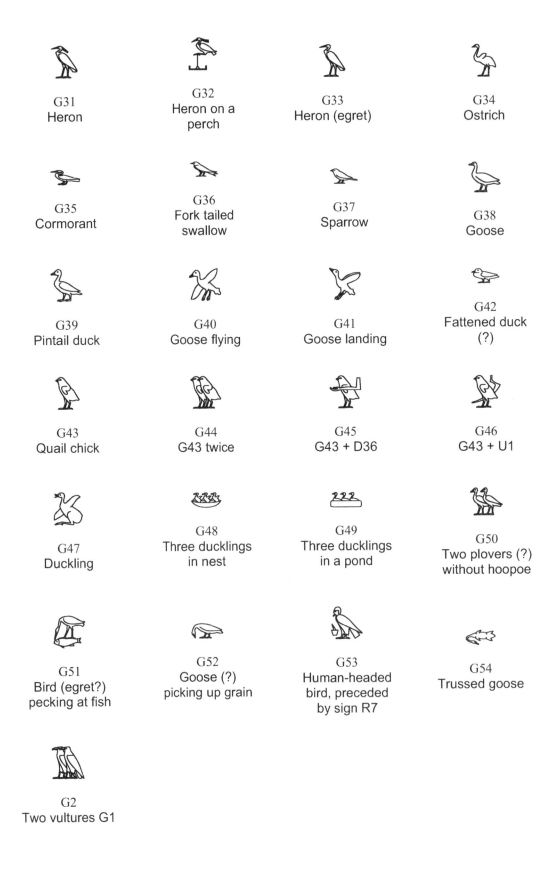

G31
Heron

G32
Heron on a
perch

G33
Heron (egret)

G34
Ostrich

G35
Cormorant

G36
Fork tailed
swallow

G37
Sparrow

G38
Goose

G39
Pintail duck

G40
Goose flying

G41
Goose landing

G42
Fattened duck
(?)

G43
Quail chick

G44
G43 twice

G45
G43 + D36

G46
G43 + U1

G47
Duckling

G48
Three ducklings
in nest

G49
Three ducklings
in a pond

G50
Two plovers (?)
without hoopoe

G51
Bird (egret?)
pecking at fish

G52
Goose (?)
picking up grain

G53
Human-headed
bird, preceded
by sign R7

G54
Trussed goose

G2
Two vultures G1

H. Parts of Birds

H1
Head of pintail
duck or goose

H2
Head of a
crested bird

H3
Head of
spoonbill

H4
Head of vulture

H5
Wing

H6
Ostrich feather

H6a
H6 + two lines

H7
Claw

H8
Egg

I. Reptiles, Amphibians, and their Parts

I1
Lizard

I2
Turtle

I3
Crocodile

I4
Crocodile on a
shrine

I5
Crocodile with a
curved tail

I5a
Mummy or
archaic image of
a crocodile

I6
Crocodile-skin
with scales

I7
Frog. Goddess
Hekhet

I8
Tadpole

I9
Horned viper

I10
Cobra

I11
Two cobras

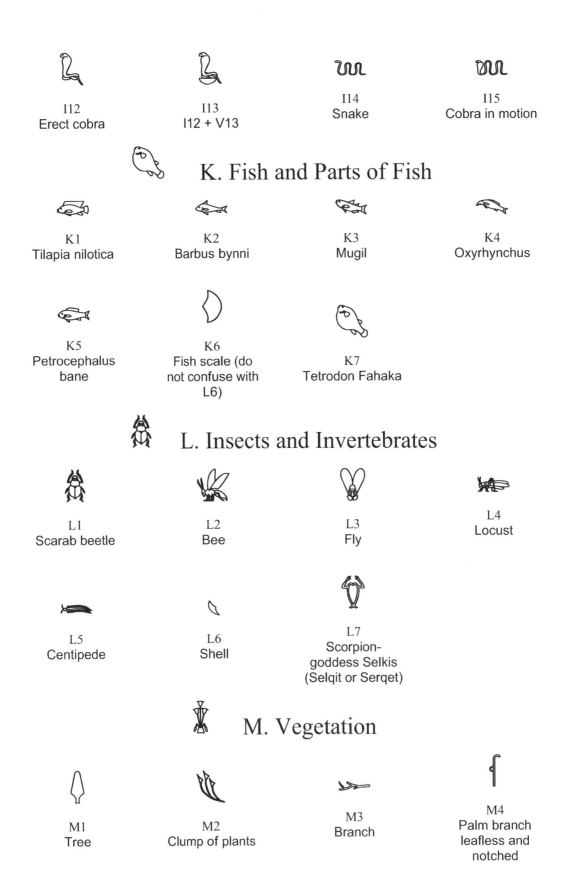

I12
Erect cobra

I13
I12 + V13

I14
Snake

I15
Cobra in motion

K. Fish and Parts of Fish

K1
Tilapia nilotica

K2
Barbus bynni

K3
Mugil

K4
Oxyrhynchus

K5
Petrocephalus
bane

K6
Fish scale (do
not confuse with
L6)

K7
Tetrodon Fahaka

L. Insects and Invertebrates

L1
Scarab beetle

L2
Bee

L3
Fly

L4
Locust

L5
Centipede

L6
Shell

L7
Scorpion-
goddess Selkis
(Selqit or Serqet)

M. Vegetation

M1
Tree

M2
Clump of plants

M3
Branch

M4
Palm branch
leafless and
notched

M5
M4 + X1

M6
M4 + D21

M7
M4 + Q3

M8
Pool with lotus
flowers

M9
Lotus flower

M10
Lotus bud

M11
Flower on a long
twisted stem

M12
Lotus plant

M13
Papyrus

M14
M14 + I10

M15
Clump of
papyrus with
buds

M16
Clump of
papyrus

M17
Reed in bloom

M18
M17 + D54

M19
M17 tied up with
U36

M20
Field of reeds

M21
Var. of M20

M22
Swamp rush

M23
Rush, heraldic
plant of Upper
Egypt

M24
M23 + D21

M25
M23 (buds
opened) on D21

M26
Plant in bloom

M28
M23 (buds
opened) on V20

M29
Pod from carob-
tree

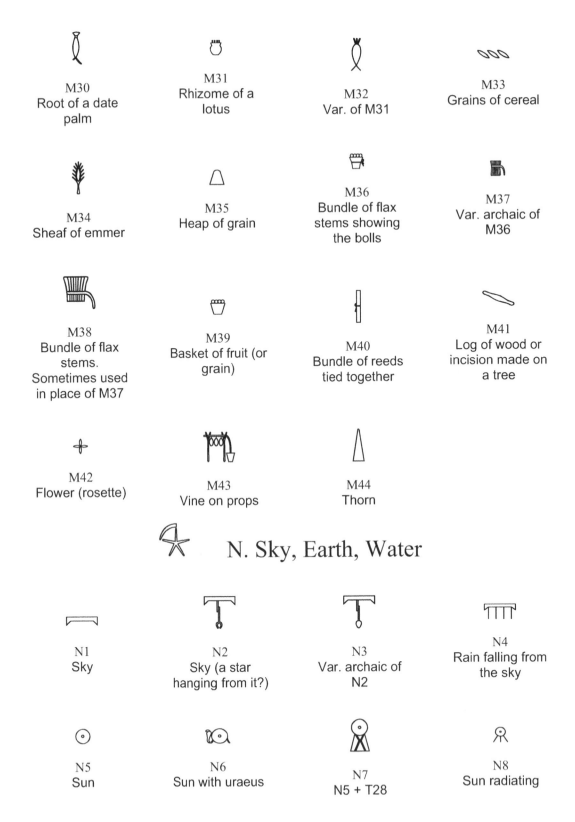

M30
Root of a date palm

M31
Rhizome of a lotus

M32
Var. of M31

M33
Grains of cereal

M34
Sheaf of emmer

M35
Heap of grain

M36
Bundle of flax stems showing the bolls

M37
Var. archaic of M36

M38
Bundle of flax stems. Sometimes used in place of M37

M39
Basket of fruit (or grain)

M40
Bundle of reeds tied together

M41
Log of wood or incision made on a tree

M42
Flower (rosette)

M43
Vine on props

M44
Thorn

N. Sky, Earth, Water

N1
Sky

N2
Sky (a star hanging from it?)

N3
Var. archaic of N2

N4
Rain falling from the sky

N5
Sun

N6
Sun with uraeus

N7
N5 + T28

N8
Sun radiating

N9
Moon obscured.
(Sometimes
written with a
simple circle).

N10
Var. of N9

N11
Crescent moon

N12
Var. of N11

N13
Half of crescent
moon and star

N14
Star

N15
Star in a circle

N16
Flat land with
three grains of
sand

N17
Var. of N16

N18
Sandy island.
Sometimes used
instead of X4
(loaf of bread).

N19
Two sandy
islands

N20
Tongue of land

N21
Tongue of land

N22
Archaic var. of
N20 and of N21

N23
Irrigation canal

N24
Land irrigated by
runnels

N25
Hills of the
desert

N26
Valley between
two sandy hills

N27
Sun rising above
the horizon

N28
Hill illuminated
by the sun

N29
Sandy slop

N30
Hill with shrubs

N31
Road bordered
by papyrus

N32
Lump of clay

N33
Grain of sand

N33a
Grains of sand

N34
Crucible

N35
Ripple of water

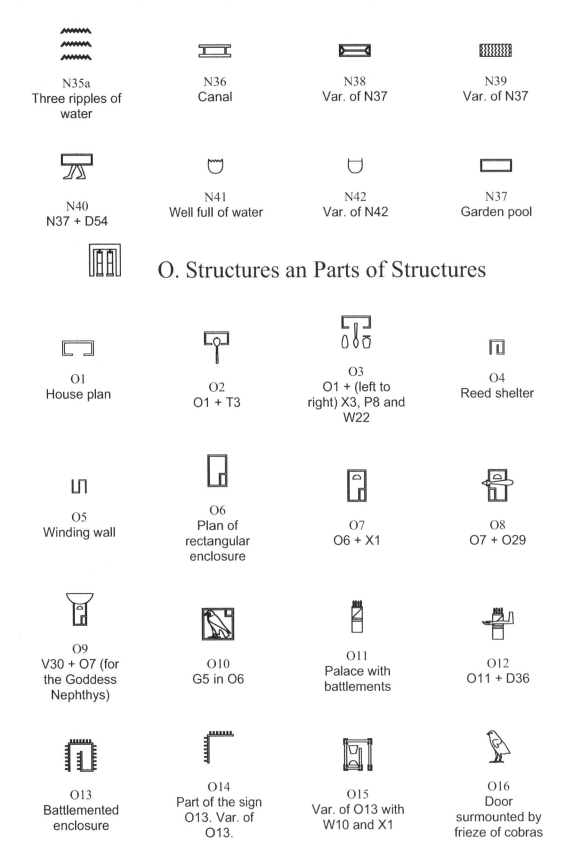

N35a
Three ripples of water

N36
Canal

N38
Var. of N37

N39
Var. of N37

N40
N37 + D54

N41
Well full of water

N42
Var. of N42

N37
Garden pool

O. Structures an Parts of Structures

O1
House plan

O2
O1 + T3

O3
O1 + (left to right) X3, P8 and W22

O4
Reed shelter

O5
Winding wall

O6
Plan of rectangular enclosure

O7
O6 + X1

O8
O7 + O29

O9
V30 + O7 (for the Goddess Nephthys)

O10
G5 in O6

O11
Palace with battlements

O12
O11 + D36

O13
Battlemented enclosure

O14
Part of the sign O13. Var. of O13.

O15
Var. of O13 with W10 and X1

O16
Door surmounted by frieze of cobras

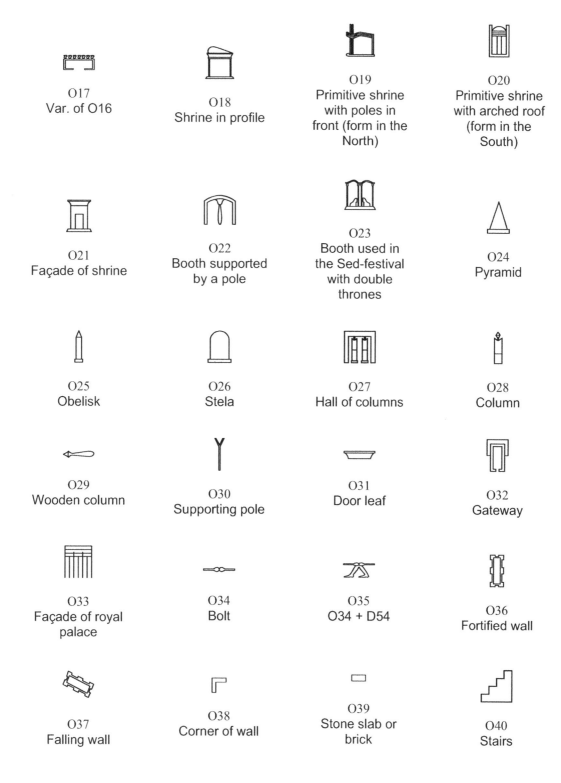

O17
Var. of O16

O18
Shrine in profile

O19
Primitive shrine
with poles in
front (form in the
North)

O20
Primitive shrine
with arched roof
(form in the
South)

O21
Façade of shrine

O22
Booth supported
by a pole

O23
Booth used in
the Sed-festival
with double
thrones

O24
Pyramid

O25
Obelisk

O26
Stela

O27
Hall of columns

O28
Column

O29
Wooden column

O30
Supporting pole

O31
Door leaf

O32
Gateway

O33
Façade of royal
palace

O34
Bolt

O35
O34 + D54

O36
Fortified wall

O37
Falling wall

O38
Corner of wall

O39
Stone slab or
brick

O40
Stairs

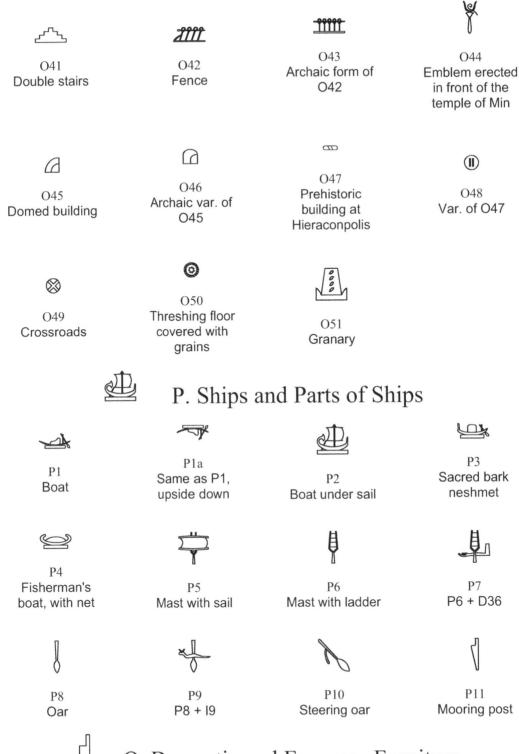

O41
Double stairs

O42
Fence

O43
Archaic form of
O42

O44
Emblem erected
in front of the
temple of Min

O45
Domed building

O46
Archaic var. of
O45

O47
Prehistoric
building at
Hieraconpolis

O48
Var. of O47

O49
Crossroads

O50
Threshing floor
covered with
grains

O51
Granary

P. Ships and Parts of Ships

P1
Boat

P1a
Same as P1,
upside down

P2
Boat under sail

P3
Sacred bark
neshmet

P4
Fisherman's
boat, with net

P5
Mast with sail

P6
Mast with ladder

P7
P6 + D36

P8
Oar

P9
P8 + I9

P10
Steering oar

P11
Mooring post

Q. Domestic and Funerary Furniture

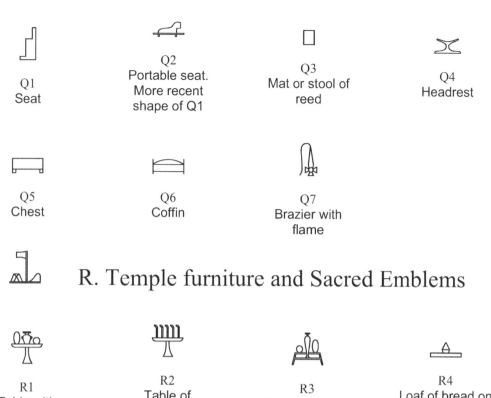

Q1
Seat

Q2
Portable seat.
More recent
shape of Q1

Q3
Mat or stool of
reed

Q4
Headrest

Q5
Chest

Q6
Coffin

Q7
Brazier with
flame

R. Temple furniture and Sacred Emblems

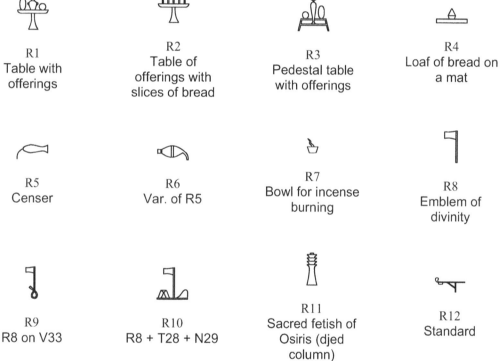

R1
Table with
offerings

R2
Table of
offerings with
slices of bread

R3
Pedestal table
with offerings

R4
Loaf of bread on
a mat

R5
Censer

R6
Var. of R5

R7
Bowl for incense
burning

R8
Emblem of
divinity

R9
R8 on V33

R10
R8 + T28 + N29

R11
Sacred fetish of
Osiris (djed
column)

R12
Standard

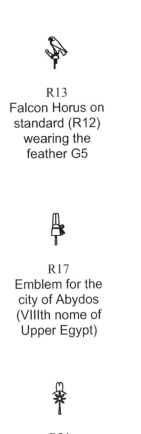

R13
Falcon Horus on standard (R12) wearing the feather G5

R14
Var. of R13

R15
Emblem of the East (in place of U23, starting with dyn. XVIIIth.).

R16
Papyrus stem surmounted by two feathers

R17
Emblem for the city of Abydos (VIIIth nome of Upper Egypt)

R18
Var. of R17

R19
Was-scepter (S40) surmounted by a feather. Emblem of the IVth nome of Upper Egypt.

R20
Emblem of the Goddess Seshat

R21
Var. of R20

R22
Emblem of the God Min

R23
Archaic form of R22

R24
Emblem of the Goddess Neith

R25
Archaic var. of R24

 # S. Regalia and Clothing

S1
White Crown (Upper Egypt)

S2
S2 + V30

S3
Red Crown (Lower Egypt)

S4
S3 + V30

S5
Pschent (Double Crown)

S6
S5 + V30

S7
Blue Crown

S8
Atef Crown

S9
Double plumes

S10
Headband

S11
Collar of beads

S12
Collar of gold

S13
S12 + D58

S14
S12 + T3

S14a
S12 + S40

S15
Pectoral of glass and faience beads

S16
Var. of S15

S17
Var. of S15

S18
Bead necklace with counterpoise

S19
Cylinder seal attached to a bead necklace

S20
Cylinder seal attached to a string

S21
Ring

S22
Shoulder knot

S23
Two flagellums united by ring V9

S24
Knot

S25
Garment

S26
Kilt

S27
Cloth with fringes

S28
Cloth with fringes

S29
Folded cloth

S30
S29 + I9

S31
S29 + U1

S32
Piece of cloth with fringe

S33
Sandal

S34
Sandal strap

S35
Sunshade of ostrich feathers

S36
Var. of S35

S37
Small fan

S38
Crook (shepherd)

S39
Crook (shepherd)

S40
Scepter, surmounted by the head of Seth (?)

S41
Var. of S40

S42
Scepter, emblem of authority

S43
Walking stick

S44
S43 + S45

S45
Flagellum (flail)

T. Warfare, Hunting, and Slaughter

T1
Mace (disk-shaped head)

T2
Mace with pear-shaped head

T3
Mace with pear-shaped head

T4
T3 with strap

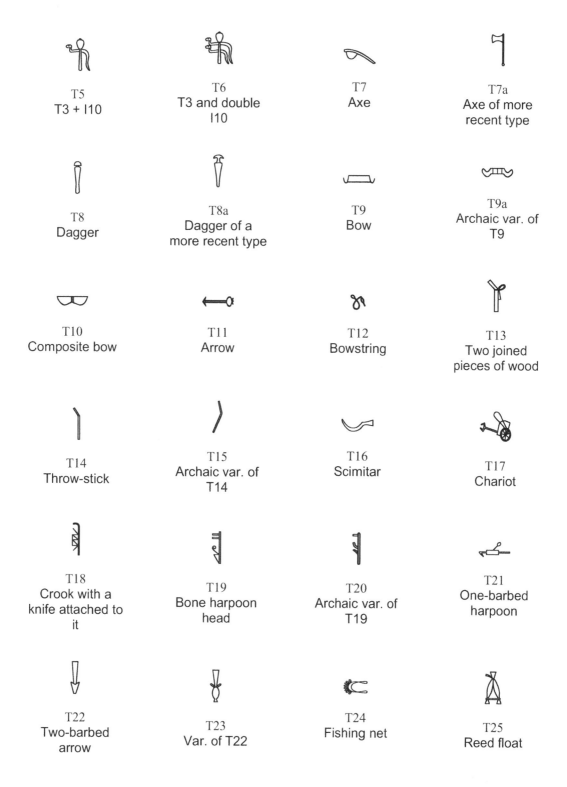

T5 T3 + I10	T6 T3 and double I10	T7 Axe	T7a Axe of more recent type
T8 Dagger	T8a Dagger of a more recent type	T9 Bow	T9a Archaic var. of T9
T10 Composite bow	T11 Arrow	T12 Bowstring	T13 Two joined pieces of wood
T14 Throw-stick	T15 Archaic var. of T14	T16 Scimitar	T17 Chariot
T18 Crook with a knife attached to it	T19 Bone harpoon head	T20 Archaic var. of T19	T21 One-barbed harpoon
T22 Two-barbed arrow	T23 Var. of T22	T24 Fishing net	T25 Reed float

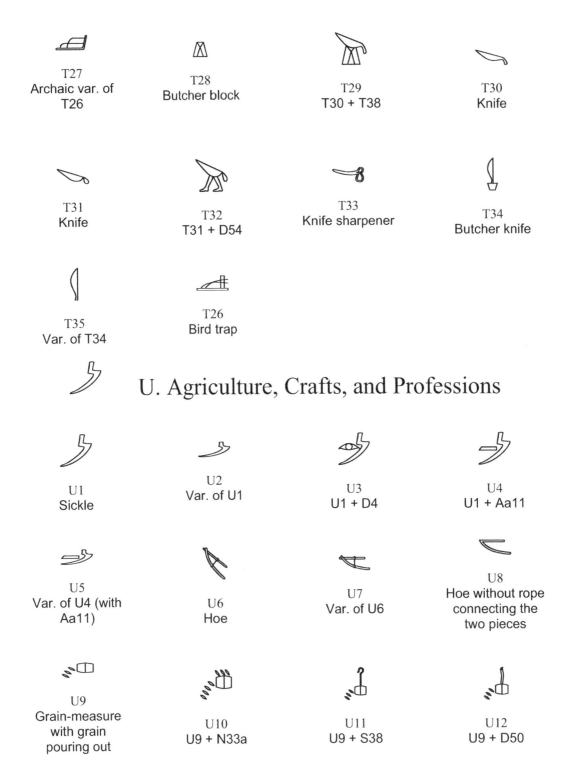

T27
Archaic var. of T26

T28
Butcher block

T29
T30 + T38

T30
Knife

T31
Knife

T32
T31 + D54

T33
Knife sharpener

T34
Butcher knife

T35
Var. of T34

T26
Bird trap

U. Agriculture, Crafts, and Professions

U1
Sickle

U2
Var. of U1

U3
U1 + D4

U4
U1 + Aa11

U5
Var. of U4 (with Aa11)

U6
Hoe

U7
Var. of U6

U8
Hoe without rope connecting the two pieces

U9
Grain-measure with grain pouring out

U10
U9 + N33a

U11
U9 + S38

U12
U9 + D50

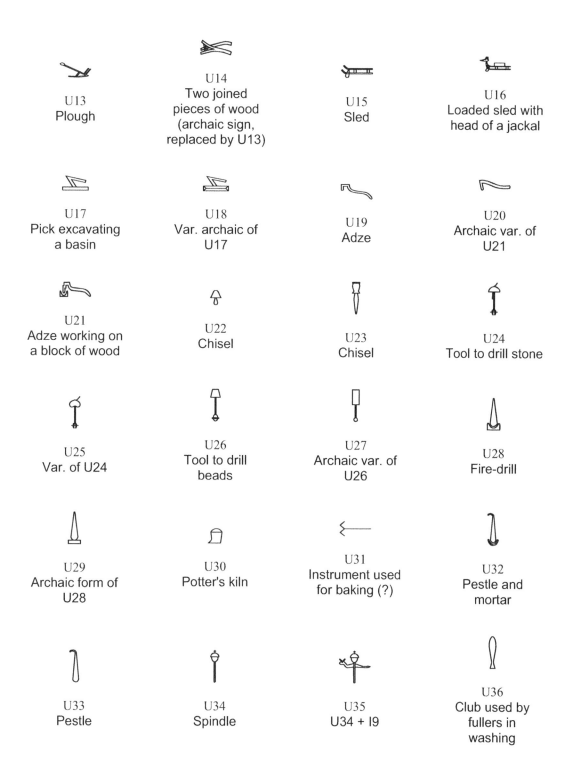

U13
Plough

U14
Two joined
pieces of wood
(archaic sign,
replaced by U13)

U15
Sled

U16
Loaded sled with
head of a jackal

U17
Pick excavating
a basin

U18
Var. archaic of
U17

U19
Adze

U20
Archaic var. of
U21

U21
Adze working on
a block of wood

U22
Chisel

U23
Chisel

U24
Tool to drill stone

U25
Var. of U24

U26
Tool to drill
beads

U27
Archaic var. of
U26

U28
Fire-drill

U29
Archaic form of
U28

U30
Potter's kiln

U31
Instrument used
for baking (?)

U32
Pestle and
mortar

U33
Pestle

U34
Spindle

U35
U34 + I9

U36
Club used by
fullers in
washing

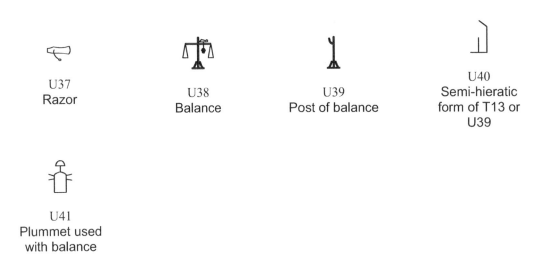

U37
Razor

U38
Balance

U39
Post of balance

U40
Semi-hieratic
form of T13 or
U39

U41
Plummet used
with balance

V. Rope, Baskets, and Cloth

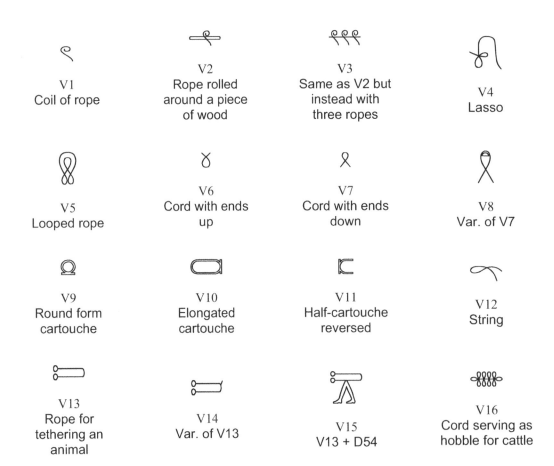

V1
Coil of rope

V2
Rope rolled
around a piece
of wood

V3
Same as V2 but
instead with
three ropes

V4
Lasso

V5
Looped rope

V6
Cord with ends
up

V7
Cord with ends
down

V8
Var. of V7

V9
Round form
cartouche

V10
Elongated
cartouche

V11
Half-cartouche
reversed

V12
String

V13
Rope for
tethering an
animal

V14
Var. of V13

V15
V13 + D54

V16
Cord serving as
hobble for cattle

V17
Shepherd's shelter, made of papyrus

V18
Var. of V17

V19
Hobble for cattle (cord with wooden cross-bar)

V20
Same as V19, without the wooden cross-bar

V21
I10 on V19

V22
Whip

V23
Whip

V24
Cord wound on stick

V25
Var. of V24

V26
Weaver's spool

V27
Archaic form of V26

V28
Wick of cord

V29
Swab made from flax fiber

V30
Basket

V31
Basket with right handle

V31a
Basket with left handle

V32
Wicker float attached to the rope of a harpoon

V33
Bag of linen

V34
Recent form of V33

V35
Archaic form of V33

V36
Receptacle

V37
Sealed bowl with attachment on top

V38
Incision (on the side of a mummy), or bandage

 W. Stone and Ceramic Vessels

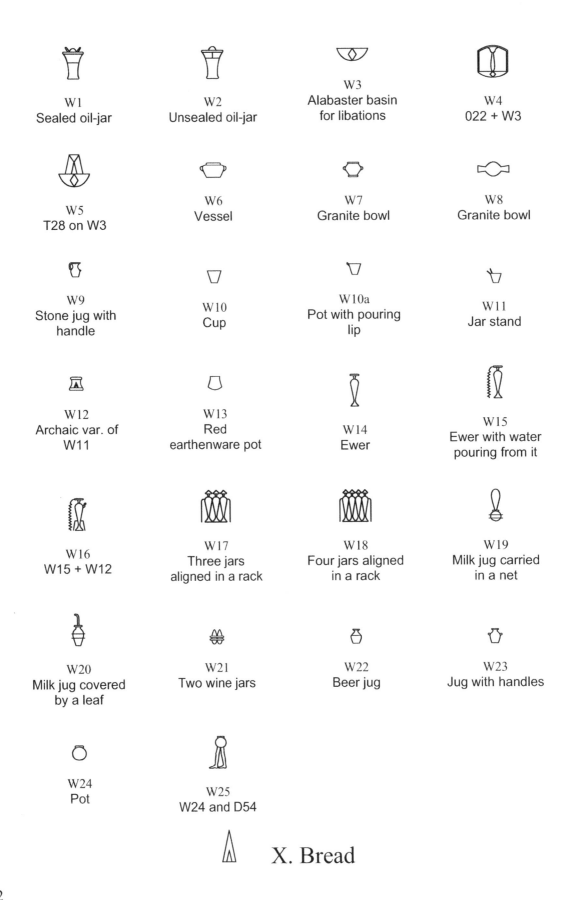

W1
Sealed oil-jar

W2
Unsealed oil-jar

W3
Alabaster basin
for libations

W4
022 + W3

W5
T28 on W3

W6
Vessel

W7
Granite bowl

W8
Granite bowl

W9
Stone jug with
handle

W10
Cup

W10a
Pot with pouring
lip

W11
Jar stand

W12
Archaic var. of
W11

W13
Red
earthenware pot

W14
Ewer

W15
Ewer with water
pouring from it

W16
W15 + W12

W17
Three jars
aligned in a rack

W18
Four jars aligned
in a rack

W19
Milk jug carried
in a net

W20
Milk jug covered
by a leaf

W21
Two wine jars

W22
Beer jug

W23
Jug with handles

W24
Pot

W25
W24 and D54

X. Bread

X1	X2	X3	X4
Bread	Bread	Var. of X2	Bread roll

X6	X7	X8	X5
Round loaf of bread, with the mark of the baker's fingers	Half-loaf of bread	Conical loaf of bread	Var. (semi-hieratic) of X4

Y. Writing, Games, and Music

Y1	Y2	Y3	Y4
Papyrus scroll, tied and sealed	Archaic form of Y1	Scribe's outfit with palette, bag for powdered pigments and reed-holder	Same as Y3, reversed

Y5	Y6	Y8	Y7
Draughtboard and pieces	Game piece	Sistrum. Read as S42 between XIIIth and XVIIIth dyn.	Harp

Z. Strokes and Figures

Z1	Z2	Z3	Z4
Vertical stroke	Three vertical strokes. Indicates the plural.	Var. of Z2	Two diagonal strokes. Indicates dual

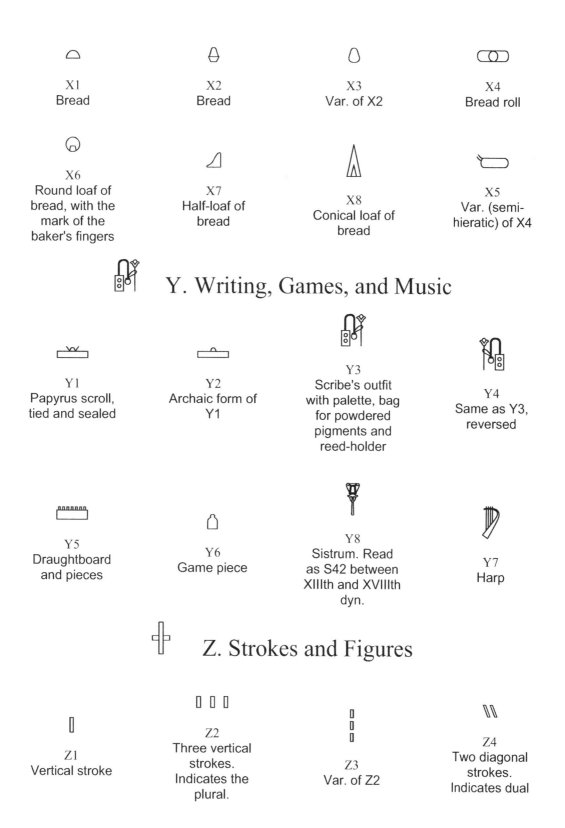

33

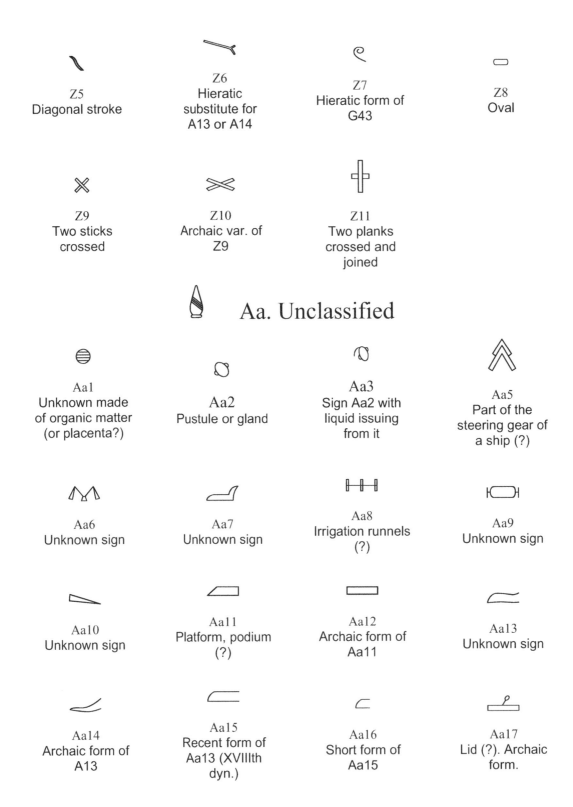

Z5
Diagonal stroke

Z6
Hieratic
substitute for
A13 or A14

Z7
Hieratic form of
G43

Z8
Oval

Z9
Two sticks
crossed

Z10
Archaic var. of
Z9

Z11
Two planks
crossed and
joined

Aa. Unclassified

Aa1
Unknown made
of organic matter
(or placenta?)

Aa2
Pustule or gland

Aa3
Sign Aa2 with
liquid issuing
from it

Aa5
Part of the
steering gear of
a ship (?)

Aa6
Unknown sign

Aa7
Unknown sign

Aa8
Irrigation runnels
(?)

Aa9
Unknown sign

Aa10
Unknown sign

Aa11
Platform, podium
(?)

Aa12
Archaic form of
Aa11

Aa13
Unknown sign

Aa14
Archaic form of
A13

Aa15
Recent form of
Aa13 (XVIIIth
dyn.)

Aa16
Short form of
Aa15

Aa17
Lid (?). Archaic
form.

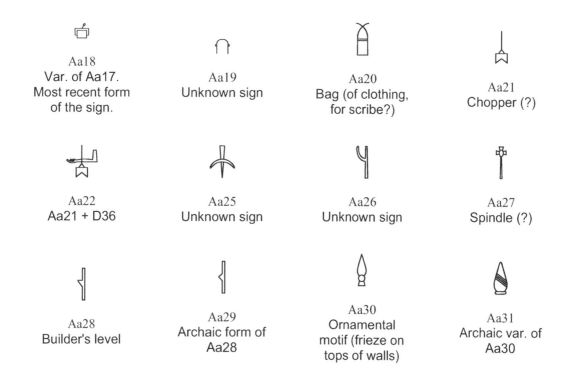

Aa18 Var. of Aa17. Most recent form of the sign.	Aa19 Unknown sign	Aa20 Bag (of clothing, for scribe?)	Aa21 Chopper (?)
Aa22 Aa21 + D36	Aa25 Unknown sign	Aa26 Unknown sign	Aa27 Spindle (?)
Aa28 Builder's level	Aa29 Archaic form of Aa28	Aa30 Ornamental motif (frieze on tops of walls)	Aa31 Archaic var. of Aa30

Seated man

I, me, my

man, men, mankind, Egyptians

Man putting his hand to his mouth

drink

Man receiving water on his hands. Purification

priestly service

Collapsed man on the ground

weariness, languor, slackness, remissness

Jubilant man

associates, family

Man holding a basket

 Load, cargo

work, construction, craft, profession

Archer, one knee on the ground

soldiers, army, infantry, gang (of workmen)

expedition

make an expedition, expedition

Man falling

fall (in military sense)

enemy

overthrow, throw down, force into place (dislocated bone)

Man falling, having been hit on the head, with dribble of blood

die, perish, death

Man bowing

bowing

Seated child, his hand to his mouth

black eye paint

be, become a child

child

small children?

boy

foster child (of king of Lower Egypt)

Old man leaning on a stick

be aged, attain old age, old age

old age

quarryman

great one, magnate

elder, eldest

Standing man, with a stick in one hand, handkerchief in the other

nobleman, magistrate

Man striking with a stick, held with his two hands

herdsman

strong, victorious, stiff, hard

Man striking with a stick, held with one hand

beat, strike, smite

Man with both arms raised toward the sky

be raised on high, uplifted

tall, high, exalted, be raised on high, uplifted
high ground, arable land

height

Man with arms outstretched in front

adoration

Man pounding in a mortar

pound, beat up, beat flat, build up, build, construct, stir

Man building a wall

build, fashion (men)

builder

Man brewing

brewer

Man brewing in a vat. Var. of A36

brewer

Man holding the neck of two fabulous animals

usae (El-Kusiyah)

Man holding the neck of two fabulous animals

Cusae (El-Kusiyah)

Seated God, wearing wig and beard

I, me, my

Seated king, uraeus on brow

King of Upper Egypt, king

Seated king, uraeus on brow and holding a flagellum (S45)

herdsman

Seated shepherd holding a stick and a rolled up mat

overseer, administrator

functionary

duty (of someone)

herdsman

await

linger, await, creep

one whose coming is awaited

guard, ward off, restrain, heed

guardian, warden

watch and ward, warding off (evil)

guardian

door-keeper

hall-keeper

bowman

keeper of the diadem

custodian of laws

overseer, administrator

Official, seating on a chair

I, me, my

nobleman, wealthy man

39

tomb-chapel

noble, august (of gods), splendid (of buildings), valuable (of plants, minerals), costly

costly offerings

noble, august, well-esteemed, rich, enrich, value (someone)

wealthy man

riches, wealth, precious things, dainties (to eat)

ritual jar

noblewoman

Official, seating on a chair and holding flagellum S45.

a noble thing (to do)

noble, august (of gods), splendid (of buildings), valuable (of plants, minerals), costly

riches, wealth, precious things, dainties (to eat)

Official squatting, holding flagellum (S45)

riches, wealth, precious things, dainties (to eat)

Erect mummy

shape, form

form, shape

statue, image, figure, likeness

Mummy on bed

corpse

spend the night, sleep, lie down, go to rest, be inert, inactive, do in the night

40

Elder of the portal

Woman giving birth

calve (of gazelle)

God with a human head and wearing the uraeus sun-disk

Re

God with the head of Seth

Seth (god)

Maat, Goddess wearing a feather

right-doing, righteousness

Seated God, arms raised, wearing the sign M4 on his head

Heh (god)

many

Head of man in profile

head, headman, chief, tip (of toe), example (mathematics), the best of

person, people

due time (to do something)

previously

Aphroditopolis (Atfih)

being upon, principal, first, high (priest)

utterance, (financial) principle, base (of triangle), radius (of circle)

utterance

(financial) principle

survivor

before (time)

who are in front of (of place), before (of place)

who had been before (of time), former (of time)

predecessors, ancestors

in front of, in the direction of, before (of time)

beside, in the neighborhood of, accompanying, escorting

a good beginning

daily

annual

the South of

the South

instructions, regulations

master

reckoning

reckoning, correct method, norm, standard (of speech, conduct), rectitude

act of rebellion?

specification

destitution

fine oil

uraeus

Beginning-of-the-Season festival

former state

journey, beginning (of region)

	utterance
	task
	roof
	dawn
	head, tip (of bow)

Face

	Nile
	terrible, terrify
	prepare, make ready, be ready
	face, sight
	a rope (aboard a ship)
	in the middle, midst of
	master
	head man
	who / which is upon, who is higher, upper, having authority over, headman
	upper
	summit of head
	epagomenal days
	Bedouin
	Master of Largess
	an offering loaf
	a breed of cattle
	Arsaphes
	Arsaphes
	terror, dread, respect
	respect
	survivor

43

terror

who is upon

who is upon, having authority over, chief, headman, master

master (of a servant)

remainder

in default?

arrears, remainder

immediately

upper part, top

on every side

apart from, besides, as well as

kind of bread

why?

loyal to him

everyone

everyone, everybody

chief of land register?

O38^c

flower

except me

upon, outside, after, in turn

why?

carnelian?

being in good state

entirely, altogether, utterly

beside, in the presence of

sky, heaven

tomb, necropolis

tomb

central hall (of temple)

44

travel by land

arrears

on behalf of

chief of land register?

garden

lump (of lapis lazuli)

Lock of hair

be destroyed

fenugreek?

hair, grass

Eye

doer (of good)

create, beget, make, construct, do, act, take action, achieve, prepare, treat

levy the cattle-tax

rejoice

work devastation among

coiffeur (do hair)

trim the nails

make provision for (someone)

cattle-tax

prepare a way for

eyes

punish

set a good example

make inspection of, look into

make inspection of, look into

do good

	obey
	read a book aloud
	I have proved it myself
	swing awry, act perversely, make a travesty of
	show less of (a bad quality)
	(evil) doer
	keep the law, carry out the law
	take care!
	get in front of
	take a wife, to marry
	make peace
	assume a shape
	meet
	do things
	stand guard against
	do trade
	deal with someone
	carry on field sports
	act as guardian to (a minor)
	achieve a (good) reputation, achieve, success
	eye
	to escort
	act properly, do as should be done, correct procedure
	look after (someone)
	do wrong
	Osiris

Eye underlined with a line of paint

	black eye paint

Eye surrounded by an ellipse (N18)

weep

Human eye surmounting the features of the falcon. The Eye of Horus

the uninjured eye of Horus

d10c

see, behold

Pupil of the human eye

eyeball?

Upper part of the face, in profile

nose

long nosed, Beaky

prison

prison, fortress

Nubian mineral (ochre?)

baker

Mouth

letter carrier

keeper of the diadem

(total of) each

foreigners

to, at, concerning, more than, from

mouth, opening, utterance, speech, language, intent

goose, goose shaped cake, goose shaped incense

fractions

(not translated)

chest

between, in the midst of

at his (proper) times

cattle-list

Re   G7c

Re (Sun god)

sun

entry (into land)

hands, actions

gate

end, limit, beside, near

combat

sun goddess (of queen)

joints (arm and leg)

consider (doing something)

path, way

dance, palpitate (of heart), clap (hands)

advance (against)

leave (a place)

go away, depart, pass away, advance (against), serve (someone)

serve (someone)

vineyard?

clap (hands)   ḏ92

palpitate (of heart)

interruption

departure

dance, palpitate

dance

gate

see under other entries

outsider, stranger

outside

two gates

strength, firmness

stairway, tomb-shaft

stairway

tomb-shaft

success

enduring, permanent

successful, succeed

bow-string

cord, bow-string

hard, firm, strong, enduring, permanent, effective, persistent

prevail (over)

prosperous, prosper

hard

sinews

agent

	hard stone, sandstone
	outside
	spokesman of every Pe-ite
	presiding goddess (of city)
	female statue
	noble, heir
	rot
	or
	temple, chapel
	foreigners
	not to be translated
	to what purpose?
	fish
	in the sight (of)
	in the sight of
	in the sight of
	weep
	likewise
	weep
	weeping
	tears
	shoulder, arm, uprights (of ladder), side
	side, gang (of rowers)
	side, half (of sheet of water)
	as well as, including
	bearer, supporter

	Meaning
	shoulder, carry, support, match, equal
	companions
	as far as
	Lebanon
	chastise
	man, men, mankind, Egyptians
	men, mankind
3^c23	according to the will of
	name
	calf
	name (of king)
	uterus
	calf
	at the proper time
	young man
$M4^b E6^c$	colt
	young, fresh (of water)
	youthful vigor
$M7^c$	herbs, vegetables
	to its end
	caress
	rejoice (over), extol
	bring up, nurse
	Renenutet (the Harvest-goddess)
	joy, exultation
	Renenutet (the Harvest-goddess)
	name of the ninth month
B5^d	(wet)-nurse
	the nurse-goddess

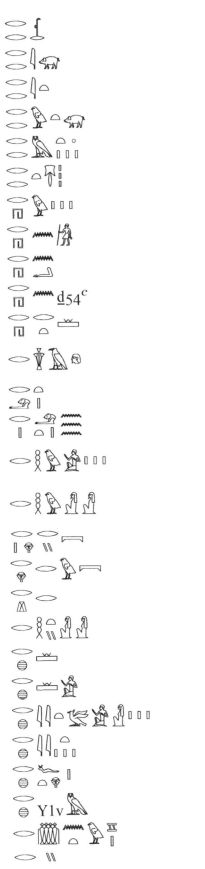

	time
	boar
	pigishness?
	sow
	mandrake?
	swine (animal)
	near
	lean (on), rely on, trust in
	rely on, trust in
	wade
	satisfactorily
	behind
	in front of, before, superior to
	river mouth
	comrades, mates
	the Two Companions, the Two Combatants (Horus and Seth)
	master, chief
	up above
	below
	the Two Female Companions (Isis and Nephthys)
	know, be aware of, Inquire!, learn
	wise man
	subjects, common folk, mankind
	subjects, common folk, mankind
	in front of, in the presence of
	know of
	out

celebrated

wisdom

wise, learned man

slaughter

knowledge

wash (clothes)

knowledge, amount, number

under the authority of

weapons

within, into

below

not translated

wake, be watchful, vigilant

be watchful, vigilant

wake

after

vigilance

as the price of, in exchange for

awakening, dream

dream

catch (of fowl, fish), affluence

catch (fowl, fish)

quite, entirely, at all

ford?

sacrificial victims?

ramp

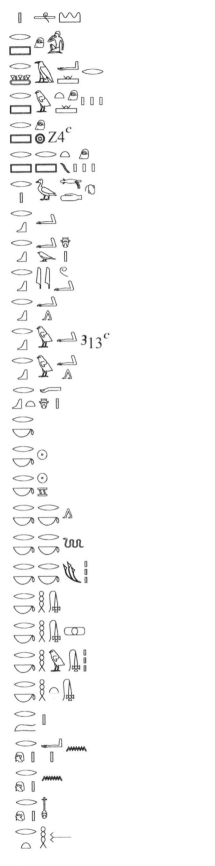

necropolis

joyful

down to

joy

rejoice

joy

fattened goose

incline, turn aside (from), defy

disaffected man

fierce?

tilting (of balance)

opponent

tilting (of balance), enmity

ill will

(not translated)

time (of king)

time (of king, of ancients)

creep

snake

a creeping plant

light (fire)

(festival of) Burning

flames

heat

beside, in the presence of

into the presence of

into the presence of

successfully

confine, restrain

	baker
	conspiracy?
	now, but
	now, but
	whither?
	Retenue (Syria)
	foot
	grow
	shoot (of tree)
	give, put, place, appoint, send (letter), cause, permit, grant
	give, put, place, appoint, cause, permit, grant
	be anxious about
	give a hand to, help
	inform
	put an end to
	a place to eavesdrop (put the temple to...)
	bury
	speak
	inform
	land (from ship), give birth, neglect, leave alone, set aside
	give in addition to
	put in the charge of
	give commands to
	incline to one side (of balance), show partiality (of judge)
	be partial, be biased, fell (an enemy)
	cast ashore (rope), cast forth, expel
	make submission to
	turn the back to

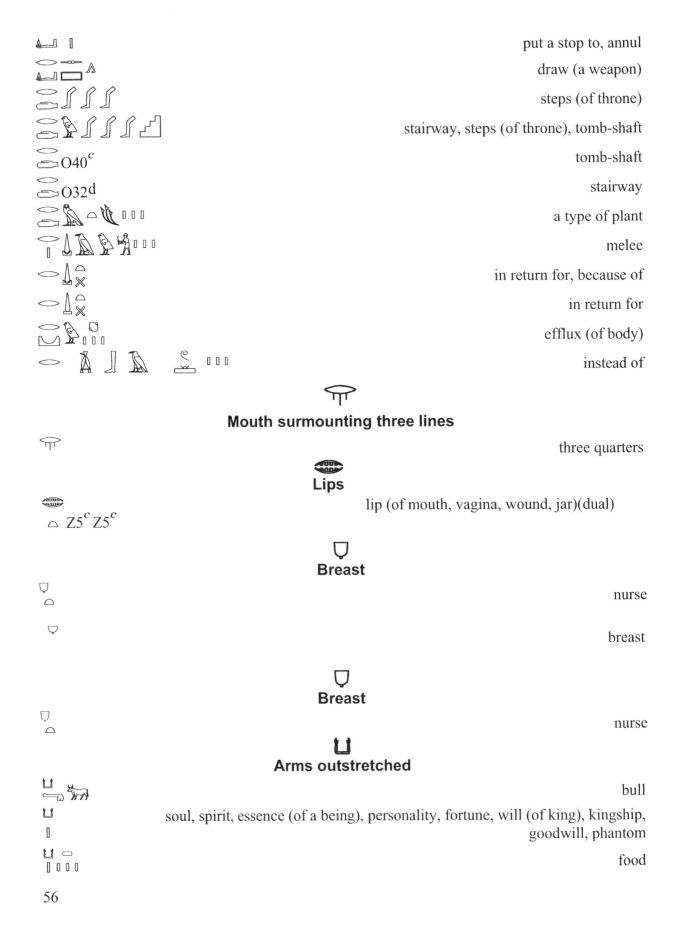	put a stop to, annul
	draw (a weapon)
	steps (of throne)
	stairway, steps (of throne), tomb-shaft
	tomb-shaft
	stairway
	a type of plant
	melee
	in return for, because of
	in return for
	efflux (of body)
	instead of

Mouth surmounting three lines

	three quarters

Lips

	lip (of mouth, vagina, wound, jar)(dual)

Breast

	nurse
	breast

Breast

	nurse

Arms outstretched

	bull
	soul, spirit, essence (of a being), personality, fortune, will (of king), kingship, goodwill, phantom
	food

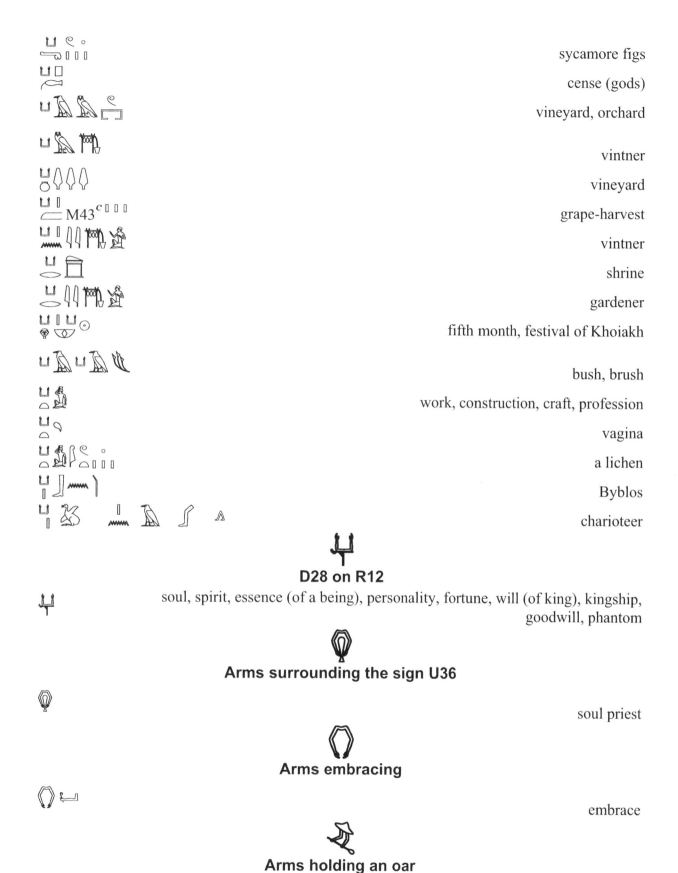

sycamore figs

cense (gods)

vineyard, orchard

vintner

vineyard

grape-harvest

vintner

shrine

gardener

fifth month, festival of Khoiakh

bush, brush

work, construction, craft, profession

vagina

a lichen

Byblos

charioteer

D28 on R12

soul, spirit, essence (of a being), personality, fortune, will (of king), kingship, goodwill, phantom

Arms surrounding the sign U36

soul priest

Arms embracing

embrace

Arms holding an oar

𓊛	row, convey by water
𓊛	row
𓊛	sailors
𓊛	sailor
𓊛	tumult, uproar
𓊛	disturb, interfere with (persons, commands), confound (truth)
𓊛	inflamed, irritated (medical)
𓊛	brawlers
𓊛	water procession
𓊛	water-procession
𓊛	statue
𓊛	living semblance

Arm holding a shield and a battle-axe

𓌡	warrior
𓌡	fight
𓌡	fish (lates niloticus)
𓌡	fight
𓌡	go to war
𓌡	arrow, weapons
𓌡 ṯ11b	arrows, weapons
𓌡	warrior
𓌡	sounding pole
𓌡	sounding-pole
𓌡	ply the sounding pole

58

	be wary of
	battleground
	warriors
	warship
	take care
	take care

Arms in a gesture of negation

	old negative particle
	who.......not, which.......not
	what is not, does not exist
	not
	drive away, rebuff
	darken (sun)
	parry (missile)
	indeed not, if not, unless
	there is/are not
	not
	there is none beside him
	there will never be his like again
	there will never be his like again
	there will never be his like again
	spleen
	never

Arm

	present (to)

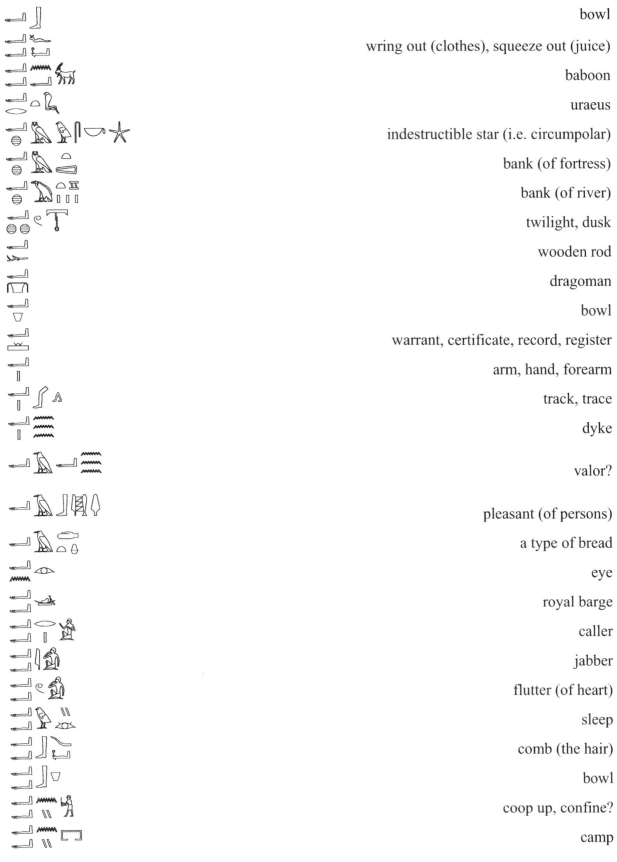

	bowl
	wring out (clothes), squeeze out (juice)
	baboon
	uraeus
	indestructible star (i.e. circumpolar)
	bank (of fortress)
	bank (of river)
	twilight, dusk
	wooden rod
	dragoman
	bowl
	warrant, certificate, record, register
	arm, hand, forearm
	track, trace
	dyke
	valor?
	pleasant (of persons)
	a type of bread
	eye
	royal barge
	caller
	jabber
	flutter (of heart)
	sleep
	comb (the hair)
	bowl
	coop up, confine?
	camp

dragoman

go bad, rot

look after, care for

steal (goods), rob (someone)

steal, rob, robbery

brigand

robber, he who is robbed

robber

reap

a fermented drink?

female robber

robbery

ring

be covetous, despoil

be rapacious, rapacity, avarice

plunderer

stave

parch (grain)

crook, scepter

men

goats

unite

meal

horn

61

offering-stone

make presentation (to)

present (to), make presentation, provide

present (to)

command (a ship)

offering-stone

glitter

provide (with)

scepter

boast, boasting, exaggeration

boast, boasting, exaggeration

become excited?

appear?, shine?

region of collar-bone

victims

purification, purity

purity

impurity

offerings

breakfast

staff of Office

lettuce

62

	forked staff
O30u	
	knock (on door)?
	use the pitchfork
W54[c]	fill up
	frog
	wine-jar
W59	wine jar
	attachment, connection(s)
	a funerary ritual object
	traverse (a waterway), pass (by)
ḥ5[c]	fly
N58	the Winged Disk
I14c	slug?
	slug
	an Asiatic people
	provide, equip (with), man (a vessel), acquire, incur (injury)
	sailors, workmen
	a type of jar
	equipment (of offerings)
	beetle
	his command
	devour?, tear off
F51[b]	devour, tear off
	encampment
	sweet clover?
	bee, honey bee

	buzz (of insect)
	fly (insect)
	fly
	cover
	royal head-cloth
š57b	royal head-cloth
Z4^c 3417	brewer
	female brewer
	lead (to), attractive?
	chest
	chest (furniture)
	swallow
	swallow, breathe in, absorb, know
	become faint, neglect, be discreet, regret, dissemble
	smear
	throw the throw-stick
	throw-stick
	throw-stick
	container (for bread etc..)
	smear
	shrew
	mud, muddy ground, mud-flat
	Brain
	beautiful, bright of face, pleasing, be kind, magnificent
	the pleasant man

beautiful

writing-board

complain, complaint

complain, complaint

chin

Ainu (a source of Limestone)

Ainu? (source of Limestone)

reed-stalk (for matting)

measure for reed-stalks

turn back

turn back, repeat again, come back, return, bring back

rump

eyebrow

Anukis

finger/toe nail, claw

ring (of gold), socket (for jar)

nail (of finger or toe)

pick

myrrh

few, scarcity, fewness, be diminished

an unguent

unguent

the few (of people)

dawn

jar

reed pen

mount up, ascend, extend, penetrate

mount up, ascend

dwelling, home

chin?

proximity

enclose

bag, combine, enclose, contain

combine

hall of judgment

gate

leaf (of double door)

lintel

know, perceive, gain full knowledge of, be wise, skilled

basket?

bent

know, perceive, gain full knowledge of, be wise, skilled (in)

don (a garment)

last day of the month

jaw

hinder part, hindquarter

jaw, hinder parts (of man), anus

roll (of papyrus)

roll (of papyrus, leather)

they who ascend?

wipe off, wipe away

rope

wipe off, wipe away

fight

attending

(proper) positions (of things)

	brazier
	desert region
	fly
	raise up, hang (men)
	image
	front of neck
	extinguish, quench (thirst)
	extinguish, destroy
	quench (thirst)
	twigs
	river-bank
	evaporate, consume
	twilight
	swoop (of falcon)
	fly, fly away
	fly, fly away
	image (of god)
	voracious (?) spirit
	audience chamber
	audience-chamber
	summon
	groan
	cedar-oil
	cedar
	obnoxious?
	lizard
	many, numerous, much, plentiful, ordinary, quantity, multitude
	voice box, larynx

[hieroglyphs]	image (of god)
[hieroglyphs] Z4^c	abundant
[hieroglyphs]	enter (into)
[hieroglyphs] Y1v	precise, accurate
[hieroglyphs]	use aright
[hieroglyphs]	a type of rope
[hieroglyphs]	precise, accurate, go straight forward, progress
[hieroglyphs] Y1v	straightforward
[hieroglyphs]	a straight-dealer
[hieroglyphs]	true balancing
[hieroglyphs]	a preparation of grain
[hieroglyphs] W78	pedestal (for vase)
[hieroglyphs]	a resinous varnish?
[hieroglyphs]	house
[hieroglyphs]	limb, member (of body)
[hieroglyphs]	room, chamber, house
[hieroglyphs]	slaughter-house
[hieroglyphs]	joints
[hieroglyphs]	cake room
[hieroglyphs]	orchard
[hieroglyphs]	brew-house
[hieroglyphs]	strain
[hieroglyphs]	brewers
[hieroglyphs]	school, school-house
[hieroglyphs]	school
[hieroglyphs]	bake-house
[hieroglyphs]	the Holy Chamber (the celestial Hall of judgment)
[hieroglyphs]	Buri fish
[hieroglyphs]	be safe, become whole

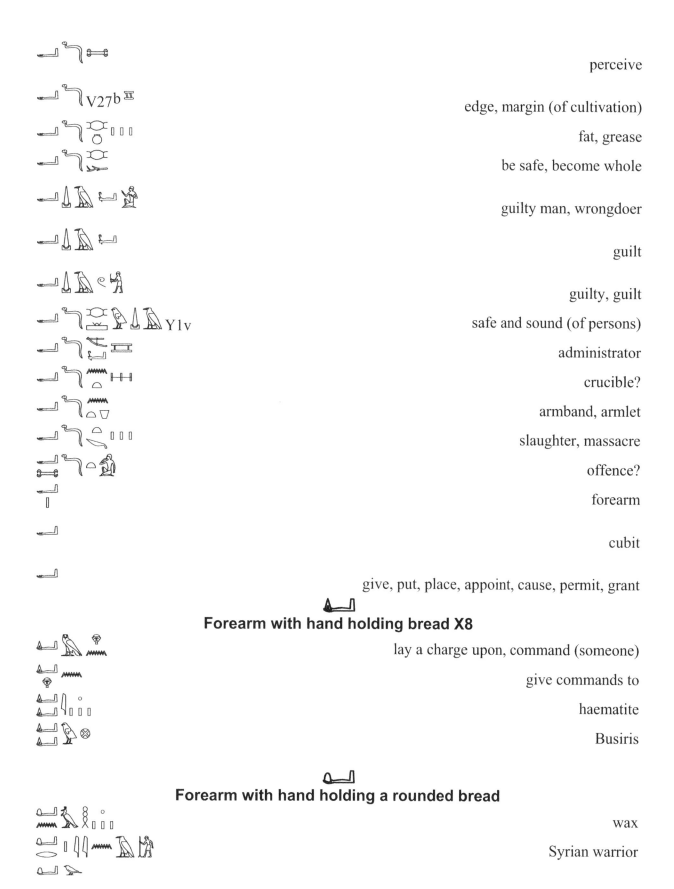

	perceive
V27b Ⅱ	edge, margin (of cultivation)
	fat, grease
	be safe, become whole
	guilty man, wrongdoer
	guilt
	guilty, guilt
Y1v	safe and sound (of persons)
	administrator
	crucible?
	armband, armlet
	slaughter, massacre
	offence?
	forearm
	cubit
	give, put, place, appoint, cause, permit, grant

Forearm with hand holding bread X8

	lay a charge upon, command (someone)
	give commands to
	haematite
	Busiris

Forearm with hand holding a rounded bread

| | wax |
| | Syrian warrior |

69

𓊛𓏦	be forgetful, neglectful
	family
	milk jar
	bring, present, bring away booty, extend (hand), take (aim)
	carriers, bearers
	give, put, place, appoint, cause, permit, grant

Forearm with hand holding the vase W24

	mother
	turquoise
	chariot
	evening
	ford
	Medjay, Police
	offer (something to)
	make offering (to)
	bed of life (where the sun sets)
	offerings

Forearm with hand holding a stick

	strong, victorious, stiff, hard
	victory
	measure, examine (patient), patrol
	treatment

Forearm with the palm of the hand downwards

	land cubit (one hundredth of one auoura)

Hieroglyph	Meaning
	underside of arm
	ostrich
	bowl
	shoulder, arm, uprights (of ladder), side
	processional shrine
	department, domain

Var. of D41, the upper part of the arm being in a vertical position

Hieroglyph	Meaning
	forearm
	cubit
	companion
	bandage
	roof

Forearm holding the scepter S42

Hieroglyph	Meaning
	bring, provide, make offering of, dedicate

Arm holding the scepter nekhebet

Hieroglyph	Meaning
	holy, sacred
	with upraised arm
	holy place
	seclusion, privacy, sanctity
	privacy
	sanctity
	seclusion
W65	strong ale
R3P	table of offerings
W65 R19^c	milky ale?
	the Western Holy Place (Medinet Habu)

71

Hand

	red linen
$\underline{d}46^c$	sweet savor, fragrance
	palm of hand
	palm (of hand), one seventh of a cubit (measurement)
	copulate
	become loose, wobble (of decaying limbs)
	shake, tremble
	subdue (lands)
	loin-cloth
	shaking, trembling
	figs
	control (temper), subdue (foes), suppress (evil), rob (someone), steal (goods)
	control (a tribe)
	self denial, self control
	copulate, masturbate, misbehave, rape, sodomize?
	gang of 5
	bellow
$Z4^c$	here, there
	papyrus plant
	give, place, put, implant (obstacle), strike (blow), cause

give, place

praise, worship

morning $Z4^{c}$

deified royal beard d156 G7c

praises

Duamutef

netherworld, nether chamber (in tomb)

netherworld

stretch out (legs, hands), stretch (bow), straighten (knees),

stretch out (legs, hands)

straighten (knees)

stretch (bow)

hippopotamus

horn (of animal), wing (of army)

stop up

go round (a place), travel round (a region)

weight (of about 91 grammes), weight (of balance)

lock of hair

ask for, beg, requisition (from)

measure for offerings

measure for offerings

necessaries

funerary meal

female hippopotamus

thump (of heart)

taste (verb), experience

Big block of stone

Dep (Delta city)

Could be a variant of dp : big block of stone. For the idea of coffin?

crocodile

taste

loins

ship

an offering

stolid

drip

be sharp

sharpen

pronounce, proclaim (name), mention (by name), be renowned (of office)

be sharp, sharpen, pierce (sky)

cut off (heads)

stretch, be stretched out

bind together

groups, classes

wing

be joined (to)

be joined (to)

touch, reach (a place)

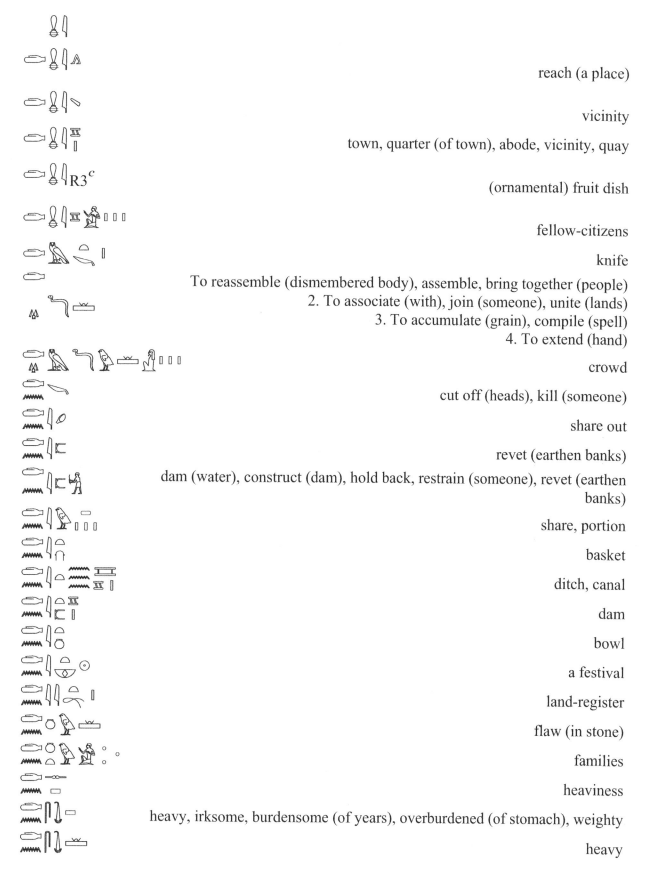

reach (a place)

vicinity

town, quarter (of town), abode, vicinity, quay

(ornamental) fruit dish

fellow-citizens

knife

To reassemble (dismembered body), assemble, bring together (people)
2. To associate (with), join (someone), unite (lands)
3. To accumulate (grain), compile (spell)
4. To extend (hand)

crowd

cut off (heads), kill (someone)

share out

revet (earthen banks)

dam (water), construct (dam), hold back, restrain (someone), revet (earthen banks)

share, portion

basket

ditch, canal

dam

bowl

a festival

land-register

flaw (in stone)

families

heaviness

heavy, irksome, burdensome (of years), overburdened (of stomach), weighty

heavy

75

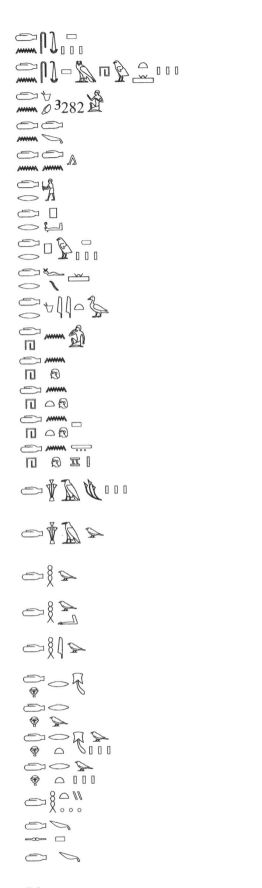

weights (of net)

guarded of speech

pygmy, dwarf

slaughter (animals)

traverse (a place, a way)

subdue (enemies), expel, drive out (people, illness)

offer to (god), feed (someone), present (dues)

offerings

writing, script, title deeds

bat (mammal)

appoint

bow (to), appoint, order (burial)

forehead

mountain-top

touch the earth with the forehead in obeisance

straw

be low

hang down

be humiliated

hang down, be low, be humiliated

leather, hide

bitter, bitterness

sickness

bitterness, sickness

lead

flint

knife

𓂝𓏲 W73	jar
𓂝𓏲𓏤𓀐	vilify
𓂋𓈖𓅦	flamingo
𓂋𓈖𓏭	red, reddening
𓂋𓈖𓅦𓏭	furious
𓂋𓈖𓅧𓅦	blood
𓂋𓈖𓅥𓏪	wrath
𓂋𓈖𓅦𓏭	furious
𓂋𓈖𓂉𓅦𓈉	the Red Land, desert
𓂋𓈖𓋔	the Red Crown
𓂋𓈖𓂉𓏭	wrath
𓃀𓏭𓈒𓏤	flour, powder
𓃀𓏭𓈖	press (against), exclude (from), a process in spinning
𓃀𓏭𓈖𓏭𓏥	fruit, fruit-trees
𓈎𓅨𓃀𓊮	walk
𓈎𓅨𓏭𓏭𓂉𓁶	starring
𓈎𓅨𓀜	hide
𓈎𓁹	look (at)
𓈎𓏭𓏭𓁹	see, behold
𓈎𓏭𓏭𓂉𓀜𓅿	a type of bird
𓈎𓏭𓏭𓂉𓅢	bat (mammal)
𓈎𓅨𓇋	castor-oil plant
𓈎𓅨𓁹	be speechless
𓈎𓅨𓏏𓂻𓂝	walk
𓂝𓃙 342c	a Nubian god
𓂝𓂉 W79	dish
𓈖𓈒𓏭	type of grain

77

(hieroglyphs)	replace, restore
(hieroglyphs)	payments, reward, compensation, bribes
(hieroglyphs)	brick, ingot, slab (of metal)
(hieroglyphs)	provisions, sustenance, victuals, (deified as) Abundance
(hieroglyphs)	territories
(hieroglyphs)	wing
(hieroglyphs)	wrath
(hieroglyphs)	be angry
(hieroglyphs)	kite (bird)
(hieroglyphs)	hand
ḏ46ḏ (hieroglyphs)	hand, trunk (of elephant), handle (of jar)
(hieroglyphs)	call (to)
(hieroglyphs)	Busiris

Fist

(hieroglyphs)	bandage

Raised finger

(hieroglyphs)	point the finger (at)
(hieroglyphs)	finger, thumb, toe, digit (one twenty-eighth cubit), 10,000 (numeral)
(hieroglyphs)	reproach
(hieroglyphs)	signet, seal

Finger in a horizontal position

(hieroglyphs)	grains
(hieroglyphs)	flour, powder

Phallus

(hieroglyph)

𓏺 𓎺	measure of capacity
	penis
𓀘	mother
	bolus, lump, pill
	strip? (of cloth)
	vessel, duct, muscle
	straightforward, precise
	strips? (of cloth)
𓀜	controller
	straightforward, precise, exact, regular (of seasons), customary (of diet), usual (of form)
	regular (of seasons)
	controller of a (priestly) phyle
	controller of (priestly) phyle
	rectitude
	semen
	semen, seed, progeny, poison, ill-will
	discuss, discussion
	reward
	reward
	testify concerning, exhibit (virtues), charge (tasks), instruct
	fame, renown
	testify concerning
	witness
	flood
	visible testimony
	midday
	testimony
	concubine

79

exact moment

affection?

arena

road, way

bull

bull calf

bull calf

bull of the herd (Head Bull?)

Legs walking

come and go

stride, journeys, movements, actions, (legal) procedure

Bended leg

quarter (of necropolis)

foot

administrative division, quarter, part

flight

administratrix

administrator, attendant

box, casket

foot

feet

splendid

gazelle

perforation, puncture

𝄮 Y24   perforation, puncture

Leg with knife (T30) across

𝄮   encroach upon (lands), cheat

𝄮   mutilator, twister (of speech)

Foot

𝄮   boast, boasting, exaggeration

𝄮   leopard skin

𝄮   leopard

𝄮   hack up (the earth), hoe (crops), destroy, devastate

𝄮   virility

𝄮   damp

𝄮 F36ᶜ   foot-ewer

𝄮   galley

𝄮   hole (socket of eye, apertures of head)

𝄮   inshore eddy

𝄮   inshore eddy?

𝄮   phallus, glans

𝄮   Bahu: a region (originally West of Egypt, later on, the East)

𝄮   Bahu: a region (originally west of Egypt, later on, to the East)

𝄮   devour

𝄮 W10b   jar

𝄮   Bubastis

oily, bright, white, be dazzled (of sight), clear of character, innocent, fortunate

moringa oil

oily, bright

fortunate

moringa oil

bright

sight?

thick (of fluids)

be weary, languid, be slack, remiss

be weary, languid

be slack, remiss

slackness, remissness

the languid ones (the dead)

thorn bush?

thorn bush

dagger

(male) genitals

bush, wisp (of corn)

ladle, dipper

good deed

metal (bronze?, iron?)

heaven

heaven, firmament

a mineral (not metal)

wonder, miracle

wonder, miracle

consisting of bronze?

consisting of bronze

firmament

miracle, marvels

miracle

miracles, marvels

mining region, a mine

the produce (of a mine)

wonders, marvels

wonders, marvels

quarry

beer vessel

marvellous person (of king)

wasp

acclamation

symptom of disease

bad, evil

evil

what is displeasing

falcon

female falcon

character, qualities

a loaf

block (of stone)

𓃀𓏤𓎺 W88	vase (in oval form)
𓃀𓏤𓎺𓏴	King of Lower Egypt
𓃀𓅞𓅆𓏪𓁹𓅿	wasp
𓃀𓉿𓃀𓎛𓈗	drink
𓃀𓉿𓃀𓊌𓈗	stream
𓃀𓈗𓎛	neck
𓃀𓎛𓆼𓆞𓀔	be detested
𓃀𓎛𓆼𓈗𓆄	abundance (as deity)
𓃀𓎛𓆼𓈖𓅞	abundance
𓃀𓎛𓆼𓇋𓌌	have abundance, be well-supplied, be inundated, flood, inundate
𓃀𓎛𓆼𓅿𓈗	inundation, flood
𓃀	place
𓃀𓅃𓆛𓏥	detest
𓃀𓅃𓈐	place (in reference to desert)
𓃀𓋁𓅃𓀭	magnate, notable
𓃀𓋁𓅃𓄤𓏥	hiding-place (for wild fowl)
𓃀𓋁𓅃𓂻𓏤𓏤	hiding-place (for wildfowl)
𓃀𓅃𓏭𓅆𓆛𓏤	those who are abominated
𓃀𓅃𓌳	truth
𓃀𓅃𓎰	everyone
𓃀𓅃𓎰𓀀𓀭𓏤𓏤𓏤	everyone, everybody
𓃀𓄤	good

84

	good, goodness
	evil
	detest, abominate
	detest, abominate, abomination
	abomination
	region of throat, hollows above collar-bone
	collar-bones
	wig (shoulder length?)
	Babel
	region of collar-bones
	herb
	hole, cavity
	negative particle
	date-wine
	date-wine
	heron
	hard sandstone, corn-rubber
	Benben stone (the sacred stone of ON)
	stem (of ship?)
	pyramidion
3^c3b	gall
	beget, become erect (of male), overflow
	become erect (of male), overflow
	bead, pellet
	pellet
	sweet, pleasant
	globe of the eye

dates

confectioners

sweetness

dates

doorpost

harp

pair of breasts, nipples

two baboons (which greet the morning sun) E35

deep-bosomed (of women)

eyes

flee

fugitive

flabellum

forced labor

drive off (foes)

cut off (limbs), drive off (foes)

howl (of dog)

hunt

calf

country mansion

basalt? greywacke?

basalt?, greywacke?

pylon O21b

pylons O137

heat?

pride? (as a bad quality)

	introduce (someone into), install, initiate (into)
	introduce (someone into)
	install
	protect
	flow forth (of water)
	secret image (of god)
	flame
	result, consequence
	(morbid) discharges
	gypsum?
	disembowel
	entrails
	malted barley?
	spit, spit out
	vomit, spittle
	rebellion
	rebels
	rebel (against)
	be hostile (to someone)?
	recalcitrance?
	spinal column
	spine
	be pregnant
	lock of hair
	tomorrow, morning
	tomorrow

𓏤𓅆𓏏𓇼	tomorrow
	pregnant woman
	hair
	shipwrecked man
	wrongdoing
	wrong, crime
	wrongdoer
	harm, injury
	disobey, defy
	insolent man
	defiant man, rebel
	squalor?
	sink (of the heart)?
	escape
	escape?
	abandon, forsake
	run
	incurable (disease or person)
	natron
	become faint, weak, exhausted
	downcast, faint-hearted
	weakness
	emmer
	water melon
	water-melon
	jar
	stiff roll of linen

𓂻𓄿𓅢𓈖	stiff roll of linen
𓂻𓄿𓅢𓈖𓏤𓏥𓅯	mast-head

D58 + D36

𓃀𓂝	boast, boasting, exaggeration
𓃀𓃀𓂝	threshold?
𓃀𓂽	purification
𓃀𓏲𓅨	inundation, flood

Foot topped with a vase from which flows water

𓎿	pure, purify oneself, bathe, cleanse, purification, purity
𓎿	serve as priest
𓎿𓈗	pure, purify oneself, bathe, cleanse, purification
𓎿𓈗𓀃	Wab priest
𓎿𓅬𓏭	sacred robe
𓎿𓏐𓈗	priestly service
𓎿𓂋𓏭𓎟	meat offerings
𓎿𓅬𓏐 F51b	meat offering
𓎿𓈗𓉴	place of embalmment, tomb, kitchen, refectory
𓎿𓌃	offering-slab
𓎿𓏐	meat-offering

Toes

𓂾	dependant?

𓅓𓄿𓇋	reach, arrive at, land (from ship), tread (the earth), go to (earth = be buried)
𓅓𓏤𓏛𓏤	grant of land
𓅓𓏤𓃀	toe
𓅓✶𓅓𓀁	Orion (constellation)
𓅓𓊖	neighborhood

𓂾 Var. of D61

𓂾 Y1v	endow (with)

𓃒 Bull

𓃒	bull
𓃒 ╳𓈖	rabble?

𓃘 Ass

𓃘	ass, donkey

𓃙 Newborn bubalis

𓅨𓅇	wrongdoing
𓅨𓀁𓃭	lament, cry out
𓅨𓀁𓃥	dog
𓅨𓀁𓅀	wrongdoing, injustice
𓅨𓀁𓏱	be boat-less, strand, leave boat-less, helpless, deprived
𓅨𓀁𓅨𓀁𓃥	Dog
𓅨𓀁𓏥𓅀𓏤𓏤𓏤	wrongdoing
𓅨𓀁𓏥𓉐	house, sanctuary, quarter (of town), public places
𓅨𓀁𓄿	inherit from (someone)
𓅨𓂻	

90

reward

troops

leg (of beef)

heir

heirs

thigh, leg (of beef)

ring

heiress

inheritance, heritage

pillared hall

sanctuary

B12   conceive (a child), become pregnant

conceive, become pregnant

beans

load

moisten, water (field-plots), inject, flood

moisten

inundation

balance (of scales)

U91   balance

gruel

corruption

ground, floor, flooring

separate (x from y)

separation

kindly disposed, pleasant

Ram

ram

Pig

pig

E14b Y1v train (troops)

Canine recumbent (the God Anubis)

royal child

a priest

make secret, mysterious, make inaccessible, secret, confidential matter, (religious) mystery, problem

Jackal

dignitary, senior (in titles)

jackal

senior warden of Nekhen

Animal of the God Seth recumbent

Seth (god)

Lion

lion

92

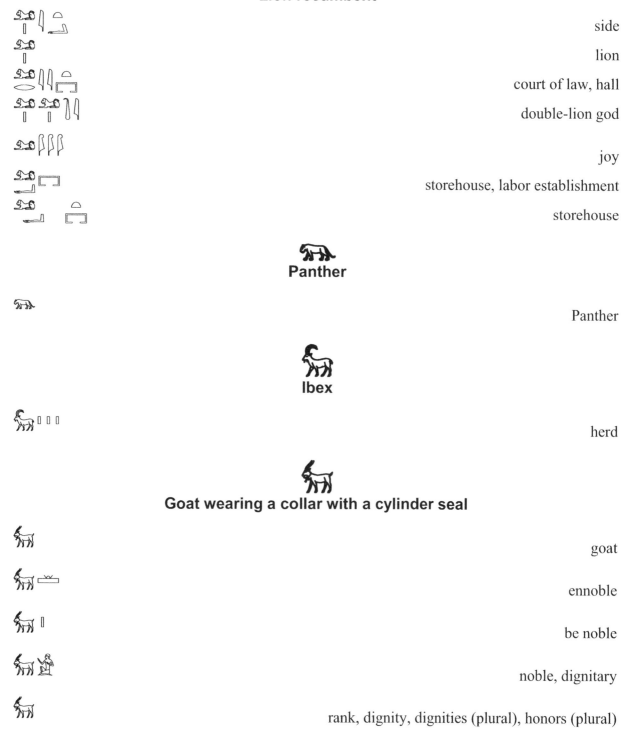

Lion recumbent

	side
	lion
	court of law, hall
	double-lion god
	joy
	storehouse, labor establishment
	storehouse

Panther

	Panther

Ibex

	herd

Goat wearing a collar with a cylinder seal

	goat
	ennoble
	be noble
	noble, dignitary
	rank, dignity, dignities (plural), honors (plural)

Hare

	be stripped off (of branches of trees)

𓄿	be stripped off (of branches)
𓄿	fault, blame
𓄿	open, open up, rip open
𓄿	open up (quarry etc)
𓄿	Hare
𓄿	hasten, hurry, pass by, pass away
𓄿	hasten, hurry, pass by, pass away, neglect
𓄿	baldness (of eyebrows)
𓄿	foetus
𓄿 390	travel about
𓄿	sway to and fro, nod, travel about, move about, traverse
𓄿	staff (of workers)
𓄿	hour
𓄿	duty, service
𓄿	priesthood
𓄿	hour-watcher, astronomer
𓄿	hour watcher, astronomer
𓄿	flower
𓄿	triumph
𓄿	be joyful
𓄿	be frivolous
𓄿	fattened ox?
𓄿	eat
𓄿	true being, reality
𓄿	true being, reality
𓄿	be, exist
𓄿	Onnophris
𓄿	Onnophris (a name of Osiris)
𓄿	indeed, really

94

open the sight of, be skilled, clear vision, public appearance

be clothed, don (clothing), assume (ones body), dress (a vase)

roll of cloth

be clothed (in)

mummy-cloth?

clothing

jackal

sledge

that

neglect

sanctuary (in temple)

hollow, depression

hold (of ship)

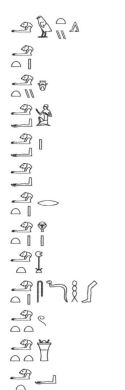

Forepart of lion

the foremost

forehead, forepart (of animal), prow (of ship), vanguard (of army)

heart, central chest, thought

local prince, nomarch, mayor

the finest of

beginning

starting with

forehead

herdsman

shinbone

bow-warp (of ship)

unguent

local princess, female nomarch, mayoress

Head of bubalis

be conversant (with)

(medical) prescription

Forepart of bubalis. Var. of F5.

be wise

Head of ram

majesty, respect

ram-headed figure (of Amun)

Forepart of ram. Var. of F7

majesty, respect

Head of leopard

(physical) strength, power (of god, king)

Head of bull on a long neck

know

Head and neck of canine

powerful

strong

strong, powerful, wealthy, influential, rich (in years)

wealthy man

oar

strength, power

	neck

Ox horns

	judge (contestants, petitioners)
	open, open up, inaugurate, part, separate, divide, judge, discern, distinguish, take
	cut off
	decision
	Wepwawet
	except
	household, crowd
	message, business, mission, behest, task, news?
	business, mission
	task
	inventory, schedule
	message
	except
	messenger, agent, commissioner, bystander
	except, but
	specify it (details of it)
	strew, scatter
	top knot (of hair)
	judgment
	horns, top, brow, top-knot, head-dress, zenith
	the space between anus and genitals
	center of torso (vertical)
	farthest South

Horn

	horn
	breakfast

| | horn (of animal) |

Horn + vase pouring liquid

	impurity
	offerings
	breakfast

Elephant tusk

	tooth
	calf
	Behdet (town in the Delta), Edfu (in Upper Egypt)
	He of Behdet (the winged Sun Disk)
	food
	roar (of lion)
	armpit
	funerary meal
	altar

Tongue

	Overseer of weavers
	Overseer of weavers
F51b	tongue
	lap up, lick
	type of bread

Ear

	proxy
	deputy
	serve as lieutenant-commander
	deputy

𓄿𓏤	ear
𓂧𓅭𓁹	paint (eyes, body)
𓂧𓅭𓁹	eye-paint
𓂧	hear (voice etc), hear of something), listen (to), obey, understand, judge, satisfy (conditions)
𓂧𓅓	hear (voice etc), hear of (something), listen (to), obey, understand, judge, satisfy (conditions)
𓂧𓅓𓏲𓀀	judge, hearers
𓂧𓅓�𓀀	servant
𓈖𓏤𓀀	deputy
𓂧𓐎	share out
𓂧𓏤	leaf

Hindquarters of lion

𓄟	reach (a person or place), attain (wealth), finish (doing something)
𓄟	reach, attain, finish, end by, attack, contest, spear, hit, surround, caught
𓄟𓅓𓏭𓏤	hinder parts, hind quarters
𓄟𓅓𓏭𓅓𓈖	end
𓄟𓏥𓏤	hinder-parts, hind-quarters, back (of jaw, house etc)
𓄟𓅓𓏥𓏭𓏤𓏤	stern-warp (of ship)
𓄟𓏭𓏤	rectum
𓄟𓄟𓏭𓏭	marshlands
𓄟𓅭𓅭𓏤𓏥	the far north
𓄟𓅭𓅭𓏤𓏥𓅭	northward to
𓄟𓏭	(physical) strength, power (of god, king)
𓄟𓏤𓏤	ending at
𓄟	god of Magic

99

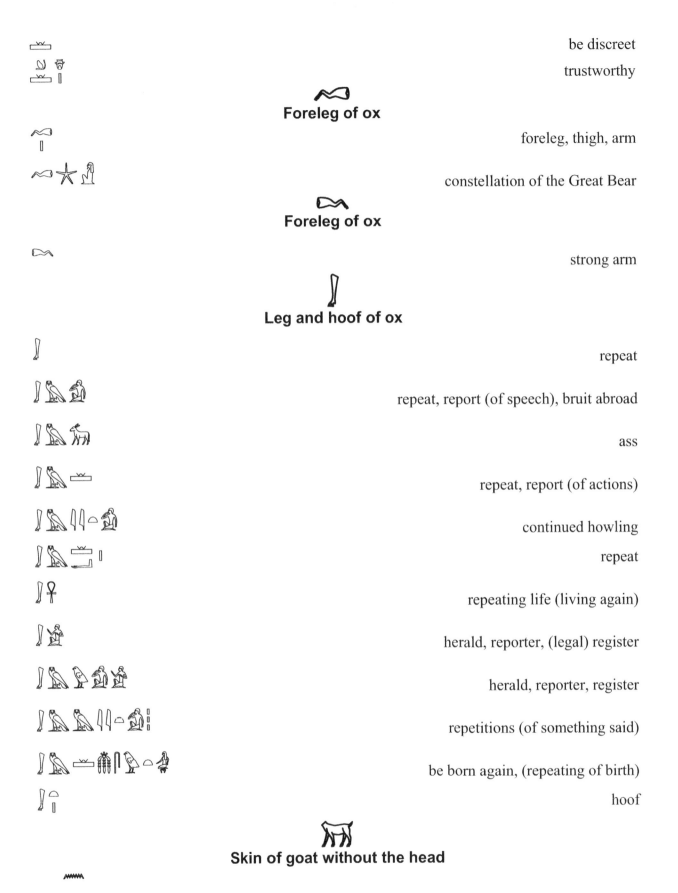

be discreet

trustworthy

Foreleg of ox

foreleg, thigh, arm

constellation of the Great Bear

Foreleg of ox

strong arm

Leg and hoof of ox

repeat

repeat, report (of speech), bruit abroad

ass

repeat, report (of actions)

continued howling

repeat

repeating life (living again)

herald, reporter, (legal) register

herald, reporter, register

repetitions (of something said)

be born again, (repeating of birth)

hoof

Skin of goat without the head

𓃀𓈖𓂝	approach
𓃀𓈖𓏏	tent
𓃀𓈖𓊖	Residence
𓃀𓅓𓈖𓈖𓈖	brook
𓃀𓅓𓇯	interior, home, abode, Residence
𓃀𓏏𓂝	embrace
𓃀𓅓𓅆𓀀𓏥	skin-clad people
𓃀𓆰𓅆𓈖𓈖𓏤	basin (for irrigation)?
𓃀𓈖𓄛	hide, skin
𓃀𓈖𓉐	burial chamber? (of tomb)

Cowskin

𓄛𓂟𓂟	go forth
𓄛	leather, hide

Cowskin

𓄜	dappled (of calf)
𓄜𓏭	many colored of plumage (of Solar Horus)

Skin pierced by an arrow

𓄟𓂝	impregnate (female), beget, ejaculate
𓄟𓂝𓏭𓈖	pour (water)
𓄟𓂝𓁹	stare, stare at
𓄟𓂝𓅅𓀀𓏥	Asiatics
𓄟𓂝𓏭𓂝𓏥	seed, posterity

101

	target
	arrow, dart
	rays (of sun)
	shooting pains
	ground
	drag

Water-skin

	vulva
	artificial lake
	mortar (for pounding drugs)
	poultice
	read, read aloud, recite
	take away, remove, cut out, dig (lake), rescue, salvage (boat)
	suckle, educate
	ditch
	rubble
	Used to emphasize a preceding word or phrase
	waterfowl
	skin, water-skin
	plot (of land)
	raft
	plot (of land)
	disturb
	public proclamation
	pomegranate wine
	disturbance
	protuberance on standard (of Wepwaret)

R62[c]

Crocodilopolis

dough

He of Crocodilopolis

Three skins tied together

 child

calf

surely, indeed

bouquet

nostril

be born

bear, give birth, calve (of gazelle), lay (of bird), be born

bear, give birth

spermatic cord

waterfowl

a festival

supper

the First Mesyt (a Festival)

the First Mesyt (a Festival)

prospector?

type of bread

children, offspring, young (of animals)

 birth

 children, offspring

	birthday of Isis
	birthday of Osiris
	girl child
	turn (to)
	turn (to), serve (someone), deal (with)
$_{E92}{}^{c}$	serve (someone)
	spin?, plait?
	harpooner
	rotate, turn backwards, turn away
	abode (of gods)
	necropolis
$d68$	birth-place
	bearing-stool?, birth-place?
	Meskhenet (goddess of birth)
	abode (of gods)
	young (boys) of the tomb
	adze (used in Opening-of-the-mouth)
	constellation of the Plough
3330	totter
	tunic
	shirt of mail
	mail-shirt
	leather
	the Milky-Way?
	the Milky Way

𓄿	skin, leather, animal hide
𓄿	slander?
𓄿 š107	armlet
𓄿	mother
𓄿	apron of fox-skins
𓄿	Sort of liquid
𓄿	offspring
𓄿	offspring
𓄿	portable shrine
𓄿	rival
𓄿	black eye-paint
𓄿	black eye paint
𓄿	haunch, thigh
𓄿	rival
𓄿	dislike, hate
𓄿	ear
𓄿	what is hateful (of conduct)

Belly of a mammal

	measure, allowance (of milk)
	approach
	shave
	barber
	navel-string, navel
	chew
	figures (inlaid in metal)

fat

approach ⸢

bend (the back in respect)

be blistered

child

calf (of gazelle)

childhood

children

children

be unanointed

type of spice

weak, feeble, humble (of rank), mean (of conduct), vile (of enemies, speech))

vile (of enemies)

coward

wrongdoing

dispel

incompetent

cowardice, impurity

be adorned

coiffeur

be injured

the injured Eye (of Horus)

insignia

ornaments

panoply, insignia, ornaments

panoply, insignia

coiffeuse, concubine

belly (of gods or men)

𓄹𓐍𓏏𓏏	belly, womb, body, sole (of foot)
𓄹𓐍𓏏𓀀𓏥	body (of gods or man), generation, people
𓄹𓐍𓏏𓏥	people
𓄹𓐍𓏏𓄹	bellies, wombs, bodies
𓄹𓐍𓂡𓀒	overthrow
𓄹𓐍𓂝𓏤	pluck (plants), to prey on
𓄹𓐍𓂡𓀀	kill
𓄹𓐍𓏏𓂻	rescue?
𓄹𓐍𓏏𓅂	be in discomfort

Heart

𓄣

𓄣𓏏	heart, mind, understanding, intelligence, will, desire, mood, wish
𓄣𓏏𓂧𓂡𓈗	weak in action

Heart and windpipe

𓄥

𓄤	good, beautiful etc......
𓄤𓂸	penis
𓄤𓆑𓂋	beautiful, fair, kindly (of face), good / fine / goodly (quality)
𓄤𓆓	crown of Upper Egypt
𓄤𓏏	beauty, good, kindness, goodness, happiness, good fortune
𓄤𓏏 Y1v	goodness
𓄤𓆑𓏏𓏏𓏤	end, bottom
𓄤𓆑𓏏𓏏𓃭	tiller-rope
𓄤𓏏𓏏𓏤	end, bottom, low
𓄤𓆑𓏏𓏏𓏤	down to
𓄤𓏤𓅡	ground level, base

107

	beauty, goodness, young people (Book of the Dead)
	end, back part (of building)
	deficiency
	young men (of army), recruits
	goodness
	fair women
	not
	not, there is not
	it is well with
	not
	diadem
	pleasing
	crown of Upper Egypt
	good things
	cattle
	good things, good, what is good, kindness
	Nefertum (the lotus god)

Lung and windpipe

	priest (who clothed the god)
	unite, join (a company), associate (with), arrive (in), partake (of), make ready (a boat),
	unite, join (a company), associate (with), arrive (in), partake (of)
	scalp, side
	companion, confederate
	(royal) consort

𓂝𓅃𓏭𓎱	(royal) consort
𓂝𓅃𓏭𓎱𓀀𓀂𓏥	association, confederacy
𓂝𓅃𓅱𓏤𓏥	branches (of tree)
𓂝𓅃𓏏	twilight
𓏭𓏭𓏭	lungs?
𓏤𓈖𓎱	union
𓂝𓅃𓈖𓏭	unite (the land), land (at), be interred (in), interment
𓂝𓅃𓈖𓏤𓏰	land (at)
𓏤𓎱𓊨𓊖	an offering
𓏤𓎱𓈖	a textile fabric

Backbone, with marrow and ribs

𓄹𓎱	Back, spine (of man, animal) : Middle (of river, lake)
F37^c 𓎱𓏪𓏏𓏏	Ennead (of gods)
F37^c 𓇋𓅃𓆙𓏤𓏥	herb

F39^c
Var. of F39

F39^c 𓏤	honor, veneration
F39^c 𓏤	spinal cord
F39^c 𓏭𓏭𓅃 351^{c}𓏤	revered ones (of the aged living)
F39^c 𓊨𓏭𓏭𓎱	revered one (of dead women)
F39^c 𓎱𓏤	honor

Var. of F39, flow of marrow at both ends

𓄿𓅃	Long (time, space) : Length (time, space)
𓄿𓏌	Death : Harm, injury

𓂝 𓄿𓏺𓏺𓀜	To extend (arms) : To present-to hand out (administration) : To arouse : To announce
𓂝 𓄿𓀜	Do violence
𓂝 𓄿 𓌪	Long-knife
𓂝 𓄿 𓏭	Gift, donation (of food), offering
𓂝 𓇾	Length (time), duration
𓂝 𓄿 𓏛 𓊫 𓏥	Gift, present (as recognition)

Ribs (of beef)

𓄹 𓏛 𓏥	slaughtering, terror

Rib

𓄽 𓀜	appeal to, petition (someone), make petition
𓄽 𓂝	arrive, reach, come
𓇋𓇋 𓄽	rib
𓄽 𓅡 𓀜 𓀜	petitioner
𓄽 𓅡 𓀜 𓏛𓏥	petitions
𓄽 𓂧 𓀜	petition
𓄽 𓂧 𓀜	petitioner

Femur or tibia

𓄸 𓇾 𓏥 𓇾	inheritance, heritage
𓄸 𓅆	reward
𓄸 𓇾	representative

Uterus of heifer

𓄺 𓇾 𓃒	cow
𓄺 F51b	womb, vulva, uterus

Intestine

𓄼 𓈖	offer (to)

110

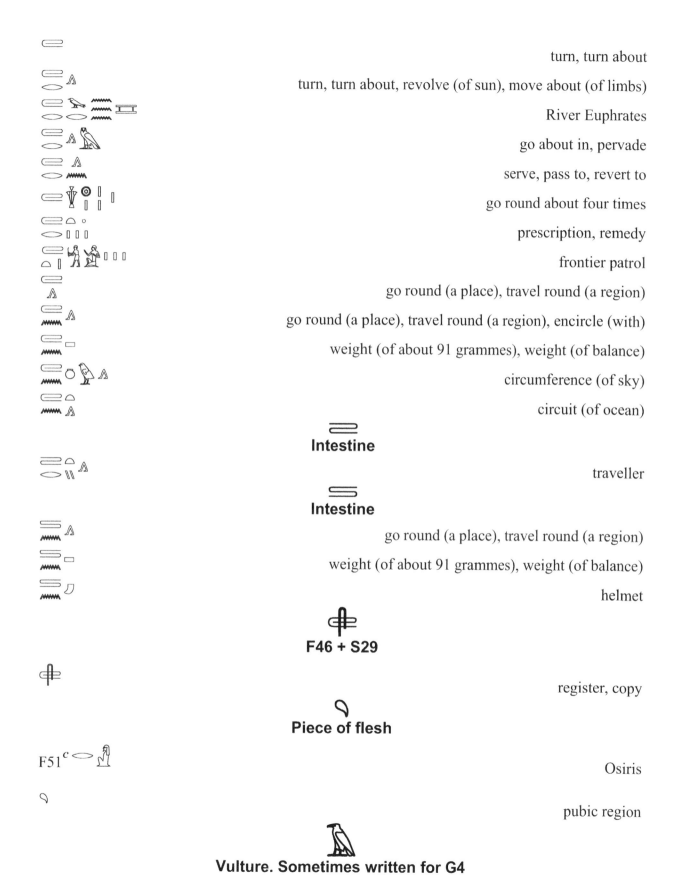

turn, turn about

turn, turn about, revolve (of sun), move about (of limbs)

River Euphrates

go about in, pervade

serve, pass to, revert to

go round about four times

prescription, remedy

frontier patrol

go round (a place), travel round (a region)

go round (a place), travel round (a region), encircle (with)

weight (of about 91 grammes), weight (of balance)

circumference (of sky)

circuit (of ocean)

Intestine

traveller

Intestine

go round (a place), travel round (a region)

weight (of about 91 grammes), weight (of balance)

helmet

F46 + S29

register, copy

Piece of flesh

F51

Osiris

pubic region

Vulture. Sometimes written for G4

	Meaning
𓄿	Used to emphasize a preceding word or phrase
	To tread a place
	Vulture : Bird (in general)
	Mound of ruins
	Ate ; a Nubian chieftain
	Atmospheric phenomenon (windy?)
	Viscera
	Blanch
	Container (for papyri)
	Oppression
	Death : Harm, injury
	To extend (arms) : To present-to hand out (administration) : To arouse : To announce
	Unite, mix, link : Join, mingle : Merge : Engage : Be filled
	swine, pigs
	rush forward
	duck, bird
	gluttony
	Glutton
	boil
	part of animal leg
	burn, burn up
	mix
	a perching bird

 𓄿𓄿�𓂝	ramus (of jaw), fork (of bone), hinged bone
 𓄿𓄿𓄿𓂝	seize, grasp, attack
 𓄿𓄿𓄿𓂺𓏥	gripings (medical)
 𓄿𓄿𓄿𓂝	grasp, fist
 𓄿𓇋𓏲𓏥	falsehood
 𓄿𓇋𓏲𓂡	club, mace, wield the Ams
 𓄿𓏏𓀜	drive away, oppress
 𓄿𓏏𓏭𓏏𓏌	staff
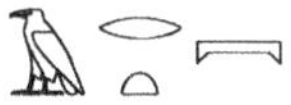 𓄿𓏏𓏏	heaven, sky
 𓄿𓊪𓏭𓂻	descend
 𓄿𓊪𓅡𓅯	Misery, trouble : Injury, illness : Pain
 𓄿𓊪𓅡𓀢	sufferer
 𓄿𓊪𓏏𓅩𓏥	sorrow
 𓄿𓊪𓏏𓅯	quiver, palpitate, be weak
 𓄿�axh𓏥	type of bread
 𓄿�axh𓏭𓈖𓈖𓈖	wave (flood)
 𓄿�axh𓂸𓉔𓊖	tomb-shaft
 𓄿�axh𓊖	field, arable land, earth, mound
 𓄿𓇳𓆰	papyrus thicket
 𓄿𓇳	spirit
 𓄿𓇳𓇰	the spirit-state
 𓄿𓇳𓄿𓇳𓆰	grow green
 𓄿𓇳𓄿𓂋𓏥	spars (of ship)?
 𓄿𓇳𓄿𓇳𓇼𓇼𓇼	stars

[hieroglyphs]	sunlight, sunshine
[hieroglyphs]	Chemmis
[hieroglyphs]	fever (of appetite)?
[hieroglyphs]	be fiery
[hieroglyphs]	Inundation-season
[hieroglyphs]	horizon-dweller
[hieroglyphs]	scratch, scrape, carve, engrave
[hieroglyphs]	scratch, scar
[hieroglyphs]	swallow
[hieroglyphs]	bald, viscera
[hieroglyphs]	bald-headed vulture
[hieroglyphs]	hurry, flow fast, hasten, overtake, quickly
[hieroglyphs]	a type of cake, bread
[hieroglyphs]	testicles
[hieroglyphs]	fierce, glowing (of radiance)
[hieroglyphs]	fierce, glowing (of radiance)
[hieroglyphs]	flames
[hieroglyphs]	heaven, sky
[hieroglyphs]	reap
[hieroglyphs]	sickle
[hieroglyphs]	Isis
[hieroglyphs]	a type of drink
[hieroglyphs]	roast, roast meat, a roast
[hieroglyphs]	roast joint

	perish, come to grief
	ruin, misfortune
t73	battle-axe
	a type of garment
	a star
	be bent (of elbow)
E128	Aker, the earth, earth-gods
	earth-gods
	The striking-power
	moment, instant, time in general
	coffer
	Load, cargo
	Load, cargo
F7d	be crowned
	Atef crown
B5d	To nurse
	nurse
	bed
	To load (ships etc...) : To be heavy laden (with trouble)
	decay
	quiver, palpitate
	be savage, be aggressive, be angry, attack, anger
	aggressor
	prepare (a sleeping place)
t30^c	bind (the sacrifice)
	bald

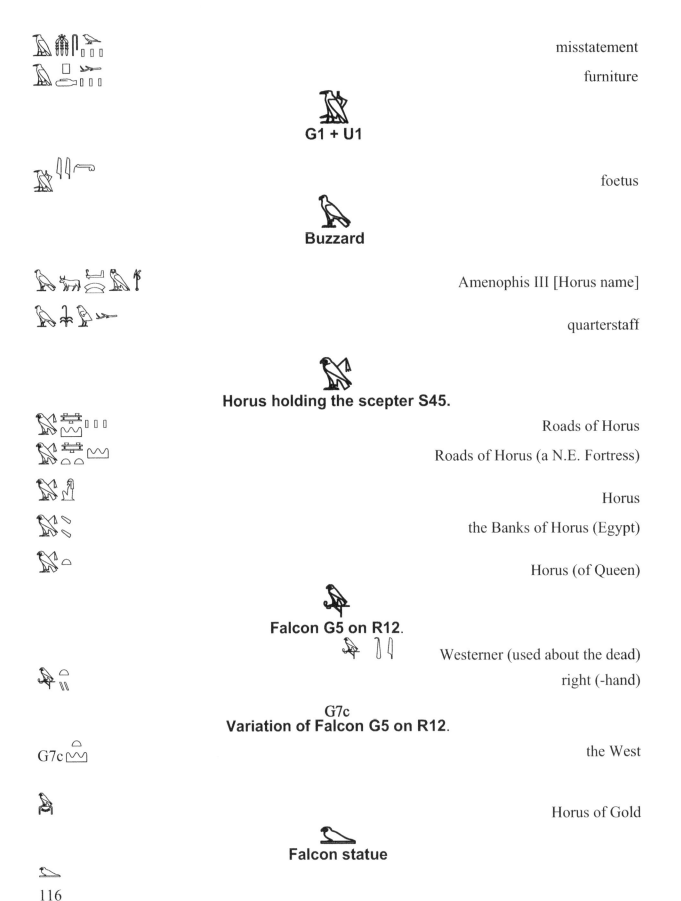

misstatement

furniture

G1 + U1

foetus

Buzzard

Amenophis III [Horus name]

quarterstaff

Horus holding the scepter S45.

Roads of Horus

Roads of Horus (a N.E. Fortress)

Horus

the Banks of Horus (Egypt)

Horus (of Queen)

Falcon G5 on R12.

Westerner (used about the dead)

right (-hand)

G7c
Variation of Falcon G5 on R12.

G7c

the West

Horus of Gold

Falcon statue

116

⌓ breast

Vulture

mother

weight

placenta

G14 and I12 on V30

The Two Ladies (Nekhbet and Edjoyet)

Owl

overseer

those of later times, posterity

member of the administration

caravan leader

Overseer of horn, hoof, feather and scale (livestock)

district-superintendent

steward

overseer of herds

member of the bodyguard

forewoman (of gang)

with, by means of, from, out of, as, namely, when, as, though, together with

do not

(not translated)

behold

	ladder
	come!
	spines
	waters
	do not
	liver
	seed-corn
	seed corn of emmer?
	(speak) boastfully
	oar
	harpoon
	pendant
	seeing that
	day bark (of sun god)
	day-bark (of sun god)
	fortunate, successful, flourishing
	success
	fortunate, successful
	tomb, cenotaph (above ground level)
	exactly
	Brave, bold
	type of boat
	Muu class of Ritual dancers
	(palace) guard
	garrison, (palace) guard, protector (of poor)
	unhindered, with free access

𓅓𓏏𓀠	mother
𓅓𓏭	in the presence of, in front of, in front, formerly
𓅓𓏭𓏤	in the presence of
𓅓𓂝𓀀	no
𓅓𓂝𓏭𓏤𓀀	no
𓅓𓂝𓏏	all together
𓅓𓆷	turquoise
𓅓𓅓	among, therein
𓅓𓂭𓏤	truly
𓅓𓂝𓏤	newly, anew
𓅓𓏥	as if
𓅓𓏥	likewise
𓅓𓅓	giraffe
𓅓𓈖	at the fixed rate of
𓅓𓈖𓇳	daily
𓅓𓈖𓀀	in order that
𓅓𓈖𓀀	unwillingly
𓅓𓈖	awry
𓅓𓈖	wrongfully
𓅓𓈖𓀀	take to yourself
𓅓𓈖	Syrian warrior
𓅓𓈖	absent from
𓅓𓈖	chariot
𓅓𓈖	let not
𓅓𓈖	in the neighborhood of

𓄿𓍿𓅱𓏤	the heart is forgetful (has defective action)
𓄿𓍿...	humbly
𓄿𓍿𓂜𓃾	milch cow
𓄿𓍿	be forgetful, neglectful
𓄿𓍿𓏏	be forgetful, neglectful (of)
𓄿𓍿	coffer
𓄿𓍿	milk jar
𓄿𓍿𓂜𓏭	forgetfulness, negligence
𓄿𓍿	negligence (of poor heart action)
𓄿𓆓	back of the head
𓄿𓆓	in excess of
𓄿𓆓	in addition to, except
𓄿	in front of, before
𓄿	drown
𓄿 396	swim, launch (a vessel)
𓄿	overflow (of Nile)
𓄿	guardian
𓄿	coil (of serpents)
𓄿	partner?
𓄿	above
𓄿	above, in advance of
𓄿	in readiness for
𓄿	with ingenious mind
𓄿	(coming) to meet him
𓄿	in very good peace (a greeting)
𓄿	respect (someone), match, equal, adjust, counterpoise, make level

120

[hieroglyphs]	match, equal, adjust, counterpoise, make level
[hieroglyphs]	make fast, bind
[hieroglyphs]	like in disposition to
[hieroglyphs]	shed
[hieroglyphs]	balance
[hieroglyphs]	in the absence of, without
[hieroglyphs]	carnelian?, jasper?
[hieroglyphs]	face, upper part of face
[hieroglyphs]	indoors
[hieroglyphs]	low-lying land
[hieroglyphs]	business
[hieroglyphs]	peg (to secure net)
[hieroglyphs]	at the approach of (in meeting)
[hieroglyphs]	into, as one thing, altogether
[hieroglyphs]	an ornament (of gold)
[hieroglyphs] V97	a closed (or) sealed receptacle
[hieroglyphs]	backwards
[hieroglyphs]	downstream
[hieroglyphs]	a boat
[hieroglyphs]	within, at, in the house of
[hieroglyphs]	within
[hieroglyphs]	ferry boat
[hieroglyphs]	ferryman
[hieroglyphs]	low lying land
[hieroglyphs]	storehouse, barn
[hieroglyphs]	a low place

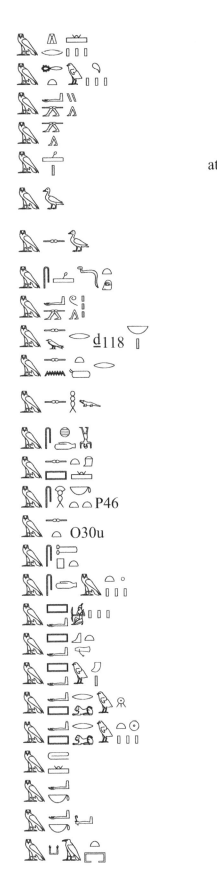

dealings, business, ordinance, arrangement (of building)

intestines, colon

bring, present, bring away booty, extend (hand), take (aim)

bring, present (to), bring away booty, extend (hand), take (aim)

at the back of, following after, having charge of, wearing (sandals)

bring, present (to), bring away booty, extend (hand),, take aim

bring, present (to), bring away booty, extend (hand), take aim

nostril

carriers, bearers

drinking bowl

in the likeness of, in accordance with

crocodile

head downwards

framework? (of chariot)

night-bark (of sun god)

a staff

portable shrine

black eye paint

soldiers, army, infantry, gang (of workmen)

shoulder blade

sword

evening

evening meal

doubled

behold

protector

support, pedestal

(glyph) O230 (glyph)	support, pedestal
(glyph)	guard, protect, look after (horse)
(glyph)	guard, protect
(glyph)	indeed
(glyph)	back of the head
(glyph)	back of the head
(glyph)	guarded and protected
(glyph) W78^c	Used to emphasize a preceding word or phrase
(glyph) R88^c	scepter
(glyph)	bowing
(glyph)	proper station (for standing)
(glyph)	protection, correct position (of limbs), proper station (for standing)
(glyph) F51^b	correct position (of limbs)
(glyph)	thoracic spine
(glyph)	protector, guardian
(glyph)	quietly
(glyph)	headlong (of flight), prostrate
(glyph)	die, perish, death
(glyph)	dead man
(glyph)	die, perish (of ship), death
(glyph)	seed, progeny
(glyph)	from.......down to
(glyph)	sheikh
(glyph)	reward
(glyph)	dead woman
(glyph)	dead woman
(glyph)	penis

𓅂𓃒𓅂𓀀	flout, vex
𓅂𓃒𓅂𓀀𓏤𓏤	disagree with someone
𓅂𓂝𓅪𓎰	land-heritage?
𓅂𓎡𓈘𓃥	arena
𓅂𓎡𓈘𓌕	road, way
𓅂𓎡𓈘𓏏𓅯𓌕	course
𓅂𓎡𓈘𓌳	Mitanni
𓅂𓎡𓈘𓅯𓌕	road, way, course
𓅂𓌆𓈖	(the land was) in drought
𓅂𓎿𓈘𓂻	straight on
𓅂𓎡𓏤𓏛	sharp (of knife), acute (of vision), forceful (of character)
𓅂𓎡𓏤𓏛𓂋	firm-planted (of foot)
𓅂𓎡𓏤𓏛𓂝	spiteful
𓅓𓊨𓅓𓌳	Medja
𓅓𓊨𓅓𓀀𓏤𓏤𓏤	Medjay, Police
𓅓𓊨𓂝𓂝𓎡	expel (foes)
𓅓𓊨𓂋𓎱𓅯	drainer (for bilge?)
𓅓𓊨𓅂𓎱	bailer (of boat)
𓅓𓊨𓎱	letter, dispatch
𓅓𓊨𓎱𓏏	chisel
𓅓𓏤𓎱𓏏𓏏	bonds
𓅓𓐍𓎱𓍿	shut out (storms), wall in (treasure)
𓅓𓏤𓎱𓍱	fillet
𓅓𓊨𓎱𓍱𓂋	hew (timber), build (ships)
𓅓𓈖𓌳𓏤𓏤𓏤 𓊌𓏤𓏤	in private

𓄿𓏲𓂧𓏥	depth
𓄿𓏲𓂧 W1ᵇ	oil
𓄿𓏲𓂧	byre
𓄿𓏲𓂧	chisel (used in Opening-of-the-mouth ceremony)
𓄿𓂡 3ᶜ24	press hard on, hit, strike (the mouth in funerary ritual)
𓄿𓂡 3ᶜ24	be loyal, obedient to
𓅭𓏏𓀾	sacred image
𓄿𓇋𓇋𓈖	in the face of, within, out of
𓄿𓏤𓀜𓏪	judge, hearers

Sign G17 twice

𓅓𓂝	among, therein
𓅓𓏮𓂝	giraffe

G17 + D36

𓅓𓏭𓅱𓈖	semen, seed of man
𓅓𓂋𓂻	march, travels

𓅮
Guinea-fowl

𓅮𓏤𓀢	pray for, prayer
𓅮𓏤𓂋𓂡	harness, yoke, appoint, combine (attributes), provide, requisition
𓅮𓏤𓂋𓎡	bud (of lotus plant)
𓅮𓏤𓂋𓂝	bud (of lotus)
𓅮𓏤𓇳𓏤𓏌𓏥	(sesame) oil
𓅮𓏤𓇳	eternity, for ever

prayer

Hoopoe

brick, ingot, slab (of metal)

target

Lapwing

subjects, common folk, mankind

Crested Ibis

spirit

be a spirit, become a spirit, glorious, splendid, beneficial, useful, profitable, fame

the spirit-state

still-room?

sunlight, sunshine

power (of god), mastery (over work)

eye (of god)

uraes-serpent

flame

what is good, profitable, useful

horizon, (tomb (of king)

horizon-dweller

Sacred ibis on standard

a type of herb

Thoth (god)

festival of Thoth

126

festival of Thoth

Flamingo

wrath

the Red Land, desert

the Red Crown

red pot

Black Ibis

type of wine

found destroyed

weakness

mourning

weakness

black ibis

catch sight of, espy, look (at)

far-sighted, perspicacious

hawk

candle

plaited hair

smash (boxes), tear up (books), break (of trees)

smash (boxes)

Jabiru

possess a soul, be a soul

soul, BA

	soul, BA
	Bahu: a region (originally west of Egypt, later on, to the East)
	jar
	moringa oil
	tree (moringa arabica)
	bright
	servant
	work, work (for someone), pay taxes, work (horses), carry out (a task), enslave
	work, task
	work, task, workmanship, execution (of a design), revenues, taxes, impost, wages
	a cake
	maidservant
	work, task, works (of craftsmanship), labor (of captives), revenues, taxes
	revenues, taxes
	symbol of Hathor
	a loaf
	bed (of gourds etc....)

Three jabirus

	souls (of dead)
	power

Heron on a perch

	abundance
	inundated land

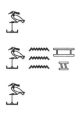

inundated land

basin (for irrigation)

inundation, flood

Cormorant

enter (into)

enter, charge, come in, have the entree, set (of sun), run aground, be noticed

become intimate

intimate friend

intimate friend

female servant

provisions, food

friends

loaves, provisions, food, income, revenue

come in and go out, come and go

one over-familiar in speech?

wedding

Fork tailed swallow

swallow (bird)

great one, magnate, chief, ruler (of foreign land)

portion (of meat)

portion of meat

insolent

door posts

cloth for straining liquids

Greatest of Seers

roofing, awnings

[hieroglyphs]	magnate of the Tens of Upper Egypt
[hieroglyphs] M27	magnate of the Tens of Upper Egypt
[hieroglyphs] M27	magnate of the Tens of Upper Egypt
[hieroglyphs]	magnate of the Tens of Upper Egypt
[hieroglyphs]	great, much, many, eldest, important
[hieroglyphs]	chariot, wagon
[hieroglyphs]	chariot
[hieroglyphs]	crown
[hieroglyphs]	anoint Someone with....), smear on
[hieroglyphs]	ointment
[hieroglyphs]	anoint (someone with....), smear on
[hieroglyphs]	anointer
[hieroglyphs]	Great of Magic
[hieroglyphs]	ointment
[hieroglyphs]	Greatest of the Master Craftsmen
[hieroglyphs]	Master Craftsman
[hieroglyphs]	head-rest
[hieroglyphs]	master physician
[hieroglyphs] Q43	wake, be awake
[hieroglyphs]	watcher, sentry
[hieroglyphs]	greatness (of rank), what is important, very
[hieroglyphs]	Great One (of uraeus, of goddess)
[hieroglyphs]	Crown of Upper Egypt
[hieroglyphs]	Crown of Lower Egypt
[hieroglyphs]	sacred cow
[hieroglyphs] P13	sacred bark
[hieroglyphs]	Great of Magic (of uraeus)
[hieroglyphs]	Great of Magic (of crowns)

𓅡𓏲 𓏼	Greatest of the Five
𓄿𓏏𓀉𓅪	weariness
𓄿𓏏𓀉𓅬	be weary, grow weary, tire
𓄿𓆓ḏ81	be weary, grow weary, tire, die

Sparrow

𓅪	little / small (of size), dim (of eyes), dull (of ears), poor (of appetite)
𓅪	little, meager, younger, junior, short

Goose

𓆭𓃀𓀭	Geb (the Earth god)

Pintail duck

𓅬	duck, bird
𓅬𓏤	fly
𓅬	fatten
𓅬𓆛	catch (of fish and fowl)
𓅬𓀔	son
𓅬𓏤𓆙	maggot
𓅬𓏠𓏤𓏼	guards
𓅬𓏤𓄜𓀀	a son who loves (ritual impersonator of Horus)
𓅬𓇳	son of Re
𓅬𓏏𓁐	daughter
𓅬𓏏𓆙	snake
𓅬𓅬𓆤𓆤𓏏𓀀	the royal twins (Shu and Tefnut)

𓅬𓏤𓃀𓂾𓂾	son of Geb
𓅬𓈖𓏤𓏪	ground, earth, soil, floor
𓅬𓂋𓐠	floor boards, flooring
𓅬𓈎𓅃𓄿	locust
𓅬𓌦	hurry
𓅬𓐖𓏲	egg-laying duck

Goose flying

𓆶𓅆	this, the
𓆶𓅆𓏏	fly, fly up
𓆶𓅆𓏭	he of
𓆶𓅆𓏭𓀀	my
𓆶𓅆𓏭𓎺	yours
𓆶𓅆𓊨𓅆𓊛𓏥	the fleet
𓆶𓂾𓊗	irrigable land
𓆶𓅆𓊨𓏥	offerings
𓆶𓎼𓏭	man of ancient family
𓆶𓎼Z4𓏌	primaeval god
𓆶𓅆𓊖𓏤	men of ancient families
𓆶𓊗𓅃𓅆𓏭	primaeval gods
𓆶𓏌𓌪	be turned upside down, be turned over (of sole of foot)
𓆶𓅆𓏌𓂡	be turned over (of sole of foot)
𓆶𓅆𓏲V102	water pot
𓆶𓊗𓏌	a flat thin cake or biscuit

fine linen

Primaeval time, prehistory

knee-cap

ball or cone (of incense)

results of labor

Goose landing

burden (of illness)

shell (of turtle, of skull), flake (of stone), potsherd

collection, summary, assemblage (of troops), list

gum, resin

reminder, explanation

Fattened duck (?)

fatten

provisions, sustenance, victuals, (deified as) Abundance

Quail chick

come, return

succeed (someone)

property

not

district, region

they, them, their

fillet (of gold)

cauldron

133

𓄿...	Wag festival (a religious festival)
	I, me, my
	I, me
	mummy case
P4^c	sacred bark
	sacred bark for the river
	thrust aside, push away, set aside
	how!
	unique, one only, sole
	curse
	privacy
	soldier
	pure, purify oneself, bathe, cleanse, purification, purity
	bend down, subdue, be bent, curled up
	subdue (nations)
	juniper
	flee, rush forth, fly
	fugitive
	hastiness (of speech)
	flight
	desert-plateau
N11^c	earth-almond?, carob?
	stride briskly
	rise, shine, glitter, appear, overflow, be excessive
	wound

𓅃𓂋𓈖𓇳	eastern, the east
𓅃𓂋𓏏𓊖	be bright
𓅃𓂋𓄹	burn, heat, be scalded
𓅃𓂋𓄺	burn, burning
𓅃𓊪𓏤	open
𓅃𓊪𓏤×	strew, scatter
𓅃𓊪𓋴𓅱𓀭	district of Peker
𓅃𓊪𓋴𓊖	district of Peker (precinct of Osiris at Abydos?)
𓅃𓂧𓅂𓀀	support (a plea)
𓅃𓂧𓅂𓏤	lungs
𓅃𓂧𓅂𓅱𓀀	talk about, discuss, support, talk, subject (of conversation)
𓅃𓄑𓊛	gateway
𓅃𓄑𓊹𓀀𓏥	mass (of men)
𓅃𓄑𓏏𓏥	thick cloth
𓅃𓄑𓏤	thick
𓅃𓄑𓄣𓏤	stout-hearted
𓅃𓄑𓊨	thick wall, thickness
𓅃𓄑𓏭	thick wall
𓅃𓊠𓅂𓊠𓅃𓀀	arrogance?
𓅃𓊠𓂾	escape
𓅃𓊠𓅂𓅾	be undone (of heart)
𓅃𓊠𓅱	escape, miss, fail, be undone, be lacking
𓅃𓊠𓂋×	pierce, hole
𓅃𓊠𓈖𓌗	throw down (fence)
𓅃𓊠𓈖 O118	throw down (fence), fall off (of scab)
𓅃𓊠𓈖𓁶	crown (of head)

failure

hew (stone)

hew (stone), pluck (flowers), cut (crops)

cut (crops)

pluck (flowers)

cauldron

family, kindred, relatives

village

family, kindred

fish

release (someone, something)

loose (fetters)

fishermen, fowlers

disappear (of inscriptions)

cut off (hair)   kill (rebels)

night

fetish of Kos

be foolish, act stupidly

ignorant, incompetent person, fool

hall of columns

column, tent pole

throw off (earth), empty out, shake out (linen), beat (a mat), purge (the body)

seek

column, tent-pole

darkness

be painful, suffer, endure, be patient with

forbearance

crack, chink, small window

(to)saw

neglect

be slack, sluggish, neglect, ignore, sluggishness

sluggard

powerful

ornamental collar

cup

barge

Broad, wide : Extensive : Breadth

barge

pass (fluid), urinate

urinate, pass (fluid)

die out (of a race)

urine

t30c sawdust

be dilapidated, ruin, dilapidation

be dilapidated, ruin

travel freely

travel freely, be unhindered, deal arbitrarily with

137

𓅓𓊪𓈖𓊃𓂻	be unhindered
𓅓𓊪𓈖𓂺	free of hands
𓅓𓄿	be destroyed
𓅓𓄿	fall out, be destroyed, desolate (a place)
𓅓𓏤𓄿𓀀	utter (plaudits), recite (praises)
𓅓𓏤𓄿𓄿𓏴	darkness
𓅓𓏤𓄿	widgeon?
𓅓𓏤𓄿	be helpless?
𓅓𓏤𓀀	eat a morsel
𓅓𓏤𓂻𓀀	chew, eat a morsel
𓅓𓏤𓂾𓀀	answer
𓅓𓏤𓂾𓏴𓀀	answer, answer for (conduct)
𓅓𓏴𓂾𓃒	bull
𓅓𓏤𓂾𓏴	beads
𓅓𓏤𓂾𓄿𓏴𓀀	comforter?
𓅓𓏤𓂾𓏴𓀀	response?
𓅓𓏤𓅓	throat
𓅓𓏤𓅓	prove?, test
𓅓𓏤𓅓	ear of corn
𓅓𓏤𓄿𓄿	jar of metal
𓅓𓏤𓈖	wring the neck (of poultry)
𓅓𓏤𓈖	wring the neck, make an offering (of food and drink)
𓅓𓏤𓂋𓄿	poultry (for table)
𓅓𓏤𓅀	be despoiled

138

dry up, be barren, be despoiled

address (someone), question (someone), assent (to), accused

question (someone)

chew

ribs (of ship)?

ribs (of ship)

talker

jaw

rise (of sun)

triturate (grind to powder)

crush (grain), crushed grain

cut open, gut (fish etc..)

feebleness, weakness, misery

woe

bandage, bind

place of embalming

embalmer, bandager

embalm

bandages, wrappings

flee

fugitive

begetter

beget

raise, lift up, wear, weigh, extol, display, announce

lay an information, report

raise, lift up

wear (crown)

𓅓𓏤𓊽 U39^c Q2^b	raise, lift up (of voice / of crowns in coronation)
𓅓𓏤𓅓𓀢𓆈	accused person
𓅓𓏤𓆓𓀾𓅓	deliver a verdict
𓅓𓏤𓅓𓄿	offspring
𓅓𓏤𓏴	peasant
𓅓𓏤𓏴𓎡	place, put, implant (an obstacle), plant (trees)
𓅓𓏤𓎡𓏤	extend the hand (to do something), press the hand (against)
𓅓𓏤𓅓𓏤	butler, cook
𓅓𓆛𓏤	delay, be sluggish, tardily
𓅓𓆓𓏤	delay
𓅓𓈖 ḏ245	record (royal titulary)
𓅓𓏤𓈖𓎺	install, record (royal titulary)
𓅓𓏤𓈖𓎺	offer (to)
𓅓𓏤𓈖𓌗	be heavy
𓅓𓏤𓈖𓌗𓏤	be heavy, weigh, become difficult
𓅓𓏤𓈖𓌗𓏤	weigh (on someone, of affairs)
𓅓𓏤𓈖𓏤𓅓𓏤	offerings
𓅓𓏤𓈖𓏤	offering
𓅓𓏤𓈖𓌗𓏤	heavy block of stone
𓅓𓏤𓈖𓌗	region
𓅓𓏤𓄿 U50^c	pour out, pour off
𓅓𓏤𓄿𓅓 U50^c 𓎺𓏤	offering
𓅓𓏤𓈖	gall-bladder, gall
𓅓𓌗𓏤	go, set out, proceed, attain (a rank), set (of sun)
𓅓𓌗𓅓𓏤	go, set out, proceed, attain (a rank), set (of sun)
𓅓𓌗𓅓𓏤	hale, uninjured, prosperous
𓉐	storehouse

140

𓄿𓇌□	storehouse
𓄿𓇌š95	pectoral
𓄿𓇌Y1v	remain over (of balance in calculations)
𓄿𓇌𓅿Y1v	be glad
𓄿𓇌𓅿Y1v	may it please you
𓄿𓏭□	mythical abode of Amen-Re
𓄿𓇌𓅿	amulets, protective spell
𓄿𓇌𓅿	well-being, prosperity
𓄿𓇌Y1v	well-being, prosperity
𓄿𓇌□□□	amulets
𓄿𓇌𓅿	go to the horizon (die)
𓄿𓇌𓅿	the uninjured eye of Horus
𓄿	cut off (head)
𓄿	cut off (head)
𓄿	cut (cords), cut off (head), be parted (of lips of wound), cut out (sandals)
𓄿	discern
𓄿	judge
𓄿	judgment, divorce by judgment
𓄿	divorced woman
𓄿	fold over, turn (away from), turn back, revert (to)
𓄿N21ᶜ	turn
𓄿	turn the hand away, desist, compose oneself, turn oneself about
𓄿	flood, inundation
𓄿	wean

141

𓅭𓄿𓏭𓏏   lone (star)

Duckling

𓅭𓏺   pellet

𓅭𓏤𓅆   fledgling (figurative for Child)

𓅭𓏏𓏤   able

𓅭𓄿𓏭𓏭𓂝𓀀   male, man

𓅭𓄿𓏭𓏭𓅭𓏤𓏤𓏤   pellets

𓅭𓄿𓀢   take up, seize, snatch, don (garment), rob, steal, shave, harbor (enemies)

𓅭𓄿𓂤   don (garment)

𓅭𓄿𓏛   book

𓅭𓂝𓂠   bearer

𓅭𓏏𓎿𓏤   sculptor

𓅭𓌳𓏤𓏤𓏤𓏤   weapon bearer

𓅭𓌉   fan bearer

𓅭𓊾   standard bearer

𓅭𓄿𓅆𓏏𓎡   sail

𓅭𓄿𓅆𓎡𓀢   theft, a gathering up (of things)

𓅭𓏭W66   a vessel

𓅭𓅭𓏭𓎯   loan

𓅭𓄿𓆱   foreskin

𓅭𓄿𓅆𓏏𓏤   veil

𓎟   cloak, swaddling-clothes, bandage

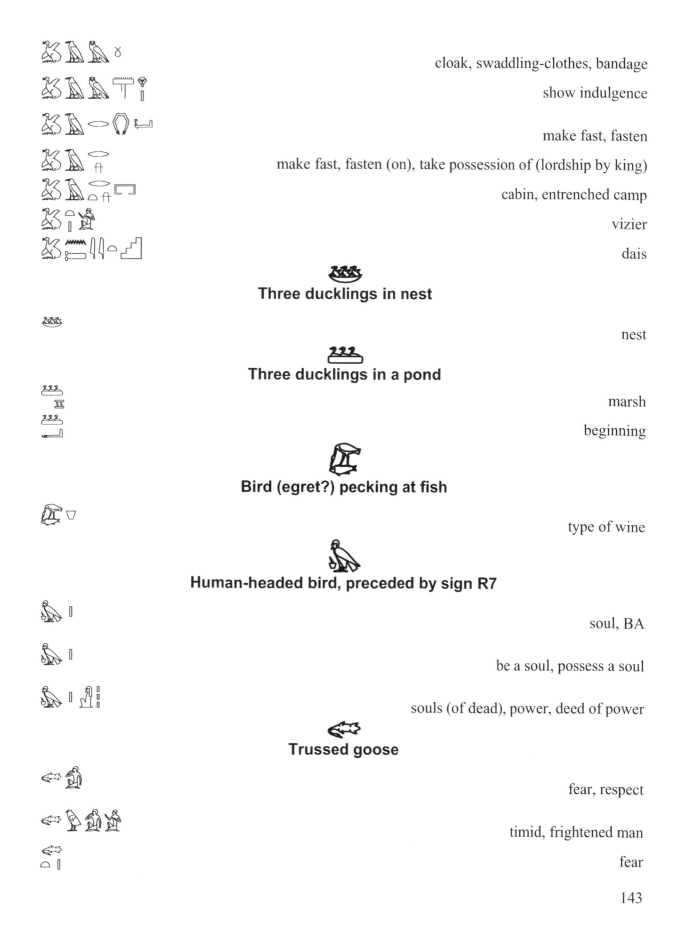

cloak, swaddling-clothes, bandage

show indulgence

make fast, fasten

make fast, fasten (on), take possession of (lordship by king)

cabin, entrenched camp

vizier

dais

Three ducklings in nest

nest

Three ducklings in a pond

marsh

beginning

Bird (egret?) pecking at fish

type of wine

Human-headed bird, preceded by sign R7

soul, BA

be a soul, possess a soul

souls (of dead), power, deed of power

Trussed goose

fear, respect

timid, frightened man

fear

143

Head of pintail duck or goose

duck, bird

Head of a crested bird

jar of metal (as beer measure)

fine linen

Head of spoonbill

a flat thin cake or biscuit

Head of vulture

fear, dread, disturbance?

man, men, mankind, Egyptians

men, mankind

Wing

Used to emphasize a preceding word or phrase

Ostrich feather

Westerners

right-doing, righteousness

pig

ascend

Shu (god of the Air)

be empty, be lacking, be devoid (of), be missing (from)

sun, sunlight

144

𓇋𓍷𓏤	blank papyrus roll
𓇋𓅓𓀜	needy man
𓇋𓏲𓅓	emptiness, default
𓇋𓅓𓈙𓏏𓇳	shadow, shade
𓇋𓅓𓆤𓏥	a type of edible vegetable
𓏭	side
𓇋𓅓𓆰	feather
𓇋𓏏𓀀𓏥	neighbors
𓇋𓏏𓅨	emptiness
𓇋𓅓𓏏𓀀𓏭	trader
𓇋𓅓𓏏𓏥	plumes (as diadem)

Egg

𓎼𓀭	Isis
𓏮	in which is
𓏮𓊽	favorite

Lizard

𓆣	many, numerous, much, plentiful, ordinary, quantity, multitude
𓆣𓄿𓏥	many, numerous, much, plentiful, ordinary, often
𓆣 G229	dove?
𓆣𓄿𓏤𓏥	chatter
𓆣𓏥𓏤𓀁	chatter, be loquacious
𓆣𓄿𓏥𓏲𓀁	noisy
𓆣𓄿𓂝𓀀𓏥	multitude (of people), company (of guests), the many, the masses

multitude (of persons)

the many, the masses

Turtle

tortoise

Crocodile

sovereign

pull together, be wary

Mummy or archaic image of a crocodile

Sobek (crocodile god)

Crocodile-skin with scales

black

total up, amount to, complete, put an end to, pay (to),

herd (of cattle)

conclusion (of book)

Bitter Lakes region

Egypt (The Black Land)

completion, final account

Egyptians

a jar

Tadpole

100,000, a great quantity

Horned viper

he, him, his, it, its

deliver (taxes, tribute)

raise, lift up, carry, support, weigh, present, deliver (taxes, tribute)

weigh

present

1) sail : the wind rose?

portable shrine

weight?

reward

food-supplies?

magnificence, splendor, magnificent

shorn man

be shorn

pubic region

financial interest?

his, its

be weak, faint

recompense?

acute?

a Syrian people

food offerings

snake, (intestinal) worm, become maggoty

snake, become maggoty

(intestinal) worm, become maggoty

nose

147

Beaky, long-nosed

loose, release

loose, release, loosen (of speech), cast off, get rid, destroy

grasp

wig?

cook

a cake

reward, wealth

be wasted (through oppression)

be empty, be wasted (through oppression)

shorn priest

defecate

disgust

leap

obliterate (inscription)

lint

fish

sweat

remove

pluck (flowers), pull up (plants), uproot (trees), pull out (hair), remove

four

fourth

sever, divide, part

sever, divide, part, waste (seed), wear out (of sandals)

waste (seed)

sweat

four (feminine), quartette

Cobra

𓅓𓂋𓁹𓏤	reversion (of offerings from temple to tomb), a reversion offering
𓆓𓇋W1b	oil
𓆓𓆙𓇳	praise, worship
𓆓𓏴𓆓𓏴	drip
𓆓𓅓𓀁	pronounce, proclaim (name), mention (by name), be renowned (of office)
𓆓𓅓𓄹𓂡	To reassemble (dismembered body), assemble, bring together (people) : To associate (with), join (someone), unite (lands) : To accumulate (grain), compile (spell) : To extend (hand)
𓆓𓈖𓏴𓎱𓏪	dam
𓆓𓈖𓌰𓂡	heavy, irksome, burdensome (of years), overburdened (of stomach), weighty
𓆓𓂧𓏴	writing, script, title deeds
𓆓𓈖𓏥	lead
𓆓𓎺	jar
𓆓𓏤𓏤𓂧𓐍	papyrus marsh
𓆓𓂧𓏐	storm, storm-wind
𓆓𓂧𓂻𓏤𓏥	spear (fish)
𓆓𓂧𓐱	a type of bread
𓆓𓂧𓊽𓏤	coal-black
𓆓𓂧𓊽𓏙	charcoal, soot
𓆓𓂧𓅆𓏤	a scepter
𓆓𓂧M3b𓂻	seek
𓆓𓂧𓏤𓏛𓏤	search out, investigate, seek, probe, palpate (wound), plan (work), take thought (for)
𓆓𓂧𓏤𓂋	search out, investigate
𓂧𓏤 𓐎	

lock (on door)

vein (of ore)

lancet, surgical knife

serfs

finger, thumb, toe, digit (one twenty-eighth cubit), 10,000 (numeral)

pole (of chariot)

be provided, abound (in supplies)

a well-provided man

penetrate

penetration

provisions, sustenance, victuals, (deified as) Abundance

provisions, sustenance, victuals, (deified as) Abundance

pupil (of eye)

drop (of liquid)

avocet

cripple

crooked

an offering loaf

deflect

territories

skull

upper part of hind leg, ham

wing

wing-rib

	subdue
	be angry
	angry man
	be infuriated
	be angry
G144	kite (bird)
	Thoth (god)
	leather lacings
	(him)self, by (him)self, (his) own
	call (to)
	separate (from)
	holy, sacred, splendid, costly
	privacy
	steer
	milky wine?
	estate
	cobra
	papyrus stem
	eternity, for ever
	body, image, bodily form (of god, statues), self
	forever
	say, speak, speak of, utter (speech), recite (spell), tell (to), expect
	stable, enduring
	fat

𓎛𓏤𓆓𓄿𓅅𓏌𓏤	I say something important
𓎛𓏤𓆓𓄿𓈖𓈖𓈖	I speak in exactness
𓎛𓏤𓆓𓊗𓅅𓏭	Busiris
𓎛𓏤𓆓𓅅𓊖	Mendes (Tell er-Ruba)
𓎛𓏤𓆓𓂝𓏤	incite
𓎛𓏤𓆓𓂾	sting, incite
𓎛𓏤𓆓𓅅	creep (of flesh)
𓎛𓏤𓆓𓏤	stand on end (of hair), creep (of flesh)
𓎛𓏤𓆓𓆙	snake, (internal bodily) worm
𓎛𓏤𓆓𓏥	recitation
𓎛𓏤	words to be spoken, to be pronounced
𓎛𓏤𓆓𓀀	shut up, imprison
𓎛𓏤𓆓𓅅𓈖𓈖	canal, channel
𓎛𓏤𓆓 M1c	Olive

Mugil

	administrator

Oxyrhynchus

	crookedness
	widow
	corpse
	marsh
	clothes peg?
	resolute
	thwart (someone)

(hieroglyphs)	heap of corpses
(hieroglyphs)	clavicle
(hieroglyphs)	sickle
(hieroglyphs)	crooked, crookedness, crookedly
(hieroglyphs)	curl (on Red crown)
(hieroglyphs)	bend down (arms in respect)
(hieroglyphs)	a type of beer
(hieroglyphs)	type of offerings
(hieroglyphs)	sack, leather bag
(hieroglyphs)	storm
(hieroglyphs)	disaffected persons
(hieroglyphs)	disease
(hieroglyphs)	oxyrhynchus fish (mormyrus kannume)

Fish scale

(hieroglyphs)	scales (of fish)

Tetrodon Fahaka

(hieroglyphs)	be discontented, angry

Scarab beetle

(hieroglyphs)	exist, be, come into being, become, change (into), occur, happen, come to pass
(hieroglyphs)	children
(hieroglyphs)	form, shape
(hieroglyphs)	form, shape, modes of being

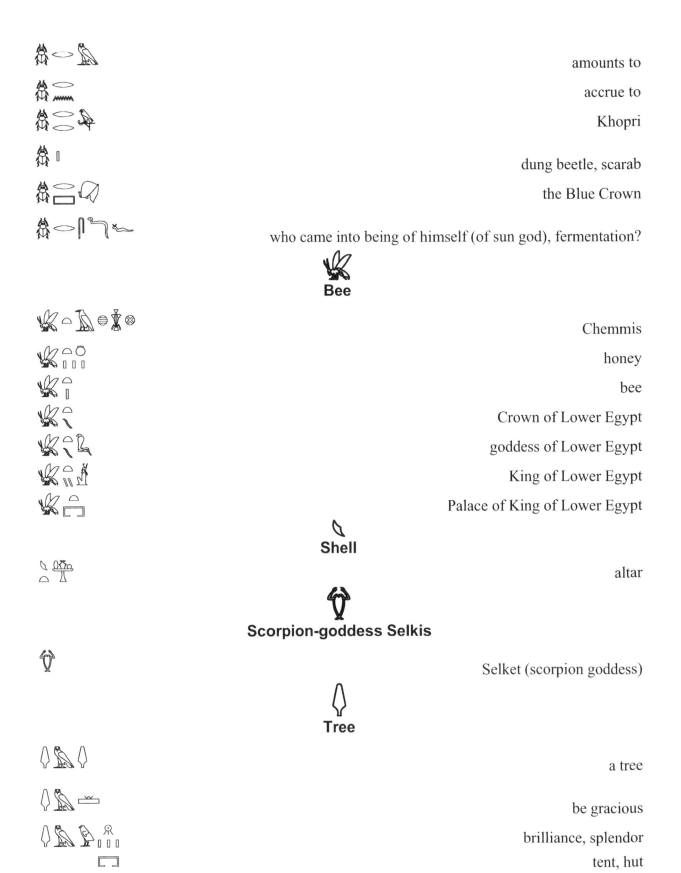 amounts to	
accrue to	
Khopri	
dung beetle, scarab	
the Blue Crown	
who came into being of himself (of sun god), fermentation?	

Bee

Chemmis	
honey	
bee	
Crown of Lower Egypt	
goddess of Lower Egypt	
King of Lower Egypt	
Palace of King of Lower Egypt	

Shell

altar

Scorpion-goddess Selkis

Selket (scorpion goddess)

Tree

a tree

be gracious

brilliance, splendor

tent, hut

𓇋𓄿𓂋𓏤	tent, hut
𓇋𓄿𓉐	tent
𓇋𓄿𓏛	gracious of countenance
𓇋𓄿𓂋𓊌𓏤𓏥	charm, kindliness, graciousness

Clump of plants

𓇥	I, me, my
𓇥𓈖	cultivator

Branch

M3b 𓁨	judgment, divorce by judgment
𓆱𓏤	wood, timber, tree, woodland, mast, stick, pole, rod (measurement)
𓐍𓏤𓆱𓂻	retire, retreat
𓐍𓏤𓆱𓂡	carve, engrave
𓐍𓏤𓆱𓄿𓏤	threshing-floor
𓐍𓏤𓆱𓊅	platform, dais, terraced hillside
𓐍𓏤𓆱𓄿𓏥𓏤𓏤	who pervade the land
𓐍𓆦	an edible bird, poultry
𓐍𓏤𓆱𓄿𓏥	menials
𓐍𓏤𓈗𓂻	free moving pole?
𓐍𓏤𓆱𓏤𓆱𓆱𓏤𓏤𓏥	furniture
𓆱𓏤𓂻𓈗𓏤 Y1v	fruit tree
𓆱𓏤𓈗𓋹𓏤	embodiment of food
𓆱𓏤𓈗𓋹𓏥	staff-of-life plants
𓆱𓏤𓈗𓏥𓍁	100 cubits (a rod of cord)
𓆱𓏤𓈗𓏥𓍁	rod of cord (linear measure of 100 cubits)
𓆱𓏤𓏥	a type of tree
𓆱𓏤𓆱𓏤𓄿	turn back, nullify, reverse (a contract), come and go (of pain)

[glyphs]	through
[glyphs]	house-servant
[glyphs]	mast
M3b [glyph]	search out, investigate, seek, probe, palpate (wound), plan (work), take thought (for)

[glyph]

Palm branch leafless and notched

[glyph]	year
[glyph]	regnal year
[glyph] Z4^c [glyph]	the five epagomenal days
[glyph]	last year

[glyph]

M4 + X1

[glyph]	time
[glyph]	time, season

M7^c
Var. of M7

M7^c	young, fresh (of water)
M7^c [glyphs]	herbs, vegetables

[glyph]

Pool with lotus flowers

[glyphs]	Inundation-season
[glyphs]	pig
[glyphs]	ordain, order, predestine, assign, settle, decide
[glyphs]	field, meadow, countryside, marsh, swamp
[glyphs]	assign
[glyphs]	bundle? (of flax)
[glyphs]	dues, taxes
[glyphs]	

156

𓏺	beginning
	container (for corn)
	begin, be the first, spring, originate
	space, volume
	as far as
	void
	weight, worth, value
	coriander
	fate
	meals, food
	be hot, burn
	soiled linen
	travel
	travel (intransitive), tread on (enemy) (transitive)
	bedouin
	desert North East of Egypt
	avoid
	bosom
	necklace
	bag
	dig, dig out
	persea tree
	ushabti figure
	a jar
	father-in-law

157

𓄎 𓏺 E131   rhinoceros

Lotus flower

𓆸   lotus

Flower on a long twisted stem

𓎯   offer (to)

𓎯   offerer

𓎯   offerings

Lotus plant

𓆼 𓈗 ⌒ M54   variety of date-palm

𓆼   1000

𓆼 𓄿 𓀀 𓅊   be young, little

𓆼 𓄿 𓉻   office, bureau

𓆼 𓄿 𓃀   measure, examine (patient), patrol

𓆼 𓏭 𓃀   measure, examine (patient)

𓆼 𓄿 𓏭 𓊪   altar

𓆼 𓄿 𓏭𓏭 𓂝   plumb-line, rule (of conduct)

𓆼 𓄿 𓏭𓏭 𓏴   measurements

𓆼 𓄿 𓏭 ⌒𓈖 𓅊 𓏮   disease

𓆼 𓏭 𓂧   slaughter, massacre

𓆼 𓂝   strike down (with disease)

𓆼 𓄿 𓂝   throw, strike down (with disease), cast off (bonds), abandon (property)

𓆼 𓄿 𓂝   drip (sweat)

𓆼 𓄿 𓂝   urination

	throw
	discharges (medical)
	plants, flowers
	plants
	bowl
	thousands
	night
	benighted traveller
	altar
	hippopotamus
	the starry sky
	crookedness
	bend (arm in respect)
	bolt (of horses)?
	be wifeless
	Khorian
	Khor
	widow
	be speedy, swift
	spear (fish)
	be speedy, swift, hasten, hurry
	winnow
	impatient
	scramble?
	creek? runnel?

𓇋𓅃𓏊𓏛	curl on front of Red Crown?
𓇋𓅃𓏊𓏭𓏛𓏥	bryony?
𓇋𓈖𓈉	hill country, foreign land, desert
𓇋𓅃𓈖𓏥	corpse
𓇋𓅃𓈅𓏤	marsh
𓇋𓈗𓏤	land measure (approx 10 Arouras), type of Crown land
𓇋𓉐𓏭	office
𓇋𓅃𓆓𓏮	dough
𓇋𓅃𓆓𓂡	grasp, make captures (in war)
𓇋𓅃𓆓𓂡	grasp
𓇋𓈖𓏏	reins

Papyrus

𓇅𓅓𓏙	a green stone, malachite
𓇅𓆓𓇏	green, pale, fresh, raw, hale, sturdy, fortunate, happy, make green, make to flourish
𓇅𓆓𓇏𓀀	fortunate man
𓇅𓇏	fresh
𓇅𓏤	wadj amulet
M13ᶜ 𓏤 𓆰	papyrus plant
𓇅𓏭𓂝𓆗	Edjo (Cobra goddess)
𓇅𓂝𓆗	cobra goddess
𓇅𓏭𓉐	hall of columns
𓇅𓆗𓆗𓏌	the two serpent goddesses of Upper and Lower Egypt
𓇅 ḏ7ᶜ	green eye-paint

𓅃

	the sea
	rawness
M13^c	(command etc)
	weaned child (of royalty)
M13^c	command, decree

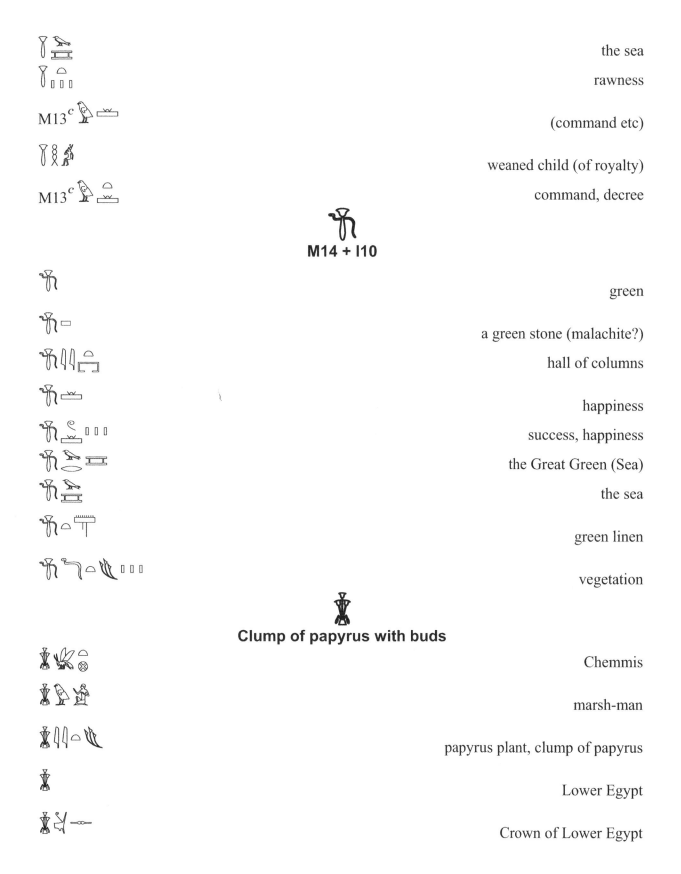

M14 + I10

	green
	a green stone (malachite?)
	hall of columns
	happiness
	success, happiness
	the Great Green (Sea)
	the sea
	green linen
	vegetation

Clump of papyrus with buds

	Chemmis
	marsh-man
	papyrus plant, clump of papyrus
	Lower Egypt
	Crown of Lower Egypt

Clump of papyrus

	Lower Egypt
	Crown of Lower Egypt
	in attendance
	would that!, O!
	back (of ear), behind, around
	outside
	go ashore, run aground (of ship)
	outer parts? (of house)
	screech (of falcon)
	protector
	carrion-birds
	flood water
	bandage
	mourning
	strife
	touch (of ship on land)
	mourners
	wealth, increase, excess, surplus
	naked man
	the lower orders

most of

(the Aegean) Islanders

more than

surpassing in beauty

a special offering

nakedness

secret place?

secret, mysterious, (to) hide

keep silence about

open mouthed

catch (fish), fish (waters)

fishermen

decoy-duck, bait (in general)

go astray, stumble

stumble

plunder (goods), capture (towns), carry off (captives)

plunder

plunderer

captives

plunder

touch (of ship on land)

rejoice (over)

tomb

food

cloudiness (of sky)

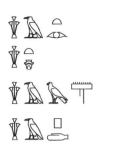

blleariness (of eyes)

heart

fine linen

open (mouth)

Reed in bloom

Viscera

Brand, stamp : Burn, fix : Branding-iron, brand sign

drive away, oppress

Misery, trouble : Injury, illness : Pain

sunlight, sunshine

I, me, my

O! : To say : Utterance

flesh

reeds, leaves (of reeds)

mounds of rubble

rod, reeds, rushes

adore

old woman

adoration

old man

be aged, attain old age, old age

old age

old age

herds

the east wind

the East

east, eastern, left-hand

offer (to)

bind (the sacrifice)

rushes (plants)

be dim, be weak (of heart)

grapes

vine

lock of hair

sunshine, radiance

bald

call, summon

leap 332b

leeks, vegetables

the aged

mourning, wailings

mourners B77

Back, spine (of man, animal) : Middle (of river, lake)

a milk-goddess

165

𓄿𓅆𓊌	mound, ruin
𓄿𓅆𓊃	standard (for cult objects)
𓄿𓅆𓊌𓏭	office, function
𓄿𓊌𓅀𓃀	mutilation
𓄿𓅆𓍱𓃀𓅪	be injured, be distorted, be missing (from), abate (of fever)
𓄿𓅆𓍱𓃀𓅪𓊋	shambles
𓄿𓅆𓂝𓏭𓏤	tract (of land)
𓄿𓅆𓂋𓅀𓏭𓏭	intruders
𓄿𓅀𓂝𓏏𓏏	dew, pouring rain, pestilence, affliction, influence
𓄿𓅀𓂝𓏲	net
𓄿𓅄	welcome
𓇋𓂝 O24^c	tomb (mastaba)
𓇋𓂝𓈗	wash
𓇋𓂝𓈗𓂡	wash, wash out (an inscription etc)
𓇋𓂝𓅆𓂡	cover up
𓇋𓂝𓅆𓈗	washing
𓇋𓂝𓈗𓇳	breakfast
𓇋𓂝𓅆𓈗𓏌𓏏𓎯	breakfast
𓇋𓂝𓂾	heap up (corn with a pitchfork)
𓇋𓂝𓂾𓐎	be united
𓇋𓂝𓂾𓎯	bowl
𓇋𓂝𓂾𓎯 š36c	assemble (of persons)
𓇋𓎯𓂾𓏤	be united, assemble, join, unite, present
𓇋𓂝𓃀	wring out, squeeze out

166

𓇋𓃭𓏤𓀀	greeting?, woe to
𓇋𓃭𓇲𓏤	greeting
𓇋𓃭𓊁	uraeus
𓇋𓃭𓉐	abode (of god)
𓇋𓃭𓆓 C114[c]	moon
𓆓𓏺 N62 G7c	moon god
𓇋𓃀𓀀	hump-back?
𓇋𓃀𓄿𓃾	ox, long-horned cattle
𓇋𓃀𓄿𓏺	beef
𓇋𓃀𓄿𓇋𓇋𓏏𓀎	female representative, substitute
𓄿𓇋𓇋 P19	strand, leave boat-less
𓇋𓃭𓇋𓇋𓏏𓀀𓏥	troops
𓇋𓃭𓆱	heir
𓄿𓃀𓏏	crumb (of bread)
𓇋𓄿𓃾𓏺	flesh, meat
𓇋𓄿𓏺	flesh (of man)
𓇋𓄿 F51b 𓏤𓏤𓏤	meat
𓇋𓆰𓏤𓀀	misstatement
𓇋𓃀𓈙	complexion, color, nature, disposition
𓄿𓏤𓃀𓀁	know not, be ignorant of
𓇋𓄿𓈙𓋔	realm of the dead
𓇋𓄿𓂝𓏤	who.......not, which.......not
𓇋𓄿𓂝𓏤	what is not, does not exist
	think, suppose

167

Hieroglyphs	Translation
	think, suppose
	thirsty man
	kid goat
	a thirsty man
	dance
	draughtsman
	Barbary sheep
	be thirsty, thirst after (something)
	refuge, shelter
	tent of purification
	refuge
	halyards (of ship)
	halyards of ship?
	labdanum
	labdanum?
	Ibhet
	Ibhet stone
	Ibhet-stone
	stream (with liquid), be suffused (with blood)
	tooth, tusk
	libationer
	headdress (of king)

168

𓏤𓃀�𓈘	thirst
𓏤𓃀𓏏𓃀	bird-trap
𓏤𓃀𓏏𓂾	part of leg
𓏤𓊪𓏤	count, reckon up, make reckoning, assess, allot
𓏤𓊪𓄿𓅡𓏏	private office
𓏤𓄿𓊪	private office
𓏤𓊪𓄿	these
𓏤𓊪𓄿⊗	Akhmim
𓏤𓊪𓄿𓏏𓏥	payments
𓏤𓊪𓁹	those
𓏤𓊪𓈘	these
𓏤𓊪𓋔𓃟	swine, pigs
𓏤𓊪𓍛𓀾	Twelfth month (name and festival)
𓏤𓊪𓂻𓎯	grain-measure of 4 heqat
𓏤𓊪𓂾	census
𓏤𓊪𓉐𓏢	Temple of Karnak
𓏤𓊪𓅯𓂾	these
𓏤𓊪𓅯𓈘	these
𓏤𓊪𓂋𓂾	those
𓏤𓊪𓂾𓈘	these
𓏤𓊪𓅯𓂻𓏪	furniture
𓏤𓋴𓂋𓏥	quadruple
𓏤𓋴𓂿	flee
𓏤𓋴𓂋	rectangular
𓏤𓋴𓂋𓏤𓏠	cloth
𓏤𓋴𓏤𓏠	couch, cloth
𓏤𓋴𓂋𓏤𓋴𓏤	couch

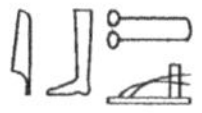

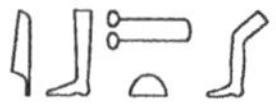

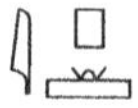

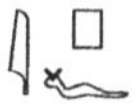

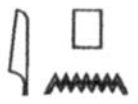

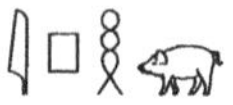

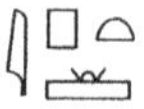

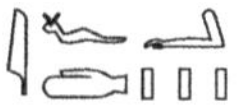

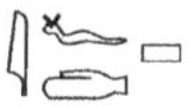

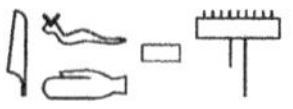

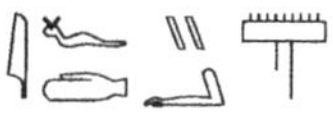

169

[hieroglyphs]	a four, quartette
[hieroglyphs] F51^b	form, shape
[hieroglyphs]	moan
[hieroglyphs]	gesso?
[hieroglyphs]	there, therein, therewith, therefrom
[hieroglyphs]	form, shape, side
[hieroglyphs]	a tree
[hieroglyphs]	pleasing (to)
[hieroglyphs]	a type of tree
[hieroglyphs]	be delighted (with), charmed (with)
[hieroglyphs]	brilliance, splendor
[hieroglyphs]	tent
[hieroglyphs] F39^c	spinal cord
[hieroglyphs] F39^c	honor, veneration, the blessed state (of being dead)
[hieroglyphs] F39^c	be honored
[hieroglyphs] F39^c	revered one (of the aged living)
[hieroglyphs] F39^c	revered one (of dead woman)
[hieroglyphs] F39^c	revered one (of the blessed dead)
[hieroglyphs] F39^c	revered one (of the blessed dead)
[hieroglyphs]	favor (toward someone)
[hieroglyphs]	charm, kindliness, graciousness
[hieroglyphs]	charm, kindliness, graciousness, favor

charm, kindliness, graciousness, favor

female ibex, female (of any animal)

give!, place!, cause!

among

between, among

belongs to (me)

who, which is in, in which is

councillor

regional officer?

favorite

aquatic animals

thoughts

snakes

of land and water

will, testament

following after(of time)

pigment

between, in the midst of

grief

ship, ship-load

ship

create

34c secret, hidden, conceal, hide

secret, hidden

Amun

right (-hand), right-side, the West

daily offerings

secret 34c

secret 34c

Amaunet

secret place

the West

Westerners

be deaf

netherworld

pleasant, kindly disposed

Imseti (a son of Horus)

Imseti

Tell el-Farun (Nebeshah)

groaning, grief

wine of Imt

foster-child

rampart

eyebrows

cordage (of ship)

by, so says

delay, hold (aloof)

chin d147

chin

pattern, model

	wall
	wall of (a place)
	be dumb
	fence, stockade
	decay
	royal child
	royal child (of princess)
	Anubis
	skin (of man or animal), hues (of sky), development, complexion
	who?
	we
	thyme?, water-mint?
	stone, rock, slab, block
	sea-shell
	shudder
	pomegranate (tree and fruit)
	eyebrows
	surround, enclose, embrace
	bright red linen
	bright-red linen
	testicles
	calf (of leg), shank, thigh, hind-leg
	unite (the Two Lands), collect, gather together
	the bulti-fish
	valley
	the bulti-fish
	hinder, linger
	hold back, restrain

𓎛𓈖𓎛	fetter
𓈖𓎛	fetter
𓎛𓈖𓄿𓀀	the afflicted man
𓎛𓈖𓅯	misery
𓎛𓈖𓀜	be afflicted
𓏏𓎟𓏭	hail to...
𓇋𓂋	as to, if
𓇋𓂋𓇋	companion
𓇋𓐍𓀜	(female) companion
𓇋𓏥	thereof, thereto
𓇋𓏥𓀜	relating to
𓇋𓂋𓏊	door-keeper
𓇋𓀀𓀜𓏥	crew (of boat)
𓇋𓏤𓏤	letter carrier
𓇋𓏥𓀜𓂋𓂻	one in attendance on
𓇋𓏥𓀜𓂝	pilot
𓇋𓏏𓅓𓅆𓊪	helmsman
𓇋𓀜𓎯𓉐	keeper of cattle-pens
𓇋𓂋𓀜𓏤𓅢𓅓𓏤𓀀	functionary
𓇋𓁹𓇋𓇋𓐍 E92	milch-cow
𓇋𓁹𓇋𓇋𓐍	tax-corn
𓇋𓁹𓀁	shape, form
𓇋𓁹𓃒	cattle-tax
𓇋𓁹𓅓𓀁𓏤	shape, form, nature
𓇋𓂋𓏌𓏤𓏤𓏤𓎯𓏌	wine

174

𓇋𓆓	enclitic particle
𓇋𓏍	(enclitic particle)
𓇋𓏤	duty (of someone)
𓏤𓀀𓈖	duty, use, purpose
𓇋𓂋𓅆𓀁	mourning
𓇋𓂋𓅆𓏥	blue, color, a blue mineral
𓇋𓂋𓏭	blue-dyed linen
𓇋𓂋𓅆𓏥	blue, color, blue mineral?
𓇋𓀀𓏤𓏭𓈖𓂝	pectoral
𓇋𓏤𓈖	(enclitic particle)
𓇋𓏤𓏤𓏊	milk
𓇋𓅆𓎡	camp
𓇋𓂻𓀏	dancing ritual
𓇋𓂻𓅆𓀏𓏥	ritual dancers
𓇋𓅆𓀎	restrain
𓇋𓅆𓂾	linger, lag
𓇋𓅆𓇳	detention
𓇋𓀀𓏤𓏏	a festival
𓇋𓉐𓏭𓀀	rejoicing
𓇋𓊽𓀀	Ah!
𓇋𓊽𓃾	bull
𓇋𓊽	sistrum player
𓇋𓊽𓏭𓏭 3239	sistrum-player
	a measure of metal

175

𓄿𓆱𓅀	a measure of metal
𓄿𓆱𓅀𓅪	weakness
𓄿𓆱𓅀𓉐	stable (for animals)
𓄿𓊪𓀜	attendant
𓄿𓆱𓃾𓃓	cow
𓄿𓆱𓊪𓏮	land-tax
𓄿𓏏𓈖	then, therefore, what?
𓄿𓏺𓄿𓏏𓏪	make to flourish
𓄿𓏺𓅬𓈖	extinguish, annul
𓄿𓏺𓅬𓏪	ignorant ones
𓄿𓏺𓅬𓏪𓀔	unwearying
𓄿𓍯𓈖𓏺𓅬𓎺 37ᶜ 𓇼𓏪	the unwearying stars
𓄿𓅬𓏺𓅬𓈖𓏺𓄿𓆰𓎺𓇼𓏪	indestructible stars
𓄿𓏺𓅬𓈖𓆰𓎺𓇼	the indestructible star (the circumpolar star)
𓄿𓏺𓅬𓆰𓄿𓎺𓇼	indestructible star (the circumpolar)
𓄿𓏺𓅬𓈅	bank (of river)
𓄿𓏏𓅬𓀔	twilight, dusk
𓄿𓏏𓈅	things, offerings, possessions, property, matter, affair, something, anything
𓄿𓏤𓈖𓅯	be light (of weight), lie light
𓄿𓏤𓉐	tomb, council-chamber, workshop, archive
𓄿𓏤𓆰𓅯	lie light (on)
𓄿𓏤𓆰𓏏	old, ancient
𓄿𓏤𓆰𓉐	tomb, council chamber, archive, workshop

𓍶

176

	go!
	enclitic particle
	tomb, council chamber, archive, workshop
	light-minded
	old clothes, rags
	reward
	reeds
	ancient ones
	non-enclitic particle
d283	testicles
	ancient times
	stool
	throne
Q12	throne, stool
	hew, cut
	whip
	quiver (for arrows)
	wrong, wrong doing, falsehood
	wrong, wrong-doing, falsehood
	evil-doer
M46	tamarisk tree
	tamarisk
	easy prey
	Assyria
	hinder, linger, wait (for)
	linger

	linger
	non-eclitic particle
	lightness (of tongue)
	boundary-stone, landmark
	non-eclitic particle
	strap up, bind
	(non-enclitic particle)
	saliva
	war-cry
	the precinct of Mut at Karnak, water meadow
	what?, wherefore?
	what?
	possessions, (morning) meal
M46	Ished tree
	Balanos, Ished tree, fruit of the ished tree
M39b	fruit of the Ished tree
	sweat
	trust, trustworthy, skilful, excellent, pleasing, well-to-do, superior
	a trustworthy man, wiseacre
	battle-axe
	builder
	quarryman
	stone-quarry
	shield

W112^c	jar
	draw (water from well etc)
	cup, jar
	hoe
	councillors?
	clouds, be overcast, soar cloudwards
	also, further / anymore (after negatives)
	moreover, now
	realm of the dead
	father
	barley, corn
	sovereign
	queen-regnant
	queen of thousands
	suffocation
	Atum
	oppose
	oppose
	sun, disk of the sun
	secret, mystery
	opponent
	solar goddess
	seasons
	measure of length
	river
	row (of men, of shrubs)
O157	conclave (of Upper Egypt)
	conclave (of Lower Egypt)

𓇋𓎿𓂝𓊭	chapel, niche, box
𓇋𓂝𓎡𓀜	drag, draw, pull off, pull out, draw off, draw out
𓇋𓂝𓎡𓂻	pull out (eye)
𓇋𓂝𓎡𓉐	fortress
𓇋𓂝𓎡𓂾	drag
𓅂𓅓𓀜	steal
𓅂𓅓𓀜	thief
𓅂𓅓𓏭𓎰	take
𓇋𓎿𓅟	fly up
𓇋𓂋𓀜	assault
𓇋𓂋 ḥ25 𓃒	bull
𓅂𓂋𓀜	boy
𓇋𓂋𓅭	smooth
𓇋𓂋𓂥	be deaf
𓇋𓂋𓏭𓎿𓀜	girl
𓅂𓅭𓂋	pestilence
𓇋𓂋𓊪 N21ᶜ	river-bank, riparian land, shore (of flood)
𓇋𓂋𓃀𓏭𓏌	red linen
𓇋𓂋𓈖 F143	lay out (enclosures)?
𓇋𓂋𓈖𓂾	govern, serve as lieutenant-commander
𓇋𓂋𓈖𓃀	serve instead of, replace
𓇋𓂋𓈖𓈖	serve instead of, replace
𓇋𓂋𓈖𓂥	stitch, stitching
𓇋𓂋𓈖𓃥𓏤𓏤𓏤	herd (of animals)

180

𓀀…	withhold
𓀀…	punishment
𓀀…	nerves, tendons
𓀀…	marsh-man
𓀀…	marsh-man
𓀀…	marsh-nest
𓀀…	the Delta marshes
𓀀…	wrath?
ꜣd46ᶜ△	censing, incense-burning
𓀀…	hall?
𓀀…	sea
𓀀…	Oho!
𓀀…	Hey!
𓀀…	steal (goods), rob (someone)
𓀀…	fill up
𓀀…	mount up, ascend
𓀀…	mount up
𓀀… t24e	wipe off, wipe away
𓀀…	rope
𓀀…	entrap, snare
𓀀…	fight
𓀀…	cultivator
𓀀…	pilot

(hieroglyphs)	act as pilot
(hieroglyphs)	strain
(hieroglyphs)	messenger, agent, commissioner, bystander
(hieroglyphs)	evil doer
(hieroglyphs)	carrying pole
(hieroglyphs)	and, further
(hieroglyphs)	betake oneself (to)
(hieroglyphs)	inspection
(hieroglyphs)	also, further, any more
(hieroglyphs)	either
(hieroglyphs)	image, form, shape, figure, design, (written) sign
(hieroglyphs)	time, season
(hieroglyphs)	seasons
(hieroglyphs)	Thoth (god)

M18 + D54

(hieroglyphs)	To come, return : Welcome
(hieroglyphs)	*jj.tw*, Welcome
(hieroglyphs)	welcome
(hieroglyphs)	mishap, trouble, harm, a wrong (which is done)
(hieroglyphs)	mishap, trouble, harm, wrong

M17 tied up with U36

(hieroglyphs)	offerings

Field of reeds

(hieroglyphs)	marshland, field, country (beside town)

182

𓇋𓇋𓇋	the Fen goddess
𓇋𓇋𓇋	peasant, fisherman, fowler
𓇋𓇋𓇋	class of Cattle

𓇋𓇋𓇋

Var. of M20

𓇋𓇋𓇋	pastures, plants, herbage, vegetables, herb

𓇎

Swamp rush

𓇏𓇏	this, these, here, hither
𓇏𓇏	be weary, inert
𓇏𓇏	be weary, inert, drag (of foot), dribble (of fluid), settle (of flood-waters)
𓇏𓇏	inert ones (the Dead)
𓇏𓇏	weariness, inertness (of the dead)
𓇏𓇏	err, go wrong (of plans), error
𓇏𓇏	spleen
𓇏𓇏 N50	lower heaven
𓇑	El Kab
𓇑 G16[c]	Nekhbet (goddess)

𓇓

Rush, heraldic plant of Upper Egypt

𓇓	Temple
𓇓	be king
𓇓	priests of Arsaphes?
𓇓	Kings
𓇓	kingship
𓇓	King of Upper Egypt, king

King

king of Upper and Lower Egypt

queen

an offering the king gives

chamberlain

chamberlain

(not translated)

M33^b pill

widen, make wide, make spacious, extend (boundaries)

make extensive (of movements)

he, it, (rarely) she

scirpus-reed, emblem of Upper Egypt

Used to emphasize a preceding word or phrase

what is his

Seth (god)

Set

carry (child)

M23 + D21

southern, south of, South

Southerners

the South land

south-wind

M23 (buds opened) on D21

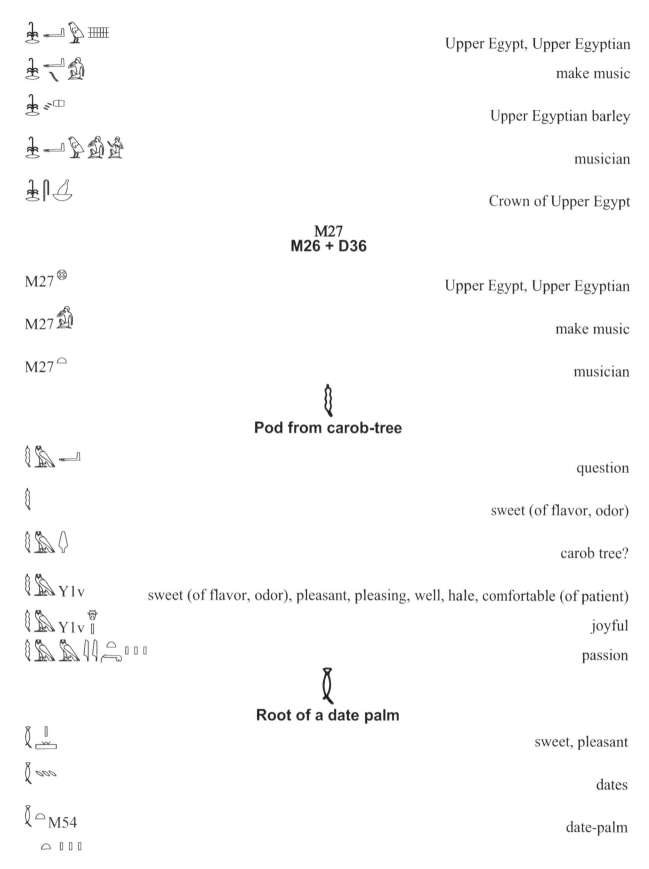

	Upper Egypt, Upper Egyptian
	make music
	Upper Egyptian barley
	musician
	Crown of Upper Egypt

M27
M26 + D36

M27	Upper Egypt, Upper Egyptian
M27	make music
M27	musician

Pod from carob-tree

	question
	sweet (of flavor, odor)
	carob tree?
Y1v	sweet (of flavor, odor), pleasant, pleasing, well, hale, comfortable (of patient)
Y1v	joyful
	passion

Root of a date palm

	sweet, pleasant
	dates
M54	date-palm

185

date-cakes

Rhizome of a lotus

agent

Grains of cereal

M33^c — barley, corn

M33^c barley, corn

M33^c barley of Upper Egypt

barley of Lower Egypt

Sheaf of emmer

emmer

Bundle of flax stems showing the bolls

offer (things to)

in, since, before, until

end (hunger), end up as, hinder, obstruct

obstacle

strong (of staff), strongly

be hard, stolid

enclosing wall

wall

kite (bird)

end, limit

walls

boundary, end, limit

paint

side, flank

wall

sarcophagus

	hall
	before, formerly
	hand, trunk (of elephant), handle (of jar)
	harm
	ancestors
	leaf
	stranger
₃280	strange

Bundle of flax stems showing the bolls

	bind together

Bundle of reeds tied together

	councillor
	gang (of workmen)
	crew (of ship)
	palace
	boundary stone, landmark
	crew (of ship), company (of soldiers), gang (of workmen)
	company (of rebels)

Flower (rosette)

	move about (of child in womb)
M96	Used to emphasize a preceding word or phrase
	eat
	Used to emphasize a preceding word or phrase
	food, sustenance

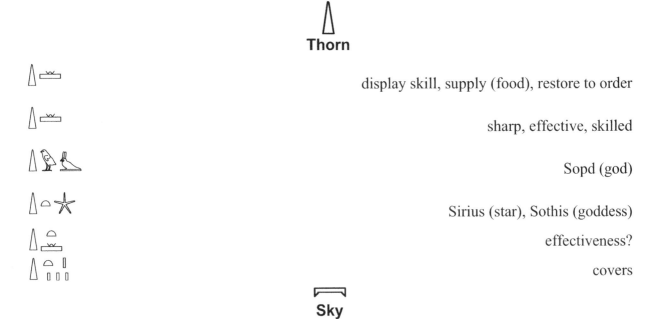

	food, fodder
	Onnophris
	be clothed (in)
	hollow, depression
	short-horned cattle
	goats
	short horned cattle
	associates
P30	ships hold

Vine on props

	fruit of various trees
M43b	vintner

Thorn

	display skill, supply (food), restore to order
	sharp, effective, skilled
	Sopd (god)
	Sirius (star), Sothis (goddess)
	effectiveness?
	covers

Sky

	The sky, heaven
	portal
	troop commander

188

foreman of weavers

Sky (a star hanging from it?)

night

Rain falling from the sky

dew, pouring rain, pestilence, affliction, influence

Sun

Re

everyday

day, daytime

birthday of Nephthys

Sun with uraeus

Re

Sun radiating

sunlight, sunshine

sunshine, radiance

wound

the sun-folk of Heliopolis, mankind

dry, dried

Moon obscured

the new moon and its festival

Ennead (of gods)

Crescent moon

 month

189

 monthly festival

⌒⦶ earth-almond?, carob?

Var. of N11

⌒ Z3^c Z1^c Z3^c Z1^c ⛵ a ship

Star

★⌓ hour

★⌓ priesthood

★⌓𓀁𓏤𓏤𓏤 priesthood, staff

★ hour watcher, astronomer

★𝕀 star

★𓅃𓀀 teach, teaching

★𓊈 door

★𓏭𓏭𓂬𓏤𓏤𓏤 (written) teaching, instructions

★𓂬 pupil, student

★𓀀 praise, worship

★𓅃☉ rise early

★𓅃𓏭☉ morning

★𓅃𓅃☉ dawn, morning, tomorrow, the morrow

★𓅪^c☉Z4^c dawn, morning

★𓎟𓅃𓅃☉Z4^c tomorrow, the morrow

★𓅨 Used to emphasize a preceding word or phrase

𓅨

190

☆🐦	adze (for Opening the mouth)
☆🦅𓀎═🦅𓆓	Duamutef
☆🦅⌢𓀀	Duamutef
☆⌢𓀀	praise, worship
☆🦅▢	netherworld
☆🦅▢𓀀𓏥	dwellers in the netherworld
☆♉	grand total

Star in a circle

⊛	netherworld

Flat land with three grains of sand

⊟𓏏	earth, land, ground
⊟𓏏🐂𓏤𓏤𓏤	Farafra Oasis
⊟⊟	flat lands (as opposed to Hill countries)
⊟⊟	the Two Lands, Egypt
⊟⌢⌢⊗	ends of the earth
🦅⌢𓀀	the Thinite nome
🦅⊟⌢	larboard
⌢🦅⌢〰	Egypt
⌢🦅𓀀🦅	Lower Egypt
〰🦅𓏤〰	Nubia
⌢⌢𓊨	stairway
⌢⌢𓊨 O40[c]	stairway
⌢♉🦅═	landing place
⌢3[c]32⌢	Nubia
⌢⌐𓏦	Used to emphasize a preceding word or phrase

191

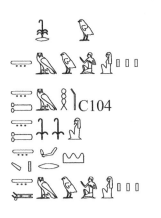

all men

southern Libya

Memphite earth-god

the Sacred Land (necropolis)

Used to emphasize a preceding word or phrase

Var. of N16

larboard

Egypt

Lower Egypt

all men

totality of men, everyone

Sandy island

island

aroura (of land), sheet (of metal)

loin-cloth

Tongue of land

turn (to)

reversion (of offerings from temple to tomb), a reversion offering

Tongue of land

arable land

the Two Banks (Egypt)

N21^c 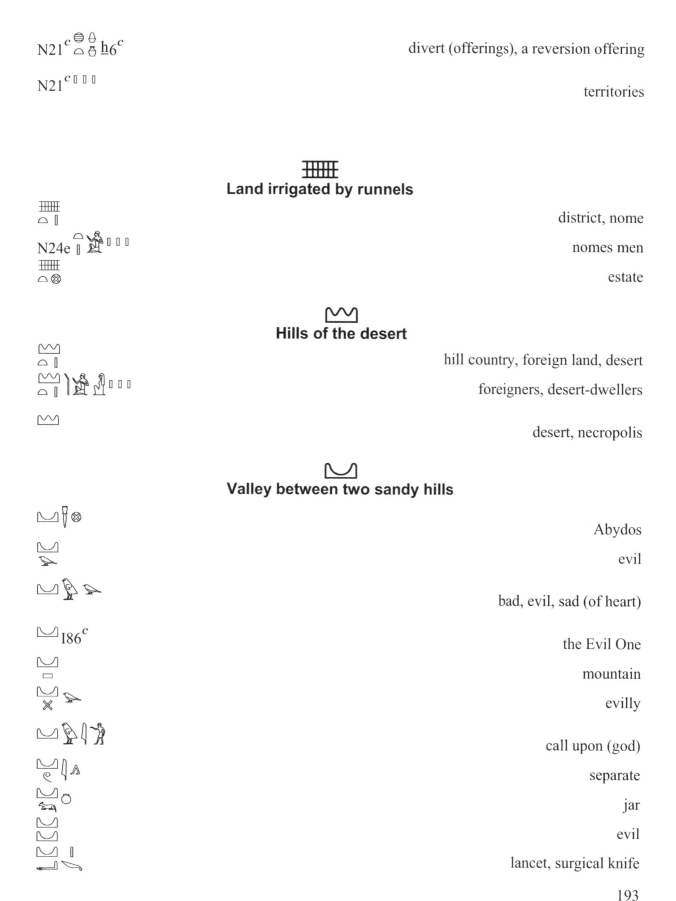 $\underline{h}$6^c divert (offerings), a reversion offering

N21^c territories

Land irrigated by runnels

district, nome

N24e nomes men

estate

Hills of the desert

hill country, foreign land, desert

foreigners, desert-dwellers

desert, necropolis

Valley between two sandy hills

Abydos

evil

bad, evil, sad (of heart)

I86^c the Evil One

mountain

evilly

call upon (god)

separate

jar

evil

lancet, surgical knife

193

evil, sadness (of heart), dirt (encumbering ruin)

Sun rising above the horizon

still-room?

horizon, (tomb (of king)

horizon-dweller

Hill illuminated by the sun

hill

rise (of sun), appear in glory (of god or king), be shining (of kings)

appearance in glory

weapons, funeral furniture, tomb-equipment, tackle (of ship), utensils, implements

crown

approach

rage

Sandy slope

moringa oil

tree (moringa arabica)

grains

hill, high ground

tall, high, exalted, be raised on high, uplifted

haughty

high ground, arable land

high throne

vomit

height, top (of voice)

interior, middle (of land)

fold over, double over, double (quantity)

intestine, interior, middle (of land)

coils (of snake)

coils (of snake)

windings (of waterway)

breast

funeral oration

bundle

door-bolt

mud-plaster

vomit

string (bow), bind (victim), tie (rope-ladder)

rope-ladder

presumptuous, overweening

bonds, rigging (of ship)

bonds

arrogant

vain glorious?

traveling barge

height

foreign foes

plaster, gypsum

form, shape, nature

vomit

195

	Cusae (El-Kusiyah)
	vomit
	elbow, arm, shoulder
	corner, bend (of stream), bight (of net)
	sunshine
F112	shoulder (of beef)
	a loaf or cake
	gold miner
	cold
	pour a libation (to)
	crown (of head)
W73	jar (for beer)
	cool breeze
W15b	be purified
	cool, cold
	cool, cold
	cold water
	foot?
	purify
	present libations (to)
	sky
	wild fowl

196

	cold water
	coolness
	fame
	bake, clot (of blood)
	a loaf
	baker
	form, appearance, nature
	form, appearance
	throw, create, beget, produce, carry out (teaching), hammer out (from metal)
	throw, create
	mourn
	nature
	winnower
	a type of soldiers
	gummed?
	reticent
	gum, resin
	a loaf
	devise, invent, mourn
V60	mat
	brave man
	fat
	offence, attack

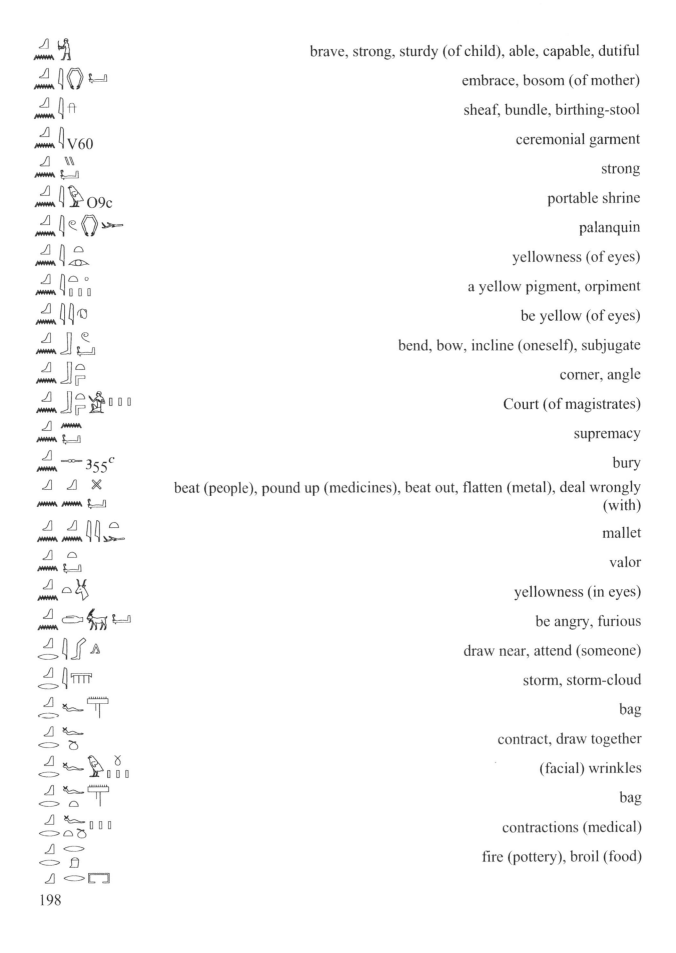

	brave, strong, sturdy (of child), able, capable, dutiful
	embrace, bosom (of mother)
	sheaf, bundle, birthing-stool
V60	ceremonial garment
	strong
O9c	portable shrine
	palanquin
	yellowness (of eyes)
	a yellow pigment, orpiment
	be yellow (of eyes)
	bend, bow, incline (oneself), subjugate
	corner, angle
	Court (of magistrates)
	supremacy
355ᶜ	bury
	beat (people), pound up (medicines), beat out, flatten (metal), deal wrongly (with)
	mallet
	valor
	yellowness (in eyes)
	be angry, furious
	draw near, attend (someone)
	storm, storm-cloud
	bag
	contract, draw together
	(facial) wrinkles
	bag
	contractions (medical)
	fire (pottery), broil (food)

198

	cavern
	serpent-spirit (as guardian of a place) (of princess of ancient family)
	vessel
	burial
	bury
	coffin
	burial
	tomb-equipment
	depression, hollow place
	axe
	a type of vase or jar
	metal-workers
	bone
	pain, troubling (by foes)
	irksome
	trouble, misfortune
	build, fashion (men)

Hill with shrubs

mound, ruin

Road bordered by papyrus

fall (into a condition)

far (from), long ago, for a long time past, go

road, way

green eye-paint

apart from, besides, as well as

basin

 Myrrh

Crucible

copper, minerals, (figuratively for Firmness of Character)

coppersmith

Ripple of water

water, rain, semen

water

be watery

urine

spittle

Muu class of Ritual dancers

cataract, rapid

to, for, to (persons), in (sun, dew, time), because, belongs to

we, us, our

This, these ; that, those

my

breeze

tress of hair

weaving room

drive away, rebuff, avoid, throw down (an enemy), turn back (evil)

throw down (an enemy)

ḏ120	
	shrink (from)
	ibex
	of (mine), belongs to (me)
	belongs to me
	primaeval waters
	ostrich
	bowl
	be glad?
N50	lower heaven
	make summons, make invocation
	summons
	he who is summoned
	call to, summon
	he will be dubbed as a
	evil doer
	a serpent demon
	wrong doing
	stammer
	impede
	therefore, for it, because of it
385	Greeting!
	be lenient
	To travel by boat, sail, traverse (waterway), convey (someone)

	mooring post
	smooth, undecorated, smoothness (of complexion), mix smoothly
	serpent
	cat-fish
	expedition
	this, these
	see, look
	hunter
	weakness
	time, for a while
	be weak
	adze of Wepwawet (used in Opening of the mouth)
	care for, take care of, collect, assemble
	bring back (someone)
	return (to a place), come (to someone), bring back (someone)
	water, flood, pool
	waters (of canal), pool, wave
	wave
390c	dishevel, be disheveled, pull (at hair)
	rope, band (of metal)
	bind (enemies)
	heat
	sheet? (of metal)
	yarn (for weaving)
	turn aside, vacillate
	vacillate
3^c23t	squeeze out (oil)
	unguents

202

	ointment
	swaddling clothes (of child)
	ointment maker
	tie
	wig?
	carrying pole
	reed, measure of 2 cubits
	flame, burn
	melt (metal)
	swim
	be hot
	flaming one (of Uraeus)
	reed
	protector
	gold collar
	guard
	zizyphus
	basket
	plait, wrap up
	the Evil One
	band (doors with metal)
	those of bad character
	tress (of hair)
	destructive

203

be wet

umbilical cord

flutter

a cake (or) a loaf

hem

grain (as god)

grain

M33 ^{c}

brim (of well), flat slab, basis

iliac region, groin, lymph nodes

slaughter

sharp knife

that, those

wrong, wrong-doing

that, those

blow (out of nose)

thus it was

creep

wrongfully

fan

remove

unroll?

slacken (bow), detach, loosen

breath, wind

detach, loosen

leap

who?, what?

who?

go wrong (of plans), rob (with), steal (with)

at the sight of him

new

shout (of people), low (of cattle)

travel, traverse

Bedouin

intruding?

be one-sided, partial, question

go to sleep

dwarf

vats

net

quake, quiver, go to and fro

in order that

be poor

orphan, private person, freeman (of low degree)

orphan, private person, freeman

stride over, traverse

slaughter house

stride over, traverse

stride, journeys, movements, actions, (legal) procedure

inert ones (the Dead)

primaeval waters

err, go wrong (of plans), error

spleen

205

	belongs to me, on my part
N50	lower heaven
	because
	charge (after enemy)
	time, return of the year
	fear (someone), overawe
	fear (someone)
	ox-herd
	ox herd
	protect
	fear, dread, disturbance?
	terrible one
	fear, dread, disturbance
	periodically
	vulture
	escape (death)
	of the environment of
	some, a little, a few
	loss
	care (for)
	copulate
	pulsate
	rise early in the morning, early morning
	mourn
	rise early in the morning, early morning
	shout, thunder (of sky)
	dance for joy?
	shout

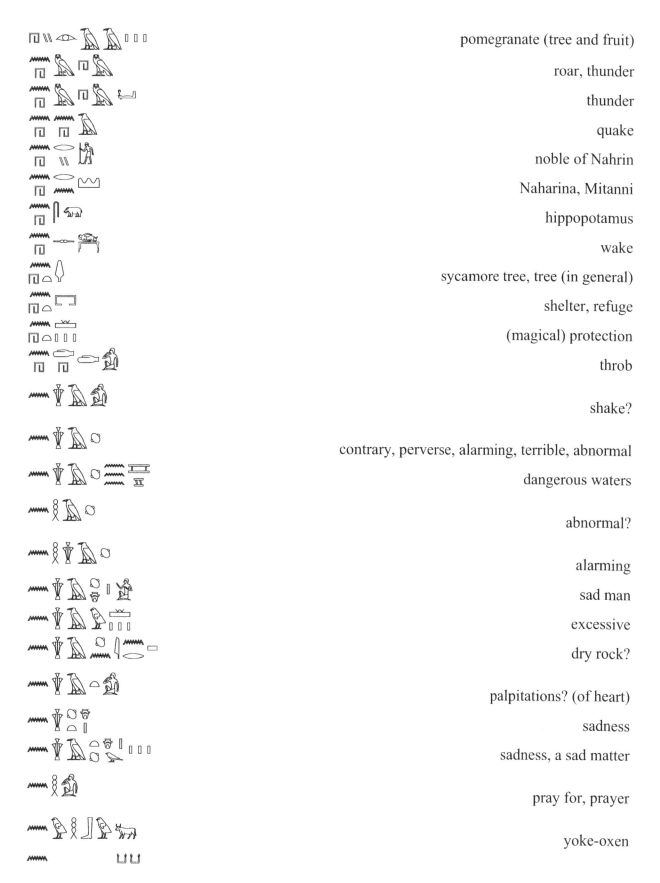

pomegranate (tree and fruit)

roar, thunder

thunder

quake

noble of Nahrin

Naharina, Mitanni

hippopotamus

wake

sycamore tree, tree (in general)

shelter, refuge

(magical) protection

throb

shake?

contrary, perverse, alarming, terrible, abnormal

dangerous waters

abnormal?

alarming

sad man

excessive

dry rock?

palpitations? (of heart)

sadness

sadness, a sad matter

pray for, prayer

yoke-oxen

the god Nehebkau and his Festival

lotus-bud scepter

neck

take away, carry off, assume (an office), save, rescue, withdraw (oneself)

surely, assuredly

rejoice

resemble

a loaf, a cake

upward

eternity, for ever

Nubian

teeth, tusks

tooth

tooth, tusk

tusk

miserable

succor, protect, protection

youthful, small?, brief? (of sufferings)

pendulous

knife

fish-shaped pendant

ruffle (hair)

flail(noun)

complaint, lamentation

open (a mine), assign (property to)

fresh land

stipulation

	draw back (door bolt), throw open (doors), crepitate (of broken bones)
	titulary
	titulary, to cover, overlaid
	young, youthful, ...the younger
	young, youthful, ...the younger
	child
	youth (abstract)
	be old, old age
	flail
	youth (abstract)
	strong, victorious, stiff, hard
	strong man, champion
	confident
	strong of arm, adult, champion
	strength, victory, hostages
	violent
	reis?
	victory, stiffness
	(bodily) fluid
	(one of the seven sacred oils)
	downwards
	tongue
	flame
	type of knife
	javelin
	King
	flame
	lap up, lick

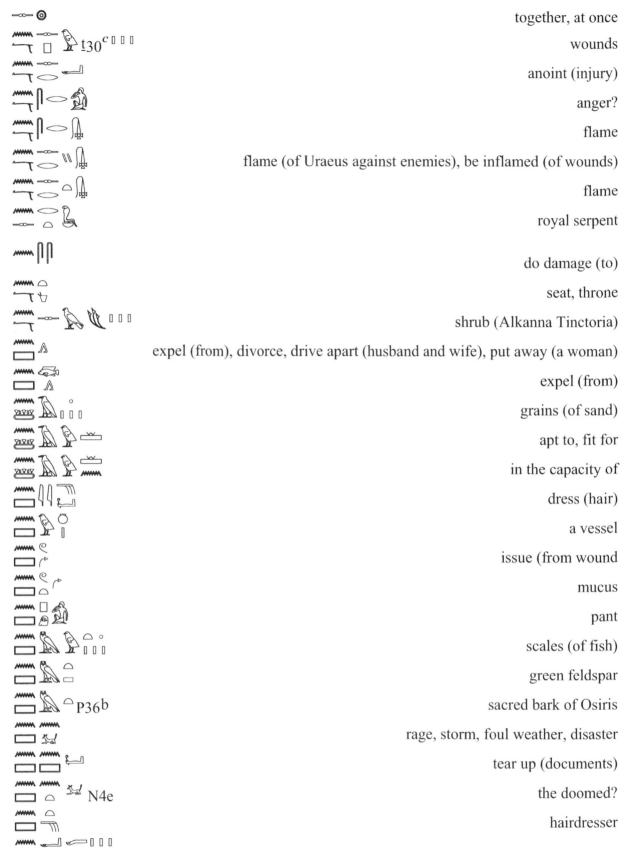

	together, at once
t30^c	wounds
	anoint (injury)
	anger?
	flame
	flame (of Uraeus against enemies), be inflamed (of wounds)
	flame
	royal serpent
	do damage (to)
	seat, throne
	shrub (Alkanna Tinctoria)
	expel (from), divorce, drive apart (husband and wife), put away (a woman)
	expel (from)
	grains (of sand)
	apt to, fit for
	in the capacity of
	dress (hair)
	a vessel
	issue (from wound
	mucus
	pant
	scales (of fish)
	green feldspar
P36^b	sacred bark of Osiris
	rage, storm, foul weather, disaster
	tear up (documents)
N4e	the doomed?
	hairdresser

	notched sycamore figs
	moisture
	suffer, be afflicted
	be bald
	affliction
	sift
	sieve
	copulate
	meditate on, think about, take counsel
	meditate on, think about
	plot
	harm, injury, be injured
	harm, injury
	sword
	some, a little, something, piece (of wood), profit, advantage
	some, a little
	long horn bull
	break open, break up
	breach (of law), crime
	loss
	turn aside, divert
	conspire
	overflow
	cackle (of goose), screech (of falcon)
	breach (in dam)
	of, belonging to
	Neith (goddess)
	Crown of Lower Egypt
	water

211

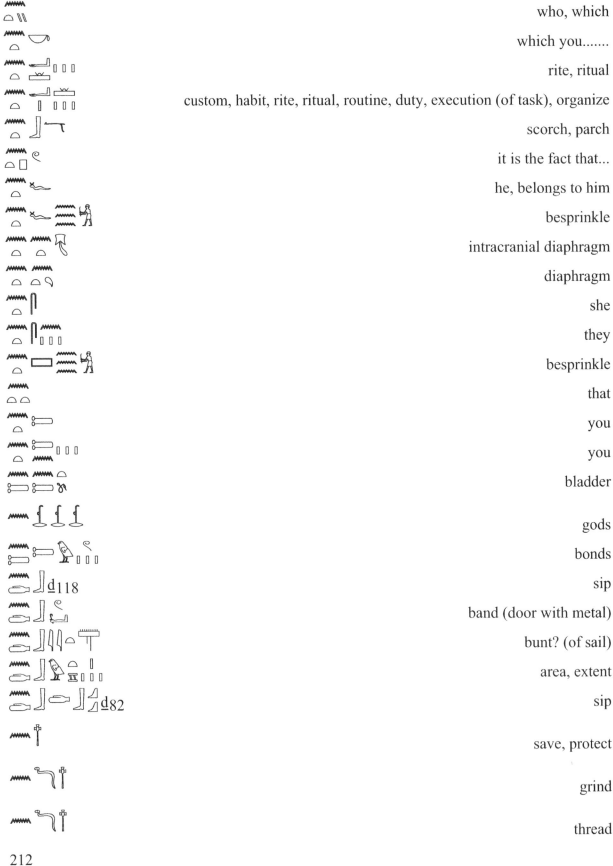

	who, which
	which you.......
	rite, ritual
	custom, habit, rite, ritual, routine, duty, execution (of task), organize
	scorch, parch
	it is the fact that...
	he, belongs to him
	besprinkle
	intracranial diaphragm
	diaphragm
	she
	they
	besprinkle
	that
	you
	you
	bladder
	gods
	bonds
	sip
	band (door with metal)
	bunt? (of sail)
	area, extent
	sip
	save, protect
	grind
	thread

212

confer (office on)

take counsel, ask advice, consult, enquire about, call upon, utter

confer (office), appoint (someone)

parch (with thirst)

measure (for loaves and dates)

chips (of stone)

baseness

counsel, consultation, oracle, greeting

pleasant, pleasing

well, hale, comfortable, joy

passion

consult (someone)

confer, take advice, consult, advice, counsel

greet

grasp, hold fast, catch, arrest, take possession, observe (regulations)

grasp, hold fast

imprisonment, suppression (of wrong)

imprisonment

greet, protect, protection

commoner, citizen

little / small (of size), dim (of eyes), dull (of ears), poor (of appetite)

commoner, citizen, good fellow (in half contemptuous address)

low estate

burn

213

 serf, serfs

protector

forever

Ripple of water, times three

water, rain, semen

water

be watery

urine

spittle

Muu class of Ritual dancers

cataract, rapid

Canal

Ekhmim

axe

liver

oar

tomb, cenotaph (above ground level)

tomb

partisan, supporter

canal, artificial lake

libation trough

R103 servants, underlings, partisans, supporters

weavers

214

bulls

weavers, servants, underlings

Garden pool

rebel (against)

coiffeur

ornaments

nest

arrow

sistra

sanctuary of Sokar

lake, pool, garden, basin (for liquids), sea

garden

cut off, cut up, cut down, hew (ship)

sand

a type of cake or biscuit

top of the Djed column

knife

slaughtering, terror

document

weight and value of a twelfth of one deben

cut, cut off, cut down

ascend

poor

poor man

a type of vegetable

persea tree

	fish-ponds
	mix, mingle with, confuse (message, words)
	necklace
	food offerings
	gullet
	knead (bread in brewing)
	kneaded bread-paste
	beer-mash (a drink)
	mix (with), consort (with)
	adjust, divide correctly, set out (design)
	value, price
	flow out, depart (of morbid fluid, evil spirit)
	be blind, make blind
	a measure of beer
	noble, august (of gods), splendid (of buildings), valuable (of plants, minerals), costly
	riches, wealth, precious things, dainties (to eat)
	blindness
	be discontented, angry
	discontent, anger
	a Nile fish (Tetrodon fahaka)
	anger
	(urinary) bladder
	swell
	respect, honor
	respect
	majesty, respect

216

	fight
	one greatly respected
	respect, awe
	the sixth month
Q19	bier
	metal object (used in ritual)
	papyrus roll, register
	foreigners
	disease-demons
	distress, disease
	walking-stick
	make music
	summer
	harvest, harvest-tax
	be warm, hot, have fever, become feverish
	fever, inflammation
	follow, accompany, serve, bring, present
	hemp?
	mother-in-law
	ring
	turn back, repulse, repel, police (district), detain, dart about (of fish)
	breast
	garment? (worn by vizier)
	slab (for offerings)

217

tear up (papers)

strife, quarrel

Nile acacia tree

kilt, apron

stop up, block

lad, younger son

daughter

little

little, meager, younger, junior, short

small, lowly man

hurry?, bolt (of horses)?

nose, nostril

type of grain

tomb garden

alabaster, vessels of alabaster

be wise, be conversant (with), be skilled (in), know

know

skill

wisdom

(medical) prescription

bubalis antelope

tongue

nightfall, night sky

take, accept, receive, assume (crown), catch (fish), purchase, wear clothes)

leather roll?, baton

sacred girdle

malachite

	refine? (gold)
	windows
	coiffeur
	panoply
	taxpayers
	assessment (of taxes)
	copse, scrub, brushwood?
	mysterious, secret, hidden, difficult
	(religious) mysteries
	secrets, (religious) mysteries
	secrets
	secrets
	stroke-oar?
	tortoise
	an offering-loaf
	leader, stroke (of bank of oars-women)
	chamber
	crate
	be quarrelsome
	hostility
	equip
	satchel
	be closed (of eyes)
	dough

N37 + D54

	pass (of property)
	go (to), walk, set out, pass, set (of sun)

𓊖𓄿𓏭	go (to), walk, set out, pass, set (of sun)
	a class of incantations?
	traveller
	babble
	walking, gait, movements, actions, business

Well full of water

	cow
	womb, vulva, uterus
	a mineral (not metal)
	a mineral (not metal)
	marshlands
	the far north
	assuredly, indeed
	coward
	retire, retreat
	steer
	helmsman
	steering oar
	steering-oar
	turn back!
	retreat
	dwell (in)

sit down

guest

guests

sloth

session

seat (in sense of Rank, Position)

homosexual

Well full of water

retreat

woman, wife

House plan

this, the

go up, ascend, be subtracted (mathematical)

house, household, palace, temple

household

go, come out, escape (from), be renowned (of name)

hero, champion

ferocious bull

crisis?

houses

be active

Great-House, Palace

House of Life (Temple Scriptorium, School)

come in and go out, come and go

get on with your work!

motion, procession, outcome, result

land emerged from inundation

excess, surplus

outcome, result

utterance

National shrine of Upper Egypt at El-Kab

more than

Palace of King of Lower Egypt

library

National shrine of Lower Egypt at Dep

height (of pyramid)

House of Gold (Treasury)

funerary workshop

Temple

National shrine of Lower Egypt at Pe

advance against (a position in war)

ascend and descend

a popular resort, thronging crowds

upper part of building

treasury

harem

ground floor

labor establishment

(ritual) procession

the month of Peret (Winter)

fruit, seed, (in sense of offspring, prosperity)

fruit, seed, (in sense of offspring, posterity)

invocation offerings

222

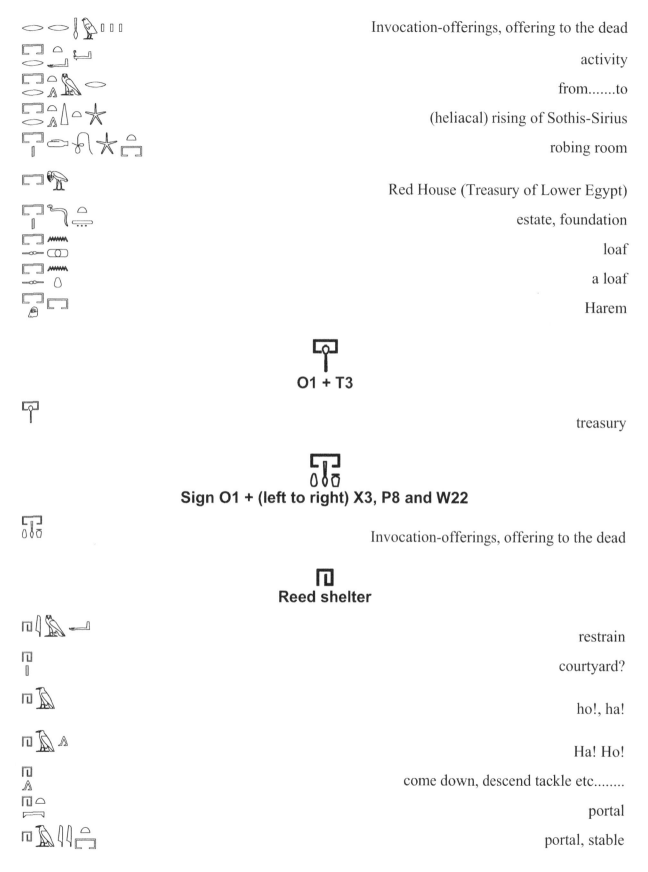

	Invocation-offerings, offering to the dead
	activity
	from.......to
	(heliacal) rising of Sothis-Sirius
	robing room
	Red House (Treasury of Lower Egypt)
	estate, foundation
	loaf
	a loaf
	Harem

O1 + T3

	treasury

Sign O1 + (left to right) X3, P8 and W22

	Invocation-offerings, offering to the dead

Reed shelter

	restrain
	courtyard?
	ho!, ha!
	Ha! Ho!
	come down, descend tackle etc........
	portal
	portal, stable

kindred, relatives

corvee

time, life-time, neighborhood, environment, belongings, circumstances, affairs

life-time

time

species of wild fowl

kindred

neighborhood, environment

ceilings

send (someone, something)

treading under foot?

send to (someone)

send to (a place), send for

dance?

rely on

herds (of game)

flag, fail, cease

a religious festival

ceiling

kind of jar

a type of jar

husband

hail!, shout

Hail!, shout

make acclamation

𓉿𓏭𓏭𓈖𓇳𓅿	jubilate
𓉿𓏭𓏭𓈖𓇳𓅿 332[c]	jubilation
𓉿𓉿𓈅	scurry
𓉿𓅿𓐍𓂾	be burnt
𓉿𓌟𓂼	plough
𓉿𓅃𓌟𓂼	tread
𓉿𓌟𓈅	tread (a place)
𓉿𓌟𓂼𓈅	tread out (grain), tread (a place), travel (to), enter (into someone)
𓉿𓌟𓂼𓈅𓏤	far-ranging of desire?
𓉿𓌟𓏢𓅝	ibis
𓉿𓌟𓈖𓏥	ebony
𓉿𓌟𓈖𓐎	a jar, measure of capacity
𓉿𓌟𓉿𓌟𓈅	traverse (country)
𓉿𓌟𓉿𓌟𓂼𓀜	drive out (pain)
𓉿𓌟𓉿𓌟𓂼𓈅	traverse (county)
𓉿𓌟𓂓	beat up, triturate
𓉿𓈖𓎬	law, ordinance
𓉿𓅿𓐍𓂾	be burning
𓉿𓅿𓂓𓏥	emolument
𓉿𓅿𓉿𓅿𓈐𓀁	war-cry, quacking (of wild-fowl)
𓉿𓅿𓉿𓅿𓈙𓏥	war-cry
𓉿𓅿𓉿𓅿𓏥	war-shout, quacking (of wild-fowl)
𓉿𓅿𓎺𓏥	fare (for conveyance)
𓉿𓈖𓎰	box, chest
𓉿𓎬	

225

𓈖𓈖𓈖	halt, cease
	praise (of god or king)
	jar, measure of about half liter
	associates, family, relatives
	waves
373	praise (of god or king)
	attend to, consider, trust (in), assent (to), approve(document), cajole?
	assent (to)
	deer
	attend to, consider
	milk
Y1v	contented
	be quiet, at peace
	day, daytime
	be pleased, satisfied, content, be quiet, at peace
	journal
	holiday, happy day
	poultry pen
	peace, pleasantness
	blast (of fire, of heat of sun, of disease)
	wade
	steal, be deficient, scanty
	call out?
	portal
	ape
E51	adoration
	female ape
	front of the head
	attack

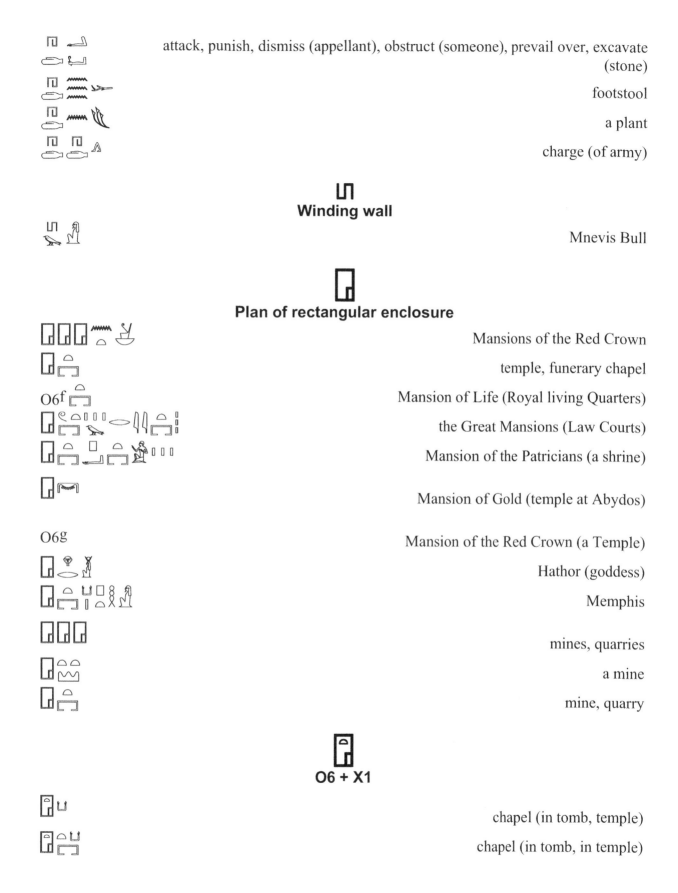

attack, punish, dismiss (appellant), obstruct (someone), prevail over, excavate (stone)

footstool

a plant

charge (of army)

Winding wall

Mnevis Bull

Plan of rectangular enclosure

Mansions of the Red Crown

temple, funerary chapel

O6f   Mansion of Life (Royal living Quarters)

the Great Mansions (Law Courts)

Mansion of the Patricians (a shrine)

Mansion of Gold (temple at Abydos)

O6g

Mansion of the Red Crown (a Temple)

Hathor (goddess)

Memphis

mines, quarries

a mine

mine, quarry

O6 + X1

chapel (in tomb, temple)

chapel (in tomb, in temple)

V30 + O7 (for the Goddess Nephthys)

Nephthys (goddess)

G5 in O6

Hathor

Palace with battlements

palace, temple

O11 + D36

palace, temple

Battlemented enclosure

hall, court

Part of the sign O13

portal

Var. of O13 with W10 and X1

hall, court

Door surmounted by frieze of cobras

the shrouded one (of Osiris)

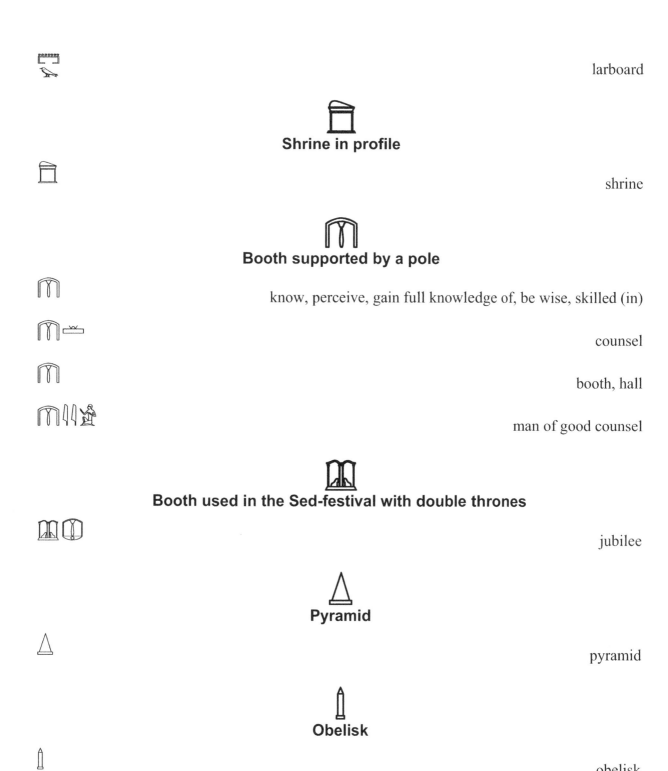

larboard

Shrine in profile

shrine

Booth supported by a pole

know, perceive, gain full knowledge of, be wise, skilled (in)

counsel

booth, hall

man of good counsel

Booth used in the Sed-festival with double thrones

jubilee

Pyramid

pyramid

Obelisk

obelisk

Hall of columns

office, bureau

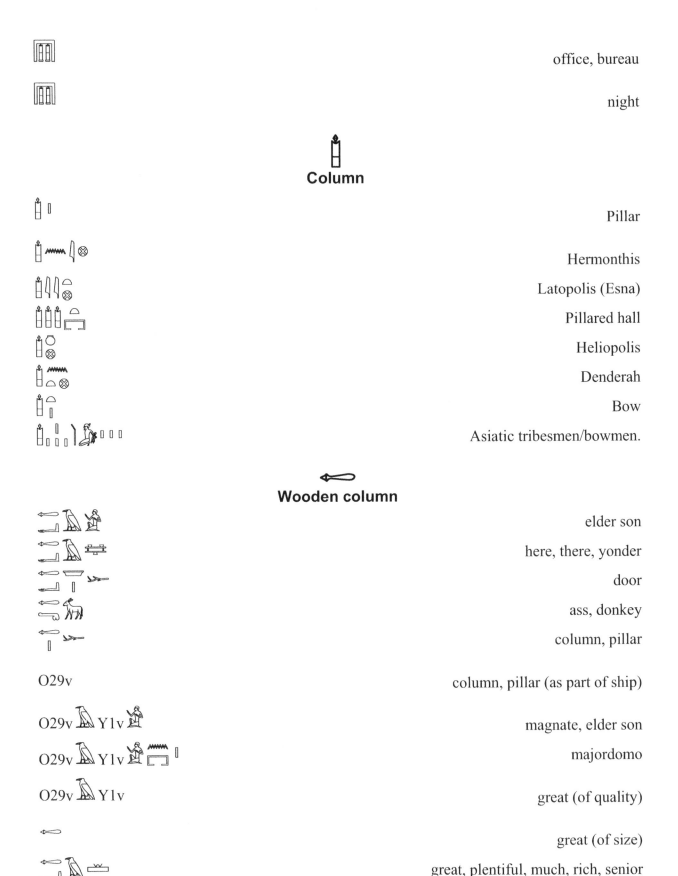

office, bureau

night

Column

Pillar

Hermonthis

Latopolis (Esna)

Pillared hall

Heliopolis

Denderah

Bow

Asiatic tribesmen/bowmen.

Wooden column

elder son

here, there, yonder

door

ass, donkey

column, pillar

O29v   column, pillar (as part of ship)

O29v Y1v   magnate, elder son

O29v Y1v   majordomo

O29v Y1v   great (of quality)

great (of size)

great, plentiful, much, rich, senior

230

Hieroglyphs	Meaning
	excess (over), difference (in mathematical)
	evil influence (causing disease)
	greatly
	the two leaves of the door
	the two leaves of the door
	stone vessels
	pleasant (of persons)
	pleasing, desirable, (of things)
	offerings
	food, provisions
	food, provisions, offerings
	selfishness
	Apep
	Asiatic
	thrash
	hoof, claw, foot
	hoof
	a great thing
	female ass, female donkey
	stone vessel
	costly stone, metal
	metal
	linen cloth
	be pale, pallid
	type of bread?
	steal (goods), rob (someone)
	many, numerous
	Great House, Palace, Pharaoh

Supporting pole

￥￥￥￥	(the four) posts (of the sky)
O30u	guilt
O30u	impediment, obstacle, (verbal) opposition, guilt, ill-will

Door leaf

	door
	the two leaves of the door
	Asiatic
	Asiatic woman

Gateway

	pylon
	door

Bolt

	night-bark (of sun god)
	man, someone, anyone, (no)-one, man of rank
t49	sheaf (of arrows)
	door bolt
	she, her, it, its
	betake oneself (to)
	weak

232

byre

linger, await, creep

be wise, prudent

one whose coming is awaited

guard, ward off, restrain, heed

beam, baulk

Sais

guardians, wardens

watch and ward, warding off (evil)

loins?

Asyut (Lycopolis)

jackal

drip

make to tarry

glorify (uraeus)

cake, loaf

prudence, wisdom

wall

ground, earth, soil, floor

floor boards, flooring

ground

make libation, pour out (water)

libation stone

rub out, obliterate

233

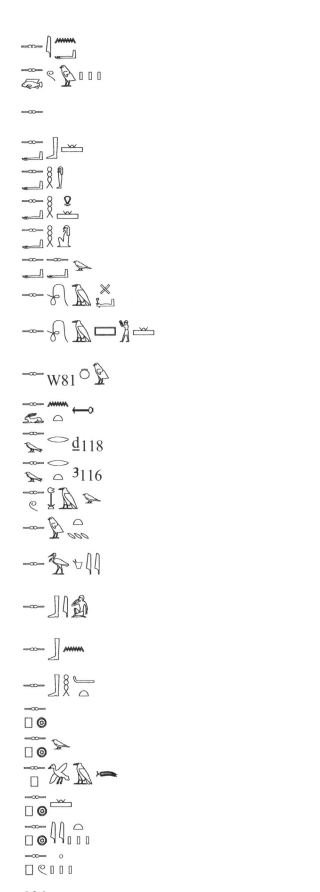

rub, rub out, obliterate, rub together

ropes

she, her, it

be equipped (with)

mummy (mummified person)

be noble

noble, dignitary

deface

break, cut (throat), cut off, cut down

pay honor to, applaud

perish

arrow

drink

drink-supply?

befool (someone)

wheat

make weary

drink

glide away (of snakes), steer off course, diverge

requisition

times, twice

misdeed, fault

centipede

remain over, be left out, excluded, abandoned

remnant

fragments, bundles

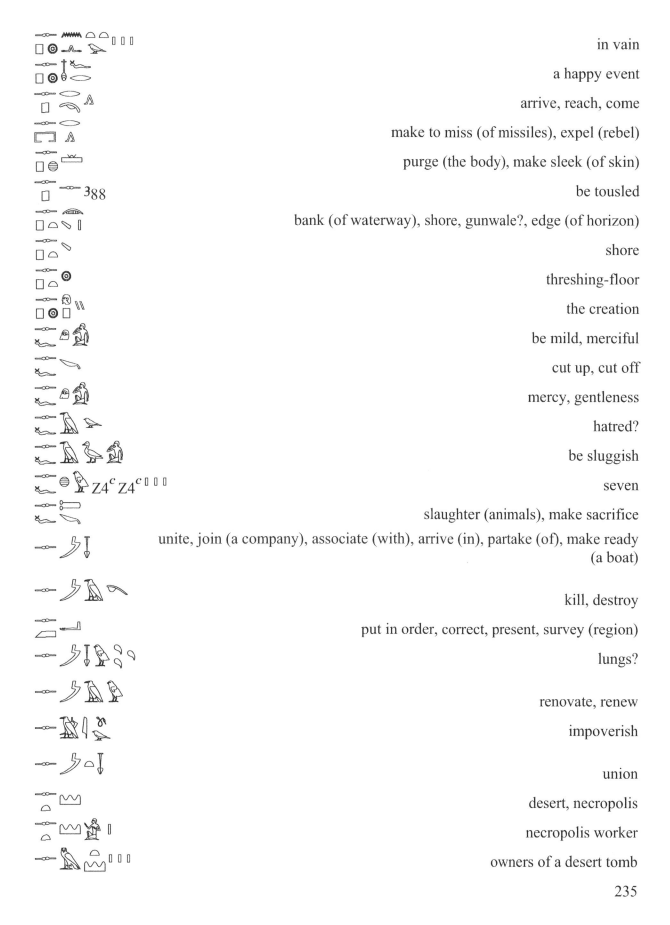

	in vain
	a happy event
	arrive, reach, come
	make to miss (of missiles), expel (rebel)
	purge (the body), make sleek (of skin)
388	be tousled
	bank (of waterway), shore, gunwale?, edge (of horizon)
	shore
	threshing-floor
	the creation
	be mild, merciful
	cut up, cut off
	mercy, gentleness
	hatred?
	be sluggish
	seven
	slaughter (animals), make sacrifice
	unite, join (a company), associate (with), arrive (in), partake (of), make ready (a boat)
	kill, destroy
	put in order, correct, present, survey (region)
	lungs?
	renovate, renew
	impoverish
	union
	desert, necropolis
	necropolis worker
	owners of a desert tomb

235

shift (boundary)

canoe

sink (ship)

eavesdrop

reveal

open

they, them, their

they, them, their

pass, pass by, surpass, transgress

cut off (heads), sever (necks)

be like, resemble, copy, imitate, conform

distress, calamity

offerings

everyone, everybody

overstep (boundary etc), overthrow (landmark)

overstep (boundaries etc), overthrow (landmark) M184

battlements M184 M184 M184

rampart O36b

jar

make to breathe, succor, unload (ships), empty out (contents)

blood

loosen, release

prayer

greed?

feed (someone), consume (food), supply (necessities)

be sad

pray (to), beg (from)

food-supply

squalls (of rain)

	pray, make supplication
	likeness, image, figure
	copy (of document)
	chariot-soldier
	suffer, be distorted
	take care of
	register, record, muster (troops), drive (birds)
	awaken
	frustrate
	locust
	phlegm
	worship
	worship
	sharpen
	tongue
	be greedy
	haughtiness
	longing
	darkness, obscurity
	Senet (a board game)
	likeness
	foundation, plan
	measure out (land), found (a house etc)
	a garment
	fear
	ram, sheep
	ewe
	goose

237

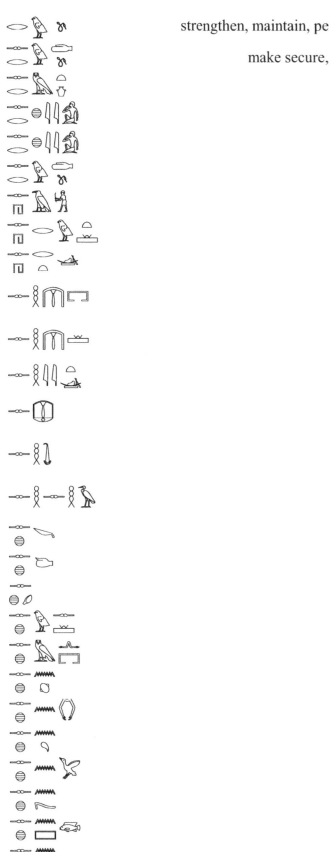

strengthen, maintain, perpetuate, make to flourish, restore (buildings)

make secure, provide, set right (a wrong), fulfill (contract)

foodstuff, beverage

accusation, reproach

accuser, complainer, evil spirit

make grow, plant (trees), erect (monuments)

hostility

make content, make peace

ship

booth, hall

council

boat (with cabin?)

make festive, adorn

crush, pound

screech (of bird)

chop off (limbs)

hit, smite, beat

be deaf

make prosperous, deck out (tomb)

fane

swelling?, gathering?

embrace, seek out, meet, occupy (a place)

kidney fat?

resting-place

bind together?

make to stink

238

M195	post
	sweep
	overthrow, throw down, force into place (dislocated bone)
	run, hurry, flee
	be neglectful
	comb (flax)
	be hasty, impetuous
	milk
	sweep, brush over, overlay (with), stroke
	a linen fabric
	ashes
	dispatch (army)
	soothe
	garments
	horse
	horse, mare
	cause to pass
	open
	cut (linen)
	writing, depiction, record, papyrus roll, letter, document
	write, inscribe, paint, draw, enroll (troops)
	pass, spread, spread out, strew, post (sentries)
	threshold
	scribe
	make progress
	prayer
	beseech (from)
	pray (to)
G48 [c]	nest

	disk (of metal)
	lead, guide
	lotus
M9b	lotus-shaped
	weave
	ropes, cordage
	arrow
	lessen
	cake
	make wise
	sistrum
	drops (of moisture)
	shrine (of falcon)
	captive, living prisoner
	strain (medicament)
	embroil (in quarrels)
	adorn, decorate
P59	Sokar (god)
	make to bow down
	destroy
	command (ship)
	cause to see, glimpse (someone)
	woman, wife
	pin-tail duck
	it, them
	injury
	strip (of cloth), rag
	choice things (of food)

	crown (king)
	woman, wife
	Seth (god)
	staff, props (plural), clouds (figuratively)
	praises
	raising up
	clothe
	trembling
	eye-paint
	ease (misery)
	punish
	break up (hailstorm), rupture (cist), inflict (wound), fracture, rupture
	break, break into, invade, breach (wall), break open (way)
	amuse oneself, take recreation
	slander
	endow (altars), provide (for someone)
	foundation, endowment
	hear (voice etc), hear of (something), listen (to), obey, understand, judge, satisfy (conditions)
	department (of the Residence)
	sleeping-place
	sleeper
	child, foster-child (of king)
	make envious
	know
	nightfall, night sky
	secret
	make secret, mysterious
	secretly

241

O34 + D54

𓊃𓂻	go!
𓊃𓂻 𓏭𓏭	who?, what?
𓊃𓂻	she, her, it
𓊃𓂻 𓅓 𓏤𓏤𓏤	day, dates (in time)
𓊃𓂻 𓃀𓏭𓂾	go, travel, attain, watch over, send, conduct (to), spend, pass (time), attain (good repute), approach
𓊃𓂻 𓅡	To wane, to dwindle away, To faint, to perish
𓊃𓂻 𓅡 𓏴𓈖𓌗	A burnt-offering
𓊃𓂻 𓃀𓏭𓆓	uraeus
𓊃𓂻 𓃀𓂝𓏤	squalor
𓊃𓂻 𓅓 𓏤𓏤𓏤	spoils (of army)
𓊃𓂻 𓅡 𓈖𓏤𓏺	crumble to dust
𓊃𓂻 𓃀𓊪𓂝𓏤𓏤𓏤	burden, cargo
𓊃𓂻 𓃀𓊪𓅡 𓏤𓏤𓏤	wrong, evil
𓊃𓂻 𓊪𓅅 𓏺	in quest of
𓊃𓂻 𓅓 𓏤𓏤𓏤	dates

Fortified wall

O36^c 𓊵	wall
O36^c 𓊶	fence, stockade
𓊵𓏤	rampart
O36^b O36^b O36^b	limits

Corner of wall

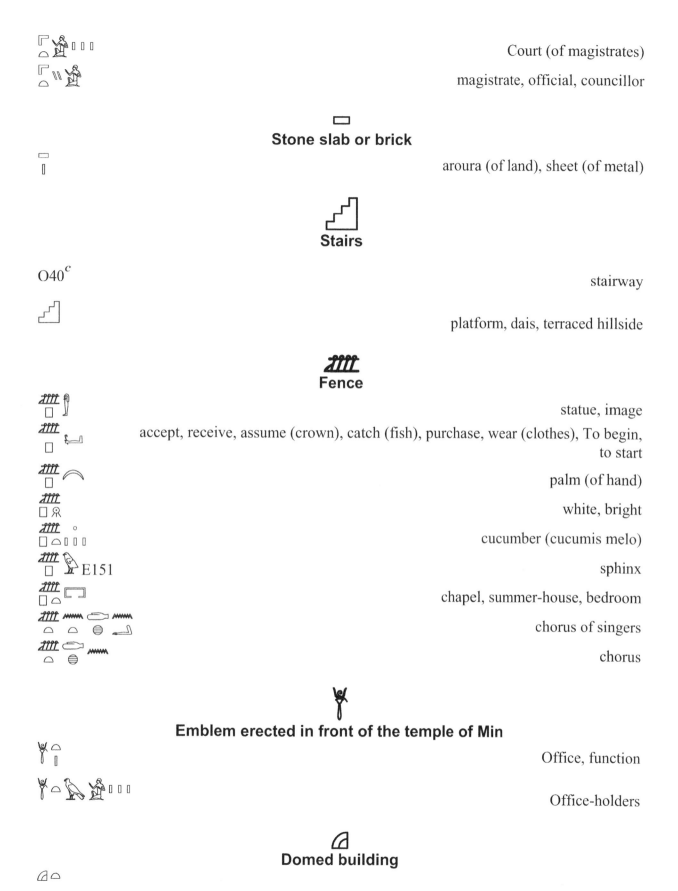

Court (of magistrates)

magistrate, official, councillor

Stone slab or brick

aroura (of land), sheet (of metal)

Stairs

O40^c

stairway

platform, dais, terraced hillside

Fence

statue, image

accept, receive, assume (crown), catch (fish), purchase, wear (clothes), To begin, to start

palm (of hand)

white, bright

cucumber (cucumis melo)

sphinx E151

chapel, summer-house, bedroom

chorus of singers

chorus

Emblem erected in front of the temple of Min

Office, function

Office-holders

Domed building

Prehistoric building at Hieraconpolis

carnelian?, jasper?

carnelian

Nekhen (Hieraconpolis)

Nekhen

(someone from) Nekhen, a Nekhenite

Var. of O47

carnelian?, jasper?

carnelian

Nekhen (Hieraconpolis)

Nekhen

shrine

(someone from) Nekhen, Nekhenite

(someone from) Nekhen, a Nekhenite

Crossroads

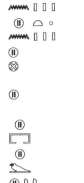

lower heaven

city, town

local (of gods)

citizens, townsmen

Threshing floor covered with grains

$Z4^c$

twice (repetition)

Granary

	granary

Boat

	ship
	turn upside down
	ships

Boat, upside down

	turn upside down
P3^c	Sacred bark

Fisherman's boat, with net

P4^c	Sacred bark
	fish (synodontis schall)
	investigate
	fisherman, fowler
	loose (fetters), release, return (from), go home
	distribute rations?
	capable, skilled
Z2^b	fowlers
	fishermen, fowlers

Mast with sail

	fan
	skipper (of boat), sailor

	the Thinite nome
	wind
	wind, air, breath
	air
	an outlying district of Egypt?
	Thinite nome

Mast with ladder

	stand
	attendant
	stand, stand by, stand erect, raise oneself, stand up, rise up, arise, attend, wait, lifetime
	heap, portion, allotment, quantity (mathematics), wealth, riches
	measure for beer
	stela
	(proper) positions (of things)
	positions (of things), (ceremonial) stations (of persons)
	lifetime, period, space of time
	ships
	attendance, service
	(ceremonial) stations (of persons)
I114	lifetime, period, space (of time)
	tombs
	ships
	Female Attendant
	spinal ridge

246

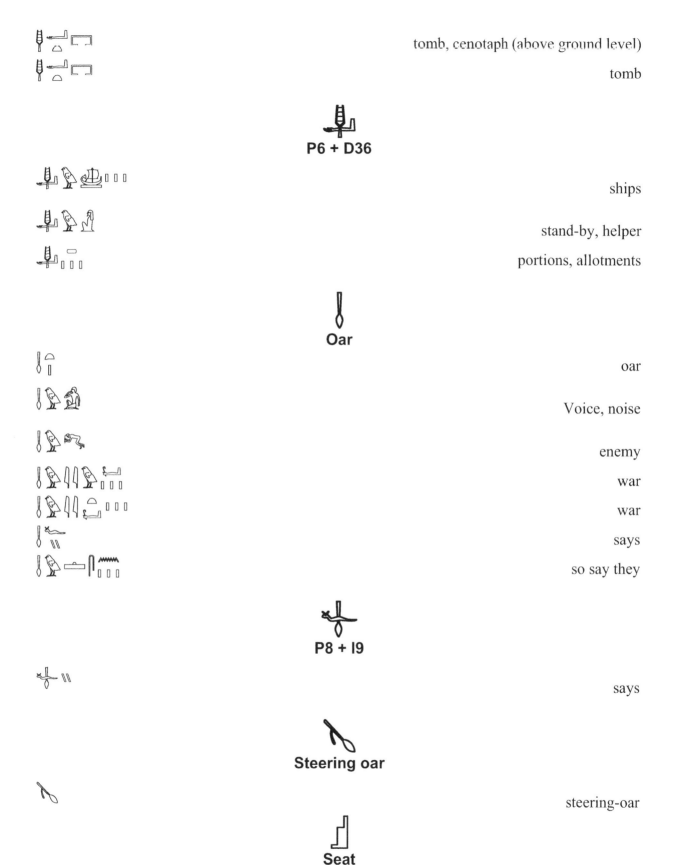

tomb, cenotaph (above ground level)

tomb

P6 + D36

ships

stand-by, helper

portions, allotments

Oar

oar

Voice, noise

enemy

war

war

says

so say they

P8 + I9

says

Steering oar

steering-oar

Seat

	Isis
	Osiris
	seat, throne, place, grounds (of house), department, office, storehouse, position, rank of official
	successor
	favorite, favorite place, wish, affection
	Place of Records
	stroke (of malignant beings)
	place of records (archive)
	(the state of) dying
F51b	speech
	dwelling-place
	divine state
	utterance
	rank, station
	rank, station
	liability to corvee
	meal
	cleanliness
	avenue, promenade
	interment
	plowing
	entertainment
	(the state of) being coffined
	(the state of) being buried
	evil case
	evil-case

---

successor

Portable seat. More recent shape of Q1

C98^c — Osiris

Mat or stool or stand

	Those
	These
	These
	slug?
	slug
	base (for statue)
	Pe
	mat
	this, the
	fly, fly up
	lock? (on door)
	irrigable land?
	quail?
	falsehood?, gossip?
	primaeval god
	primaeval god, man of ancient family
	scratch
	Pakhet (She who scratches [a lion goddess])
	lion goddess
	She who scratches (a lion goddess)
	be turned over (of dislocation of collar-bone)

249

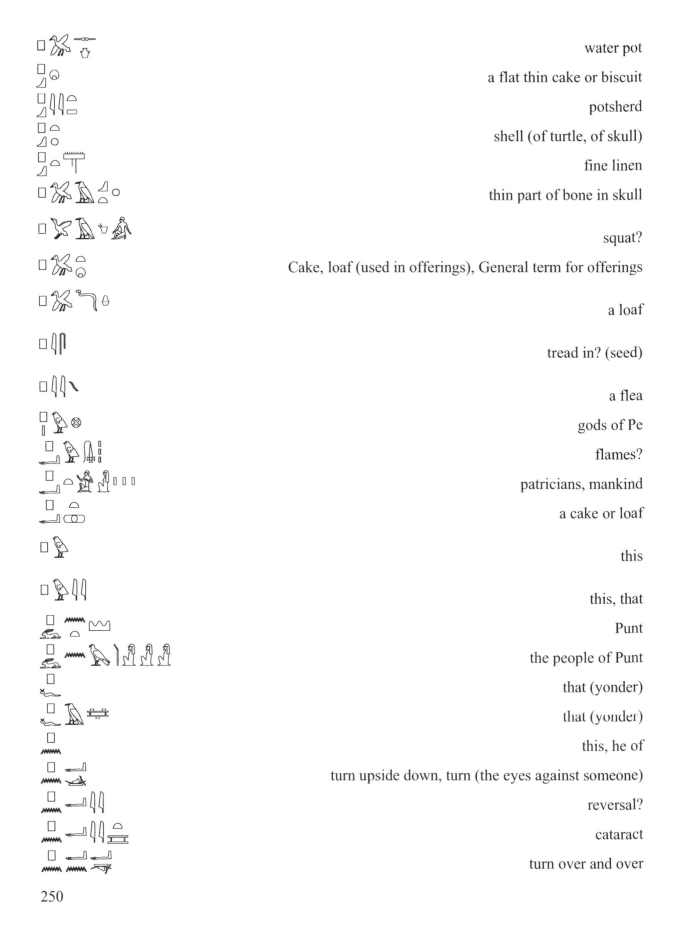	water pot
	a flat thin cake or biscuit
	potsherd
	shell (of turtle, of skull)
	fine linen
	thin part of bone in skull
	squat?
	Cake, loaf (used in offerings), General term for offerings
	a loaf
	tread in? (seed)
	a flea
	gods of Pe
	flames?
	patricians, mankind
	a cake or loaf
	this
	this, that
	Punt
	the people of Punt
	that (yonder)
	that (yonder)
	this, he of
	turn upside down, turn (the eyes against someone)
	reversal?
	cataract
	turn over and over

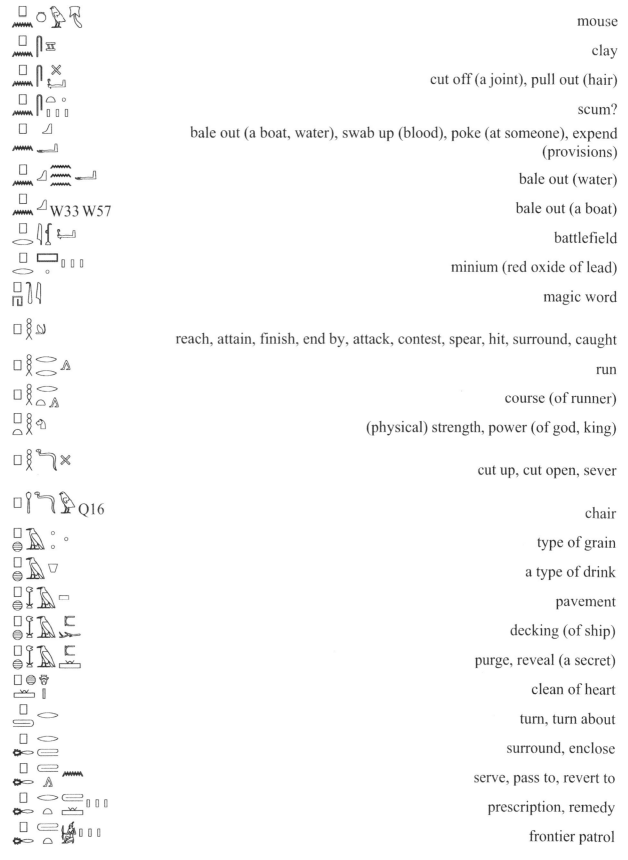

	mouse
	clay
	cut off (a joint), pull out (hair)
	scum?
	bale out (a boat, water), swab up (blood), poke (at someone), expend (provisions)
	bale out (water)
W33 W57	bale out (a boat)
	battlefield
	minium (red oxide of lead)
	magic word
	reach, attain, finish, end by, attack, contest, spear, hit, surround, caught
	run
	course (of runner)
	(physical) strength, power (of god, king)
	cut up, cut open, sever
Q16	chair
	type of grain
	a type of drink
	pavement
	decking (of ship)
	purge, reveal (a secret)
	clean of heart
	turn, turn about
	surround, enclose
	serve, pass to, revert to
	prescription, remedy
	frontier patrol

251

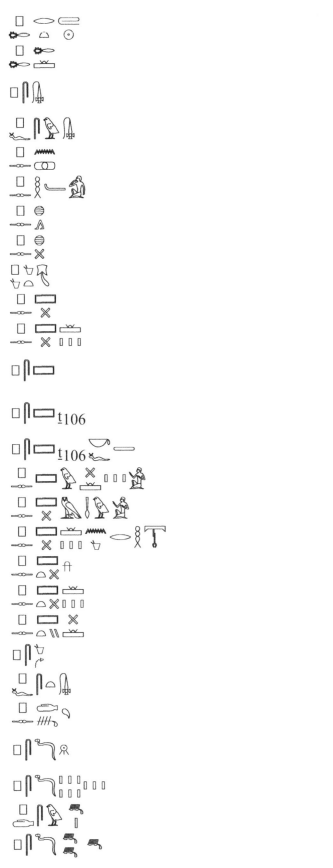

	transitory state (description of life)
	control? (horses)
	cook
	preparation (of food and drink)
	a loaf
	bite, sting
	be distraught, be strewn (with)
	be distraught
	toad or frog
	divide, share (with)
	division
	divide
t̲106	ritual instrument (for Opening of the mouth)
t̲106	ritual instrument (made from Obsidian)
	arbitrator
	break silence
	midnight
	carpet, matting (of reeds)
	sharing out, share, portion
	part, division
	spit on, spit at
	mode of cooking
	upper back
	shine
	nine
	back
	back, spine

252

the new moon and its festival

group of nine

split (metal)

split (heads, metal, wood) fracture (bones), separate (combatants), slice (bread)

split (wood)

spread (oneself over)

straddle, spread (oneself over), spread out (awnings)

straddle

precinct of Osiris at Abydos

open

mouth (of valley)

entrance (of building, of horizon), mouth (of valley), arena, battlefield

open, reveal, be open (of wounds)

entrance (of horizon)

be open (of wounds)

bowl

battlefield

open hearted

honest

The sky, heaven

trample (enemies)

tread (roads), trample (enemies)

see, behold

who?, what?

create

Ptah

cast (to the ground), put down (someone carried), be stretched out (in obeisance)

cast (to the ground)

your Queen

253

	knee
R3i	box, casket
	stamp flat, flatten
	sand dunes?
	pellet
	measure (for pigment)
	stretch out (man on ground)
	stretch (cord in foundation ceremony), stretch out (arms), stretch out (man on ground)
	stretch (cord in foundation ceremony)
	be glad
	unwrinkled, far-sighted, prescient
	foreigners
	chapel (in tomb, temple)

Coffin

	bury
	burial

Brazier with flame

	cook
	warm, warmth, temperature, inflammation, fever, mood
	be warm, hot, have fever, become feverish

R3c
Variation of Pedestal table with offerings

R3c	staff, gang, partisans

Loaf of bread on a mat

boon, offering

be pleased, be happy, be gracious, be at peace, To pardon (n : someone)

offerings

offerings

altar

be pleased (with), be happy, be gracious (to), pardon (someone)

Offering to the god

be well-disposed toward

non-combatants

non- combatants

peace, contentment, good pleasure

forecourt offerings

set (of sun), go to rest, die (of people)

bundle (of herbs)

bowl (for bread offerings)

graciousness, peace, mercy

offerings

the peaceful ones (the blessed dead)

Censer

cover, spread (with wings)

burn (incense), cense (gods), fumigate (patient)

(royal) nursery, chamber, harem

cover, roof over, hide oneself, take cover, droop (of eyebrows)

hut, hide (of fowler)

255

	roof
	Kyphi
	linen cover (of jar)
	Byblos
	(seagoing) ship

Bowl for incense burning

	ram
	precinct
	cense

Emblem of divinity

O29v	the great god
	gods of Pe
	sacred writings
	word of God, divine decree, sacred writings, written characters, script
	written characters, script
	the good god
	godhood, divinity
	god
	divine, sacred
	magic cord
	natron?
	gods

256

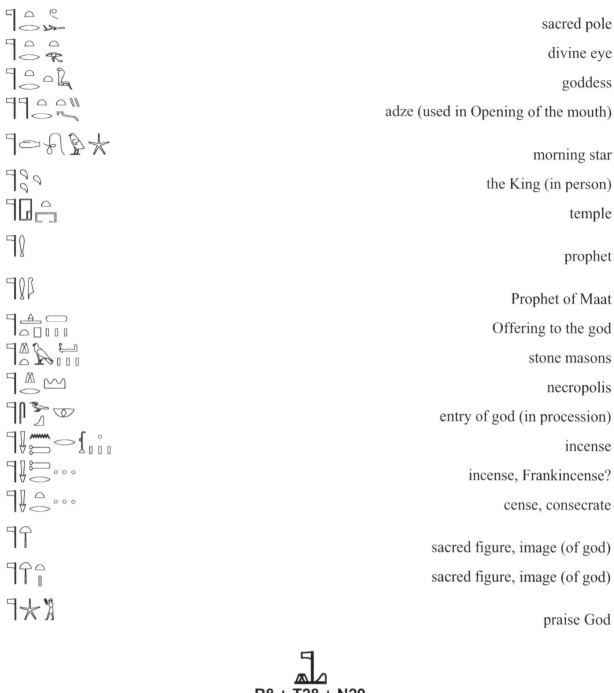

	sacred pole
	divine eye
	goddess
	adze (used in Opening of the mouth)
	morning star
	the King (in person)
	temple
	prophet
	Prophet of Maat
	Offering to the god
	stone masons
	necropolis
	entry of god (in procession)
	incense
	incense, Frankincense?
	cense, consecrate
	sacred figure, image (of god)
	sacred figure, image (of god)
	praise God

R8 + T28 + N29

necropolis

Sacred fetish of Osiris (djed column)

stable, enduring

257

stable, enduring

the djed column

Busiris

Mendes

stability, duration

Falcon Horus on standard (R12) wearing the feather G5

right (-hand), right-side, the West

the west wind

Westerners

Var. of R13

right (hand), right side, the west

the West

right (hand), western, the West

the west wind

Westerners

the West

right-hand side, right, right side of

right-hand, right side of, right

Emblem of the East

To Desire, wish for

	To Desire, wish for
	Panther
	Ivory, Elephant tusk
	A kind of fish
	finger, toe nail
	The east wind
	Left-hand, The left side of
	leopard
	The East
	the east wind
	East, eastern, The East
	, Easterners
	The east of
	*Snare, bird trap (?)
	The East
	Headress [king]

Papyrus stem surmounted by two feathers

fetish of Kos

Emblem for the city of Abydos

the Thinite nome

Was-scepter (S40) surmounted by a feather

Milk or cream

milky wine?

Thebes

Emblem of the Goddess Seshat

Seshat (goddess)

Emblem of the God Min

Min (god)

shrine

Letopolis

cow

Akhmim

Emblem of the Goddess Neith

Neith (goddess)

White Crown (Upper Egypt)

Crown of Upper Egypt

Red Crown (Lower Egypt)

of, belonging to

S3 + V30

		King of Lower Egypt
		Crown of Lower Egypt
	S5 + V30	
		the Double-Crown
	Blue Crown	
		the Blue Crown
	Atef Crown	
		Atef-crown
	Headband	
		invest (with insignia)
		hew (timber), build (ships)
		fillet?
	Collar of beads	
		ornamental collar
		breadth
	Collar of gold	
		melt (metal), cast (objects in metal), gild, model, fashion
		gild

261

	cast (objects in metal)
	goldsmiths
	Ombi (Kom Ombo)
	gold collar
	gold
	the Golden One (epithet of Hathor)
	guard
	Ombos
	gold two-thirds fine?

S12 + T3

	silver, money

Pectoral of glass and faience beads

	gleam, glittering
	Libyans
	faience

Bead necklace with counterpoise

	necklace (sacred to Hathor)

Cylinder seal attached to a bead necklace

	precious

262

seal-bearer

precious things, treasures

treasurers

Cylinder seal attached to a string

fort

seal

chest

cattle

contract

rings?

treasurers

weight and value of a twelfth of one deben

Ring

Ring

Shoulder knot

pour (water)

Asia, island of Sehel

Asiatics

larboar

Two flagellums united by ring V9

To reassemble (dismembered body), assemble, bring together (people)

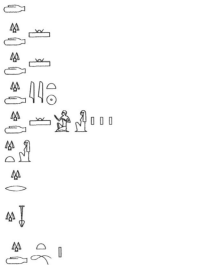

To associate (with), join (someone), unite (lands)

To accumulate (grain), compile (spell)

To extend (hand)

cycle (of festivals)

crowd

crowd

total

grand total

collection (of recipes)

Knot

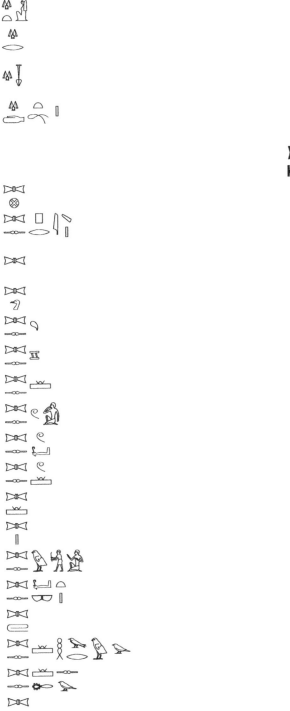

Elephantine (Island near Aswan)

fighting

model (face of sphinx)

neck

vertebra

sandbank, drought

used as a prefix to form abstracts

speech, utterance, phrase, sentence, maxim

tie (knot), tie on (fillet), weave (cloth)

speech, utterance

phrase, sentence

vertebra, spine

commander, protector (of poor)

troop captain

vice-versa

reproach

crime?

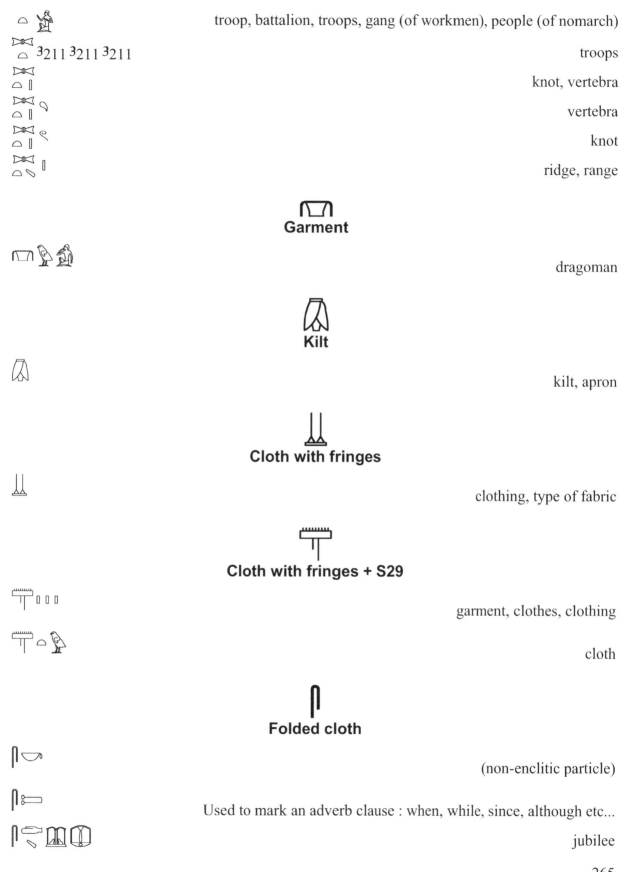

troop, battalion, troops, gang (of workmen), people (of nomarch)

troops

knot, vertebra

vertebra

knot

ridge, range

Garment

dragoman

Kilt

kilt, apron

Cloth with fringes

clothing, type of fabric

Cloth with fringes + S29

garment, clothes, clothing

cloth

Folded cloth

(non-enclitic particle)

Used to mark an adverb clause : when, while, since, although etc...

jubilee

she, her, it, its

ornamental vessel

weak

byre

wisdom

wise man

be wise, prudent

be wise, prudent, be satisfied, be sated

sift (flour etc)

be satisfied

need

prepare? (bier)

the weak of arm, weak man

beam, baulk

satiety

lengthen (building), prolong (lifetime, friendship)

make glad

keep an eye on

jackal

drip

cross (water)

many colored of plumage (of Solar Horus)

266

𓏭𓏤𓎡𓃶	variegated of plumage
	parti-colored snake
	dapoled cow
	lay out? (garden)
	lotus-leaf
	burn up
	lock of hair
	be wise
	needy man
	need
	wisdom, understanding
	grumbler?
	toe
	kick, reach, arrive at
	Orion (constellation)
	endow (with)
	neighbors, dependants
	neighborhood
	forcibly drive (into)
	spiritualize (deceased), glorify (god, name), beautify (tomb)
	(ritual) recitations
	type of bat (mammal)
	drive back, repel, force (ship over), apply (oil)
	force (ship over)
	cake, loaf

pull together, be wary

self possessed

prudence, wisdom

wall

tow boat

a festival

3363

shuffle

recognize

recognize, perceive, know, be aware of(verb)

perception, knowledge

dose? (a patient)

encroach upon

encroach upon (lands), cheat

fringed cloth

mutilator, twister (of speech), cheater

announce (someone), make a complaint (against)

, make pregnant

inundate

inspection

inspect, examine, revise, entrust, allot, assign, destine (to a fate), organize (household)

inspect

investigation

inventory

268

𓈖𓏭𓂧𓊽𓏤	make well-disposed (to)
𓈖𓂧𓅃𓅃𓊽𓏤	make well-disposed
𓈖𓏭𓆛𓈖	wait (for)
𓈖𓏭𓆛𓌪	sever (neck)
𓈖𓏭𓆛𓂺	rub
𓈖𓏭𓏤𓈖	pass away (die)
𓈖𓏭𓏤𓎱	clay
𓈖𓏭𓈖𓈖	run, pass away (die)
𓈖𓏭𓆛𓈖�舟	canoe
𓈖𓏭𓆛𓈖𓏤𓏤𓏤	clay seal
𓈖𓏭𓆛𓈖𓅆	make miserable
𓈖𓏭𓈐𓅃𓈖	hold back
𓈖𓏭𓈖𓏰	six-weave linen
𓈖𓏭𓏏𓈖𓏲𓄓	lighten (burden), lessen
𓈖𓏭𓌱𓊽𓏤	enrich (someone), make perfect (the deceased), make splendid (a building)
𓈖𓏭𓎺𓈖	subordinate (someone to)
𓈖𓏭𓊃𓀜	make impotent
𓈖	who?, what?
𓈖𓈖	she, her, it
𓈖𓏭𓈖𓏭𓈖	hurry
𓈖𓂝𓅃𓄿	gunwale
𓈖𓂝𓅃𓏭𓊽𓏤	make great (of size, rank, position), magnify (god, truth)
𓈖O29v	increase (benefits), glorify (life on earth)
𓈖O29v𓏭𓏭𓀜	tremble

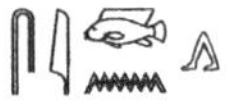

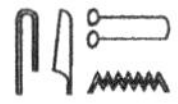

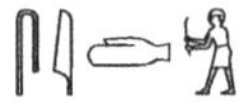

269

cause to go bad

saw out (timbers), take out, circumcise, castrate

wash down (medicine), swallow, inlay

beautify

make live, preserve, revive (dead), nourish, feed, perpetuate (name)

sculptor

make little of, lessen, diminish

cause to approach (of death), bring to an end, forward (pleas, affairs)

cause to ascend, make to rise (in rank)

bring, present, publish (report), obtain (royal bounty), report (evil)

ewer on a stand

uraerus

finish off, complete, put a stop to

kill

be noble

noble, dignitary

rank, dignity (of Royalty)

rank, dignity, dignities (plural), honors (plural)

noble

make to vie (with)

raise up, cause to stand, set up, erect, accuse, establish (against)

make numerous, multiply

police, policeman

escort

cause to enter, bring to land, bring, send in, drive (animals)

head of family

make hale

pass (on road), escape (from), surpass (someone), pass away, transgress, occur

journey

ponder

make to endure, to last, make stay (in house), lengthen (life), last long

pay honor to, applaud

what is past

make prosperous (of years), richly provide (altars), refurbish (stela)

make green (herbage), make to flourish (of person, office)

cleanse

cleanse, purify, decorate (a building), consecrate

cleanse, purify, decorate (a building), consecrate (temple servants)

day, dates (in time)

open, reveal (oneself)

open the heart (to wisdom)

instruct

make thick, make stout (the heart)

open

perish

affliction

flattery

	pain
O233	tower
II	pond
	instruct
	price
³410	drink
	promote (an official), increase (herds)
	drink-supply
	To weary someone
	break up (of ship)
	boast of, vaunt with
O118	throw down (building)
	wind
	loincloth
	egg
	coffin
	shroud
	spend the night
Z4^c	decay
	make strong, powerful
	make extensive (of movements)
	widen, make wide, make spacious, extend (boundaries)
	dry
	pulverize
	grind, pulverize
	wheat
	force (of wind)

𓅱𓂋	force (of wind)
𓅱𓂋𓅱	walk about, journey, travel, go forth
𓂋𓅱	go forth, walk about, journey, travel
𓅱	plant (with trees)
𓅱𓂋𓅱 V48	bandage
𓅱	make to linger
𓅱	hand over, pass on, assign (office etc)
𓅱	convey (to someone)
𓅱	make healthy, keep safe, calm (fear)
𓅱	die
𓅱	inform about
𓅱	wind (rope around)
𓅱	overstep (fence)
𓅱	star
𓅱	pupil, student
𓅱	teach, teaching
𓅱	door
𓅱 U97	surveying instrument
𓅱	(written) teaching, instructions
𓅱	cleanse
𓅱	give a clear character (to), commend (someone)
𓅱	make weary

	morning star
	rebel
	rebel-serpent (a demon)
	flautist?
	alienate (relatives, property)
3 15^c	rebels
	glide away (of snakes), steer off course, diverge
	fish
$\underline{d}$280 E100^b	cow in suck
	woman who breast feeds
$\underline{t}$19b	Sweet flag?
	make to flee
	cry out
	lowing (of cattle)
	close (arms around someone), shut away (from)
	jar
	pylon-shaped chest
	portal
	make to vomit
	calf (lower part of leg)
	splendid, precious
	Sobek (crocodile god)
W14^c	libation-jar

274

enclosure

rampart

laugh, laughter

laugh

friendly

make weak

birds made to fly (flushed from cover?)

district, nome

overturn, renew (skin)

appeal to, petition (someone), make petition

rib

petitioner

petition

petitioner

attain

lasso

lasso

ribs of beef

purge (the body), make sleek (of skin)

cause to circulate, brandish (weapons)

register, copy

lip (of mouth, vagina, wound, jar)

ritual? object

display skill, supply (food), restore to order

sharp, effective, skilled

Sopd (god)

triangle

	supply
	be mild, merciful
	mercy, gentleness
	mix (with)
	yesterday
	hatred?
	sluggishness
	the gentle man
	muddle
	be kindly, merciful
	afflict
	be drowsy
	purify
	lose, loosen, release, purify, remove (evil), lay aside (garment)
	part (fighting animals), offer (to god), let go (of)
	fortress
	offerings
	excretion
	The Seven-Horned (deity)
	break? (knives)
	clemency
	knife
E100	sacrifice
	oil, conifer resin?
	butcher
	oil
F37	help, succor

276

𓊪𓅃𓀀	a priest
𓊪𓏤𓏤𓏤	deed, event, affair, pastime
𓊪𓌡	priest (who clothed the god)
𓊪𓏲𓏛	scalp, side
𓊪𓏲𓃔	wild bull
𓊪𓏲𓅢𓏤𓏥	ramp?
𓊪𓏲𓅢𓏤𓏤	unite, join (a company), associate (with), arrive (in)
𓊪𓏲𓅢𓅢𓏤	partake (of), make ready (a boat), kill, destroy
𓊪𓏲𓅢𓏲	put in order, correct, present, survey (region)
𓊪𓏲𓏛𓀀	justify (the dead, the living)
𓊪𓏲𓅢𓏲𓏤	renovate, renew
𓊪𓂀𓅢𓏲	impoverish
𓊪𓎺	report, acknowledgement (of letter)
𓊪𓎺𓏲𓀀	report, make report, complain, announce, proclaim
𓊪𓎺𓏲𓏤	whip
𓊪𓎺𓏲𓀢	chastise
𓊪𓎺𓏲𓏤𓏤𓏤	curds
𓊪𓎺𓏲𓀀	charge, accusation
𓊪𓅃𓏤𓏤𓋌	desert, necropolis
𓊪𓅢𓏤	sounding-pole?
𓊪𓅢𓏤𓏤	make fortunate, cleanse
𓏐𓏐𓏐	pastures, plants, herbage, vegetables, herb

pastures, plants, herbage, vegetables, herb

vegetables

probably, surely

retire, withdraw

goose

set in place (parts of body), set up (stela), record (events), confirm (office)

make firm, establish, make to endure, perpetuate, fasten, make fast

supports of sky

rungs of ladder

settle (endowment), confirm, embellish, restore, efficiently execute

publish, make effective (words), pull, set in order (affairs),

advance, ennoble, make distinguished (a name), endow

emissaries

friend (of king)

cause pain

friends

flood (land), drown (enemy), sink (his ship)

forget, ignore

deliver (woman)

elder, eldest

hear

hammock

bear witness to (truth), examine, make enquiry

subjects, subordinates, compulsory labor

they, them, their

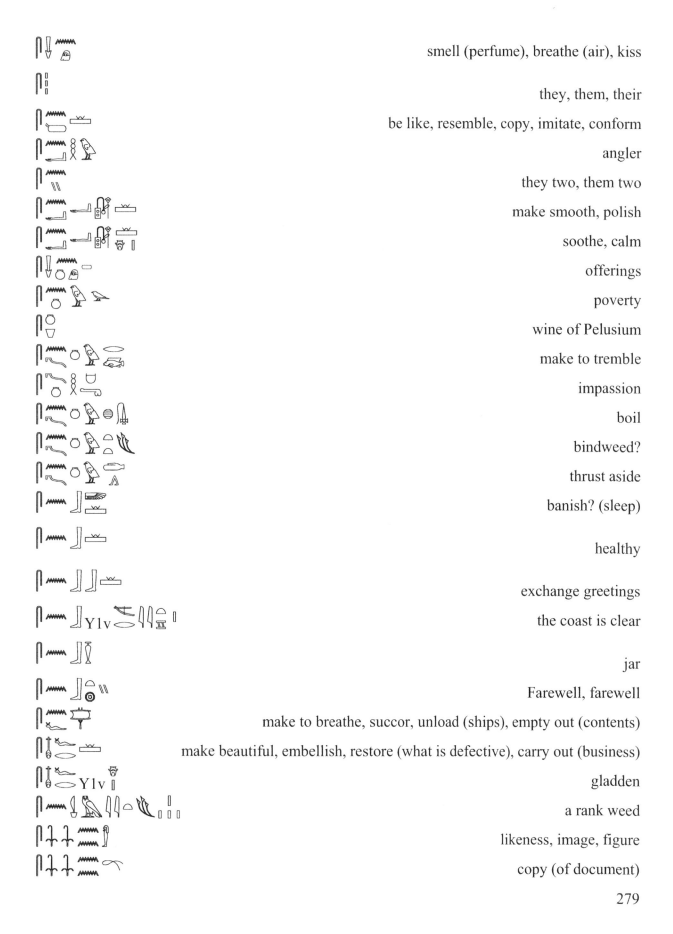

	smell (perfume), breathe (air), kiss
	they, them, their
	be like, resemble, copy, imitate, conform
	angler
	they two, them two
	make smooth, polish
	soothe, calm
	offerings
	poverty
	wine of Pelusium
	make to tremble
	impassion
	boil
	bindweed?
	thrust aside
	banish? (sleep)
	healthy
	exchange greetings
	the coast is clear
	jar
	Farewell, farewell
	make to breathe, succor, unload (ships), empty out (contents)
	make beautiful, embellish, restore (what is defective), carry out (business)
	gladden
	a rank weed
	likeness, image, figure
	copy (of document)

likeness

terrify

shelter, refuge

register, record, muster (troops), drive (birds)

set in motion

rise early

bind, entwine

prevent (movement)

nurse (a child)

control (people)

rejuvenate oneself, renew (breath)

make strong, strengthen, enrich

stiffening, stiffness (of limbs)

disturb

be brotherly

suck

nurse

suckle

injure, damage

darkness

darkness, obscurity

gossip

base (of statue)

festival of the 6th day of lunar month

measure out (land), found (a house etc), form (limbs), refix (eyes of the dead)

cabin (on vessel)

cense, consecrate

fear, respect

𓊪𓏏𓅆𓀔	sit, be seated
𓊪𓏏𓅆𓉼	rest
𓊪𓏏𓅆𓎡	make happy, make pleasant, ease (suffering), make content, please, give pleasure
𓊪𓈖𓌘𓅆𓎡	make happy, make pleasant, make content
𓊪𓈖𓌘𓈖𓌘𓈖𓌘	incite
𓊪𓂝𓀒	Nobleman, Magistrate, official
𓊪𓂝𓏛	tress, wig, hide (of animal)
𓊪𓂝�	show (something, someone)
𓊪𓂝𓃀𓀄	foretell, make known
𓊪𓃒	sheep
𓊪𓂝𓏭𓏭𓏛𓀄	cough
𓊪𓂝𓏭𓏭𓏛𓏲	standard
𓊪𓂝𓃀𓀄𓂡𓀀	challenge to battle
𓊪𓂝𓆉	goose
𓊪𓂝𓅓𓏤𓏥	remove
𓊪𓂝𓅓𓎼𓎿	treatment
𓊪𓂝𓅓𓎼	foster, cherish, treat medically
𓊪𓂝𓅓𓎿𓀒𓏪	body of magistrates
𓊪𓂝𓅓𓎿𓀔𓏪	prophecies
𓊪𓂝𓌘𓈖𓏲	strengthen, maintain, perpetuate, make to flourish, restore (buildings)
𓊪𓈖	make secure, provide, set right (a wrong), fulfill (contract)
𓊪𓈖𓇌𓅆𓌘𓎡	strengthen, maintain, perpetuate

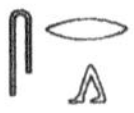

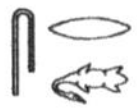

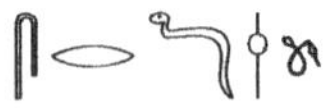

warm, warmth, temperature, inflammation, fever, mood

Rest, relief

deliberate

fever

cause to weep

foodstuff, beverage

complain, lay information against, accuse

guilty person

a government department

memorial

Serekh (palace-facade design holding the Horus name of King)

learn about (future events)

accusation, reproach

accuser, complainer, evil spirit

awaken, take command of (corps)

inhale, permit to breathe (of throats)

Selket (the scorpion goddess)

thorn, spine

make grow, plant (trees), erect (monuments)

erect (monuments)

terrorize

be in confusion

bring down, make to fall

discharge (medical)

govern

make content, make peace

strip (someone), reveal (secret)

strip (someone), reveal (secret)

conceal

gallinule (moor hen)?

acclaim

join up (boundaries)

collect, assemble

collection, summary, assemblage (of troops), list

shorten

vilify

make festive, adorn

put a stop to

crush, pound

To command, order, instruct

decorate

fly up

remove, exorcise (ill), drive away (foes), avert (face), deliver (from)

meet (someone)

cause to rule, install as ruler

make hungry

propitiate, please, pacify, satisfy (employees)

provide (for temple), make gracious (to)

please

censer

destroy

283

𓏺𓏤𓄿𓅂𓅱𓀀	destroyer
𓏺𓏤	inspector
𓏺𓏤𓏌𓇳	illumine, gladden, make clear, reveal
𓏺𓏤𓀠	shine, make illumination, make explanation, become pale
𓏺𓏤𓏌𓇳	make glad
𓏺𓏤𓏌𓇳𓅱	great light-maker (of Sun god)
𓏺𓏤𓏌𓄿	vex
𓏺𓏤𓏌	chest (furniture)
𓏺𓇋𓏏	spend the night
𓏺𓇋𓅂𓀁	remembrance, memory, mention, memorial
𓏤𓇋𓅂	hasten
𓏤𓂝	hit, smite, beat
𓏺𓇋𓅂𓀁	remember, call to mind, think about, mention
𓏤𓎺𓏭	cause to appear (of a god or king), display (object)
𓏤𓎺𓀁	enrage
𓏤𓅂�	breadth
𓏤𓅂	slaughter-house
𓏤𓀀𓏴𓀁	dispute
𓏤𓇋𓅂	enrich
𓏤𓂝	conduct (someone to someone), bring (offerings), display (decree)
𓏺𓀔	raise (a child), educate, breed (animals), bring about (an event)
𓏺𓀔	bring into being, create, make, make grow (a garden)
𓏤𓅂	forget

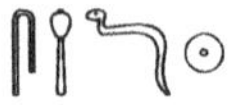

284

power, grimness

scepter, sistrum

mighty one, Power

make warm

distract the heart (of someone), take recreation, enjoyment

swelling?, gathering?

alight, rest, dwell

a class of incantation?

(the four) posts (of the sky)

advance, promote

take southward

overthrow, throw down, force into place (dislocated bone)

plan, counsel, determination, governance, conduct, condition, fortune, affair, fashion, nature, custom

captain (of ship)

those who govern

overflowing bowls?

thought

roll (of papyrus)

run, hurry, flee

runners

create opposition (against)

pursue, persecute

run

marshland, field, country (beside town)

blow

weave, mould (bricks)

trap, snare, close (net), acquire? (wealth)

ambushing?

an offering loaf

run

be upside down, be disordered (of dress)

be upside down, hang down (of breasts)

be upside down

strain, squeeze out

hare

swallow

draught (of medicine)

swallow

demolish

sweep, brush over, overlay (with), stroke

milking

decorate, adorn, burnish

ashes

hurry

burn

satisfy, make wise

provisions, sustenance

satisfaction

destroy

destroy, destruction

a metallic inlay?

honor (someone)

make to laugh

make ready, supply (with), prepare (food), enliven (the downcast), penetrate (into)

make ready, supply (with), prepare (food)

horse, mare

To breathe, To smell

preserve, heal

a costly wood

plant (garden)

destroy (enemies), shatter (heads)

destroy (enemies)

shatter (heads)

strengthen

breathe, smell

calf (of leg)

write, inscribe, paint, draw, enroll (troops)

beseech (from)

pray (to)

Seshat (goddess)

disk (of metal)

lose (by theft)

dry (something)

impoverish, deprive (of)

be white, be bright

guidance

conduct

lead, guide, rule, govern, show (the way), conduct (war, work), instruct (people)

guidance, procedure, conduct, business

lead, guide

business

statue, portrait, image, counterpart

ruler, leader

warm (someone), heat (something)

leading (of procession), guidance, governance, control

guiding serpent (of god)

guidance

dry, dry up

utter, express

linen

grain

things, actions, course, manner (of action)

make brightness, lighten (darkness)

discuss?

window

flash

thunderbolt

288

𓇋𓂝𓎛	fillet, bandage, garlands, ribbons, tether
𓇋𓂝𓎛	put a fillet on (someone)
𓇋𓂝𓉔	shrine (of falcon)
𓇋𓂧𓀠 R31	base (for shrine)
𓇋𓂧𓀠	extol (beauty, victories), prolong (lifetime, kingship)
𓇋𓂧𓄿𓀠	make high (a building), set upright (a person), exalt (a god, king)
𓇋𓂧𓄿𓊁𓀗	plaster
𓇋𓂧𓅢𓇋𓀜	bind, fetter, check, string up (fowling-tackle)
𓇋𓂧𓏤	make vomit
𓇋𓂧𓆑𓏥	double (supplies)
𓇋𓂧𓆑𓏲	type of wood
𓇋𓂧𓆑𓆑𓈖𓈖	make cool, calm (disturbed land), refresh (oneself)
𓇋𓂧𓆑𓆑𓈖𓈖𓉐	bathroom
𓇋𓂧𓆑𓊃𓈖	refresh
𓇋𓂧𓈖𓂝𓀜	enrage
𓇋𓂧𓃀	offer, present
𓇋𓂧𓃀	strike, strike down, clap (hands), grasp (hand)
𓇋𓂧𓊪𓏤	step out (of feet in dance), work (metal), set up (stairway)
𓇋𓂧𓊪𓏲	wound, injury
𓇋𓂧𓊪𓏲	knead (dough), get rid of (something), offer, present
𓇋𓂧𓏲	set up (stairway, ladder)
𓇋𓂝 ḏ235	work (metal)
𓇋𓂧𓊪𓋹𓀜	captive, living prisoner
𓇋𓄿𓈖𓅪	make miserable
𓏤	sailor, traveller

289

	sailor, traveller
	cause to build
	slope (of a pyramid)
	sail, travel (of persons)
ḏ33b	row
	sail, voyage (of boat), sail, travel (of persons)
	sail, voyage (of boat)
	builders
	sailing
	company of troops
	fell (trees)
	wipe, wipe out, wipe away
	cultivate, plough
	plough-ox
	crops
	cover up
	plough land
	perish
	destroy
	pass (time)
	battle
	troops, companies
	make complete, make up to
	be / become gray-haired
	wise

be greedy, lust (after)

destroy

type of boat

night-bark (of sun)

soften, weaken, anoint

tallow, ointment

silence

satisfy

make peaceful, pacify, satisfy

make peaceful, pacify

institute (offerings)

yard arms (of ship)?

it, them

they

heat, kindle (taper)

injury

dragging

censer, lamp

impregnate (female), beget, ejaculate

pour (water)

shoot, throw, thrust, spear, kindle (light), inspect (work), glitter (of sky)

set (fire to)

stare, stare at

Asiatics

mid-day meal

a sacred oil

hold up

keep clean

rays (of sun)

resemble, smooth over, make over, praise (craftsmanship)

resemble

hasten

choke?

cut up (animal), cut off (limbs), pick out, choose

cut up (animal)

The choicest, the pick, the elite of

protect, do escort duty

palace

choice things (of food)

liquid?, to foam up

sheet (copper)

lead astray, confusion

lead astray, confuse

ramble about

make dazzling, radiant

Seth (god)

cause to approach, induct (into), cut short, bring on (doom), execute (judgments)

shooting pains

Satis (goddess)

measure of capacity

weave, spin (yarn)

(of things) drag, pull, pull out, reduce (swelling), draw off (pus)

Hieroglyphs	Meaning
	bind up (injury)
ḏ117	strew, scatter
	Satis
	odor, smell
F29 c	sower
	leap up
	discharge (of the eyes)
	distinguish, honor, make distinctions, differentiate
Y1v	distinguish, honor, make distinctions
	raise, lift up, remove (lassitude), display (beauty)
398	be stretched out, prostrate
	kindle (light)
	jar (for beer)
	clothe
	tail
	tremble
	egret
G68	trembling
	embalm
	chew
O30u	penetrate (of injury)
	fringe (of cloth), a garment
	eye-paint
	paint (the eyes, body)

293

	paint (the eyes, body)
	punish
	attach (to)
	conceal (from)
	well?
	redden
	reddening
	hidden place
	conceal (from)
	hidden things
	weaklings
	break up (hailstorm), rupture (cist), inflict (wound), fracture, rupture
W31	break up (hailstorm), rupture (cist), inflict (wound)
	break, break into, invade, breach (wall), break open (way)
	adviser?
	travel, depart (in sense of die)
	take recreation
	amuse oneself, take recreation
	seal
	lie (with woman)
	pick
	slander
	restore (to life)
O30u	impediment, obstacle, (verbal) opposition, guilt, ill-will

294

𓊪𓏤𓃹𓅭𓏥	endow (altars), provide (for someone)
𓊪𓏤𓃹	foundation, endowment
𓊪𓏤𓃹𓅃𓅯𓀜𓎛𓏏𓂝𓂡𓅪	oath of allegiance
𓊪𓅓𓏭	hear (voice etc), hear of (something), listen (to), obey, understand, judge, satisfy (conditions)
𓊪𓏤𓈖𓏛 3406	carry (child)
𓊪𓐍𓏛	spend the night, sleep, lie down, go to rest, be inert, inactive, do in the night
𓊪𓐍𓏥𓂝 395 𓏛	slaughter
𓊪𓐍𓏛	sleeper
𓊪𓐍𓂝𓎺 𓏥	sleeping-draught
𓊪𓐍𓂝𓎻	(festival of) Laying (Osiris) to Rest
𓊪𓏤𓎡𓏏𓂈	shank, shin
𓊪𓏤𓎡𓏏𓅯	ringed plover
𓊪𓂉𓅯𓏏𓂈	shank
𓊪𓎱�	consecrate, hallow, sanctify, clear (way)
𓊪𓏤𓂝𓌪	fire, flame
𓊪𓏤𓂝𓀜	child, foster-child (of king)
𓊪𓏤𓂝𓊗	relate, recount, talk (of)
𓊪𓏤𓂝𓊗𓅯	fatten
𓊪𓏤𓂝𓊗𓅯𓀀𓏥	tales
𓊪𓏤𓂝𓀁𓂉	description, tale
𓊪𓊽𓊽	make permanent
𓊪𓊃𓌡𓂝𓇼	nightfall, night sky
𓊪𓎳𓎶𓏤	Take, accept, receive, assume (crown), catch (fish), purchase, wear (clothes), To begin, to start

𓉐𓎟𓏏𓅆𓏤	make secret, mysterious, make inaccessible

𓋴𓇋

S29 + I9

𓋴𓇋𓇳	yesterday

𓈖

Piece of cloth with fringe

𓈖𓅆𓀁	recognize, perceive, know, be aware of(verb)
𓈖𓅆𓀁𓆰	perception, knowledge
𓈖𓅆𓏥°	orpiment?
𓈖𓏤	fringed cloth

𓋴

Sandal

𓋴𓂝𓀒	sandal maker
𓋴𓈖	sandal, sole
𓋴𓋴	sandals, soles (of feet)

𓋹

Sandal strap

𓋹	swear
𓋹 3223	captive
𓋹𓈖𓏏	live, life
𓋹𓈖𓏏𓀀	Person, Soldier
𓋹𓈖𓏏𓀁	swear, oath
𓋹𓈖𓏏𓆣	beetle
𓋹𓏤	sandal strap

296

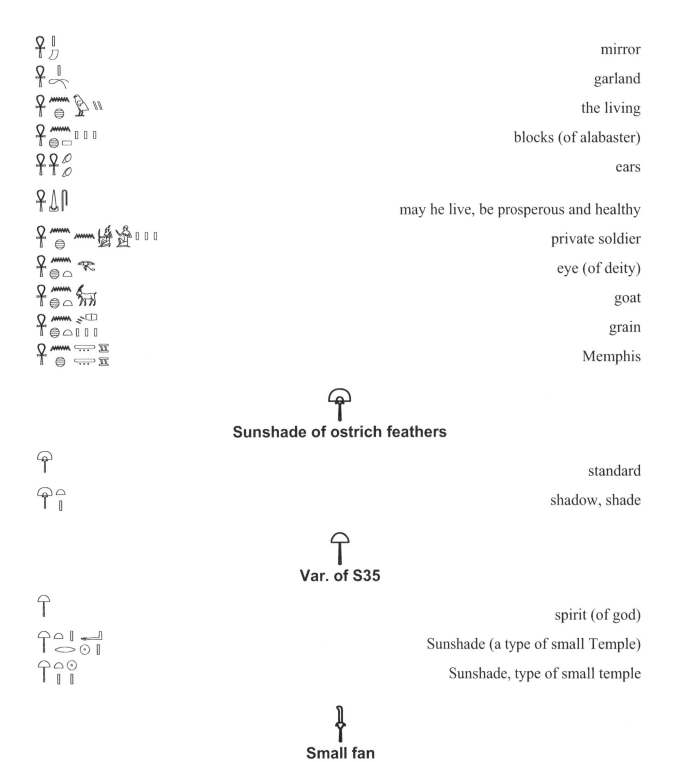

mirror

garland

the living

blocks (of alabaster)

ears

may he live, be prosperous and healthy

private soldier

eye (of deity)

goat

grain

Memphis

Sunshade of ostrich feathers

standard

shadow, shade

Var. of S35

spirit (of god)

Sunshade (a type of small Temple)

Sunshade, type of small temple

Small fan

fan

Crook (shepherd)

𓀀 (hieroglyphs)	herds (in general)
(hieroglyphs)	small cattle, goats, herds
(hieroglyphs)	desert game
(hieroglyphs)	Ruler
(hieroglyphs)	rule over, govern
Y8ᶜ	guardian of hathor? (a title)
(hieroglyphs)	district governor
(hieroglyphs)	grain-measure (4.54 liters)
(hieroglyphs)	rulership
(hieroglyphs)	scepter
(hieroglyphs)	Heqat (frog goddess)

Scepter, surmounted by the head of Seth (?)

(hieroglyph)	dominion, have dominion
(hieroglyphs)	scepter
(hieroglyphs)	ruin
(hieroglyphs)	be ruined, decayed
(hieroglyphs)	Thebes
(hieroglyphs)	the Theban

Var. of S40

(hieroglyphs)	ruin
(hieroglyphs)	fine gold, electrum

298

Scepter, emblem of authority

𓌂	offering-stone
𓌂	scepter
𓌂	baton (of office)
𓌂	controller, administrator
𓌂	district, estate
𓌂	district?, estate?
𓌂	power, grimness
𓌂	mighty one, Power
𓌂	powerful
𓌂	founder? (of ship)
𓌂	scepter, sistrum
𓌂	stout-hearted, violent, violence
𓌂	potentate
𓌂	mighty one, Power
𓌂	Sekhmet (goddess)
𓌂	power
𓌂	the Double-Crown
𓌂 š156	troops, companies

Walking stick

	speak, address (someone)
	speech, word, plea
	speak, address (someone), speech, word, plea
	staff, rod
	staff of old age (supporter of an aged parent)
	speak against
	word of God, divine decree, sacred writings, written characters, script
	dispute with
	talker, speaker
	taker, speaker
	speech, words, (legal) plea, talk, (written) word, content (of letter), matter, affair
	speech, words
	matter, affair
	goldsmiths
	recitation
	recitation by

Flagellum (flail)

	flail

Mace (disk-shaped head)

	take to yourself

Mace with pear-shaped head

	white (of the eye)
	jaw
	white, bright
	set forth at dawn
	white clothes
	silver, money
	mace
	chapel
	bird-chapel
	injure, destroy, disobey, annul, waste, eclipse, degrade
	damage, destruction
	be upset, annoyed
	onions
	cheerful
	white linen
	dawn
	white sandals
	milk
	brightness

T3 with strap

	mace

mace

white linen

T3 + I10

damage, destruction

white (of the eye)

T3 and double I10

brightness

Axe

hewer (of stone), carpenter

hew (timber), build (ships)

Dagger

being upon, principal, first, high (priest)

predecessors, ancestors

Bow

stretch (cord in foundation ceremony)

foreigners

bow

302

⌒𝕀 ⌒ ▭ ⑊⑊ 𓀀 ▭ 𓅃 𓀀 𝕀𝕀𝕀	measure (for textiles, for incense) foreigner foreigners

Bow

𓏲 ⌒ 𓏲 ⌒𝕀	bow measure (for textiles, for incense)

Composite bow

⊂⊃ ⊂⊃ ⊂⊃ ⊂⊃ ⊂⊃ ⊂⊃ ⊂⊃ ⊂⊃ ⊂⊃	the Nine Bows (traditional enemies of Egypt)
⊂⊃ 𝕀𝕀𝕀 𝕀𝕀 ⌒ 𝕀𝕀𝕀	the Nine Bows
⊂⊃ 𝕀 𓀀 𓀗 𝕀𝕀𝕀 ⌒	foreigners
⊂⊃ ⌒ 𝕀	bow
⊂⊃ 𝕀 𓀀 𝕀𝕀𝕀 ⌒	troop (of soldiers)
𝕀 ⊂⊃ 𓀀	bowman

Arrow

↤o ▭ ⌁⌁⌁	trade
↤o 𓀀 ○ 𝕀	physician, doctor
↤o ⌒ ⌁⌁⌁ ▭ 𝕀𝕀𝕀	price

Bowstring

𓍢	success
𓍢	enduring, permanent
𓍢	cord
𓍢 𓀾	prosperous, prosper
𓍢 ▱	control, administer

303

	hard
	hard stone, sandstone

Two joined pieces of wood

	wake
	The watch, guard [sentries], The vigilance
	awakening
	sacrificial victims

Throw-stick

	Asiatic
	throwstick
	small cattle, sheep, goats
	goats
	small cattle
	village
	mooring-post
	Nubian
	grain-measure (of 4.54 liters)
	throw, create, beget, produce, carry out (teaching), hammer out (from metal)
	one of the seven sacred oils
	Libya

Chariot

                                                          chariot

Crook with a knife attached to it

follow, accompany, serve, bring, present

follower, retainer

worship

following, suite

follower of Horus, righteous person

following, suite

funeral procession

Bone harpoon head

bone

painful, painfully, irksome, troubled, difficult, dangerous, wretched

trouble, misfortune

records, annals

sculptor

One-barbed harpoon

one, unique, one only

unique, one only, sole

[hieroglyphs]	be alone
[hieroglyphs]	every one of them
[hieroglyphs]	privacy, private apartments
[hieroglyphs]	private apartments
[hieroglyphs]	privacy
[hieroglyphs]	everyone, each one, each
[hieroglyphs]	unique
[hieroglyphs]	captive
[hieroglyphs]	sole, single
[hieroglyphs]	goat
[hieroglyphs]	royal uraeus

Two-barbed arrow

[hieroglyphs]	smell (perfume), breathe (air), kiss
[hieroglyphs]	brother
[hieroglyphs]	angler
[hieroglyphs]	offerings
[hieroglyphs] $Z4^c$	companion, fellow, equal, counterpart, dual contestants (in Court of Law)
[hieroglyphs] W66	jar
[hieroglyphs] $Z4^c$	contestants (in Court of Law)
[hieroglyphs]	companion, fellow, equal, counterpart, (dual) contestants (in court of law)
[hieroglyphs] $Z4^c$	two
[hieroglyphs]	brethren
[hieroglyphs]	flagstaff
[hieroglyphs]	shrine
[hieroglyphs] $Z4^c$	female companions

306

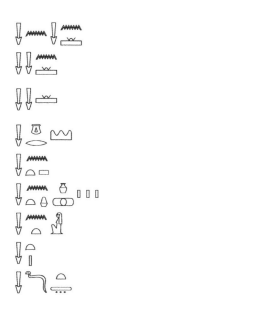

agree to (action)

be well disposed toward

be brotherly, fraternize, associate

Babylonia

base (of statue)

festival of the 6th day of lunar month

sister

flagstaff

person sharing in funerary offerings

Fishing net

cultivator

cultivators

farm land

Reed float

clothe, adorn

mat of leaves

stop up, block

Edfu

garment (worn by god)

repay, make repayment, replace, restore, clothe, adorn, provide, pad

payments, reward, compensation, bribes

floats (of net)

altars

𓉐𓄿𓂝 R40 R40	altars
𓉐𓄿𓏖	crowning
𓉐𓂝𓎳	robing-room, sarcophagus
𓉐𓎰	robing-room

Bird trap

	weave, mould (bricks)
	stone for patching?
	close (net)

Bird trap

	spider

Butcher block

	under, carrying, holding, possessing
	which is under, lower, having, possessing, suffering from (illness)
	apprentice, assistant
	halyards
	lector (priest)
	abdomen, under-side (of sky)
	the hindermost?
	under the hand of, in the charge of
	relatives (of family), underlings, inhabitants (of land), household members
	relatives (of family), underlings, inhabitants (of land)
	men
	base, lower part, underside
	testicles

	under the control of, under the supervision of
	under the control of, under the supervision of
	possessions, belongings, share, portion, requirements, due from), duty, skill
	stone masons
	deceit
	writing materials
	under the head of, beside
	(the spirits) who attend Re

T29c
Variation on T29

t29c ⬓   slaughter house

Knife

t30c   sawdust

                             kill, destroy

t30b ～～ ⌒ P2g   (seagoing) ship

                               knife

T31 + D54

                              conduct (work, war)

Butcher knife

                orphan, private person, freeman

                             free woman?

š57c   the (royal) Nemes head cloth

                         clothe with the head cloth

𓎛𓏭𓌙	clothe with the head cloth
𓄿𓂧𓏤	type of jar

Sickle

𓌙𓅭𓅭𓁻	look toward, take care of, take heed of
𓌙𓅭𓏭𓃮	lion
𓌙𓅓𓃭	lions
𓌙𓅭𓏭𓏤𓅆𓏪	misery
𓌙𓅭𓏭𓏭𓎶𓏤	sheath (of sword)
𓌙𓎡𓅆	real
𓌙𓏰𓏰𓅆	oryx
𓌙𓅭𓅭𓏴	new, be renewed
𓌙𓅆	new
𓌙𓅭𓂝𓏴t19b𓄿	shaft (of spear)
𓌙𓅭𓅭𓈇𓏪	new land
𓌙𓅭𓅭𓈇𓁻𓏥	rays (of light)
𓌙𓅭𓅭𓏴	a new thing
𓌙𓅭𓂝M195	shaft (of spear), staff, stalk (of corn), measuring-rod
𓌙𓌙M54	dom-palm
𓌙𓅭𓌙𓅭𓂝𓏴Z3ᶜ	dom-palms
𓌙𓌙𓈗𓊪𓈗𓂝M54	dom-palm
𓌙𓏰𓏰𓋁	the Western mountain
𓌙𓅭𓏭𓅪𓀒	wretched man, pauper
𓌙𓅭𓏲𓏥	pasture
𓌙𓅭𓏲𓏤	wreath

𓂝𓏤𓇋��𓃟	Fierce lion
𓂝𓏤𓃘	oryx
𓂝𓏤⊕M182	sheaf
𓂝𓅀⊷𓊨	burn
𓂝𓇋ḏ159	kneel
𓂝𓅀𓊪⊂𓂾	knee (of man), hock (of animal)
𓂝𓇋⊂𓂾	knee (of man), hock (of animal)
𓂝𓅀𓂝	ladder
𓂝𓅀𓏤⊂𓏭⊂𓊪𓏪	female mourners
𓂝𓅀𓊗𓀢	proclaim
𓂝⊷𓀠	acclaim
𓂝⊷𓎳	granite
𓂝 𓅀 ⊷ t30ᶜ t30ᶜ t30ᶜ	spines

Sickle

𓄿⌒ M46ᵇ	charm, kindliness, graciousness
𓄿⌒ M46	charm
𓄿👁F81 ⌁	oryx
𓄿⌁	stern (of boat)
𓁷𓅀𓅀	To see, look upon, regard, To take care, heed
𓄿oo	see, look upon, regard, see to, inspect, look on
𓁷𓅀𓈖	look at
𓁷𓅀𓃭𓊪𓏪	lions

311

	real
	lead, guide, direct, send, dispatch, throw out (rope from ship)
	temple (of head)
	bank (of river or lake)
	breeze
	aright
	justification, vindication, triumph
	truth
	rightness, orderly management
	just men, the righteous (the blessed dead)
	aspect, appearance
	new
	mirror
	shaft (of spear), measuring rod
	Mafdet (a cat goddess?)
	dom-palms
	wretched man, pauper
	dispossess (someone of)
	Fierce lion
	its stern (of ship)
	its bow (of ship)
	lioness
	mandrake?

Composite sign : U1 + D4

	see, look upon, regard, see to, inspect, look on

 viewing place (in sun cult)

Composite sign : U1 + Aa11

lead, guide, direct, send, dispatch, throw out, steer, extend, paddle, set out

Var. of U4 (with Aa11)

temple (of head)

bank (of river or lake)

present, offer, make presentation (to)

true (of speech), real, just, righteous, true (to), loyal (to)

breeze

products, offering, tribute, gifts

products

type of wood

deceased, be justified, vindicated, true of voice

deceased, be justified, vindicated (against someone), be triumphant, true of voice

truth, right-doing, righteousness, justice, rightness, orderly management

judgment

just men, the righteous (the blessed dead)

Hoe

to love, to want, wish, desire

𓄿	wife
𓄿	crocodiles
𓄿	a type of wood
𓄿	Mnevis Bull
𓄿	love, will, desire
𓄿	the well-beloved

Hoe

	bind
	milk jar
	sounding-pole
	run aground (of ship)
	fighting bull
	Syrian warrior
	crocodiles
	bank, shore
	bank, shore, sandbank?, quay
	a type of wood
	harbors?
	desert
	strip (of cloth)
	canals, artificial lakes
	black stork
	the coast is clear
	love, will, desire
	the well-beloved
	the well-beloved

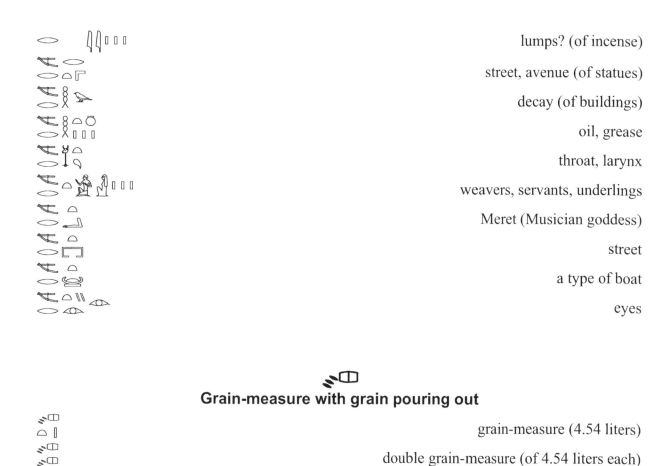

lumps? (of incense)

street, avenue (of statues)

decay (of buildings)

oil, grease

throat, larynx

weavers, servants, underlings

Meret (Musician goddess)

street

a type of boat

eyes

Grain-measure with grain pouring out

grain-measure (4.54 liters)

double grain-measure (of 4.54 liters each)

Composite sign : U9 + N33a

Barley, (grain in general)

Composite sign : U9 + S38

grain-measure (of 4.54 liters)

Plough

fruit, seed, (in sense of offspring, posterity)

court of law, hall

plough

ebony

a jar

laborer?

storehouse, labor establishment

Sled

Atum

perish, cease

(negates the sentence)

Loaded sled with head of a jackal

To wonder, to marvel

Omen, sign, Miracle, marvel, wonder, Valuables, outstanding product, treasure, Heroic dead, act of glory, (glorious) feat

wonders, marvels

grindstone

character, qualities

Pick excavating a basin

settle (crown on king)

furnish (waste lands with vegetation), settle (crown on king), provide (for), set in order,

falsehood, lie

found (a land), establish (a house), people (a place)

catch (of fish)

Adze

	time
	water, flood, pool
	pool
	adze
M171	unguents
	adze
	yarn (for weaving), cord

Adze working on a block of wood

	cut up (animal)
	be dismembered, ruined
	strip (of cloth), rag
	pick out, choose
	The choicest, the pick, the elite of
	protect, do escort duty
	palace
	choice things (of food)
	choice

Chisel

	potent (of king etc...)
	excellence, virtues (of someone)

Chisel

𓂝𓃭𓃭𓀀	Be *delighted (existence not ascertain)
𓂝𓃭𓃭	To Desire, wish for
𓂝𓃭	To tarry, stay, halt, stop, To avoid, cease
𓂝𓃭𓏭𓃡	Panther
𓂝𓃭𓃭𓅨	Elephantine (Island near Aswan)
𓂝𓃭𓅆	Cessation, stop, halt
𓂝𓃭𓃰	Elephant
𓂝𓃭𓅆	To brand, stamp, Branding-iron, brand sign
𓂝𓃭𓅆	Ivory, Elephant tusk
𓂝𓃭	To merge, To be satisfied
𓂝𓃭𓀀𓏥	Family, tribe, clan
𓂝𓃭	Brand, branding-iron
𓂝𓃭𓅨	A kind of fish
𓂝𓃭	Abydos
𓂝𓃭	Left-hand, The left side of
𓂝𓄿	sorely
𓂝𓄿	sick, ill, diseased, painful
𓂝𓄿𓀀	sick man
𓂝𓄿	pyramid
𓂝𓄿	have compassion on, be sorry for
𓂝𓄿	painful to

 painful to

be displeasing to

pains

Tool to drill

be skilled, skilful

ingenious

work

craftsman, expert, carpenter

craftsmen

craftsmen

skill

skill, craft (of sculptor)

etcetera, and so forth

magic-spell

Tool to drill

To open, To reveal, to expose

butler

open court (of temple)

maidservant

opening

Fire-drill

	go, set out, proceed, attain (a rank), set (of sun)
	pectoral
	remain over (of balance in calculations)
	fire-drill
	extend (arm), oppose (oneself), pierce, transfix
	ferry (one across), cross (sky)
	pierce, transfix
	dispute, argue, oppose (actions)
	civil war
	argument, dispute
	disputant
	opponent
	wrongdoing
	robe
	opponents
	night
	mat
	type of fisherman
	heat, burn
	young men
	young men, troops

320

𓊪𓄿𓅱𓂝𓀀𓏥	young men, troops
𓊪𓄿𓃀𓅱𓆋𓏥	Aspalathos
𓊪𓄿𓂋𓏤	be contentious
𓊪𓄿𓏤𓅓𓂜𓀀	need
𓊪𓄿𓏤𓏥	bitter gourd
𓊪𓄿𓂋𓏤𓎛	impede
𓊪𓊅𓏤𓏥	part of Palestine and Phoenicia
𓊪𓂝	hand, handful
𓊪𓏤𓅭	crane
𓊪𓄿𓂋𓏤𓏤𓏤	be busied, interfere (with)
𓊪𓏤𓈇	estate
𓊪𓄿𓏤𓅆𓏤	audience hall
𓊪𓄿𓊪𓄿𓀁	head, tip (of bow)
𓊪𓄿𓊪𓄿𓂐	pot
𓊪𓄿𓊪𓄿𓂷	lyre
𓊪𓂓𓏤𓀀𓏥	magistrates, assessors

𓊪

Fire-drill

𓊪𓏤𓏥	balance, remainder, deficiency

←

Instrument used for baking (?)

←	confine, restrain
←𓂝𓏥𓀁	baker
←𓂋𓉐	prison, fortress, council-chamber

321

Pestle and mortar

𓍜𓂋	menstruate
𓍜∘∘∘	bronze
𓍜𓈗𓂋	menstruation

Pestle

𓍜𓍜𓍜 321^c	sovereign
𓍜	(not translated)
𓍜𓏤	not translated
𓍜𓂝𓀀	yes
𓍜𓇑𓅯𓄿	quarterstaff
𓍜𓀢𓏭	Cinnamon, a tree, (and its) spice?
𓍜𓊌𓎫	pestle
𓍜𓊌 V39	an amulet
𓍜𓅻	show respect to
𓍜𓇬𓏥𓅯 𓏢𓏢𓏢	paneling
𓍜𓂓𓂝∘ 𓏴𓏥	pea
𓍜𓅆𓏥𓍜𓀀𓍜 𓏤𓏤𓏤	Libyans
𓍜𓇬𓏥𓎺𓈖	be besmeared
𓍜𓅆𓎺	red, ruddy, violet
𓍜𓇬𓏥𓏤𓅯𓎺𓅆 𓏢𓏢𓏢	injury, harm
𓍜𓊖𓂽 𓈗 𓎱	willow

322

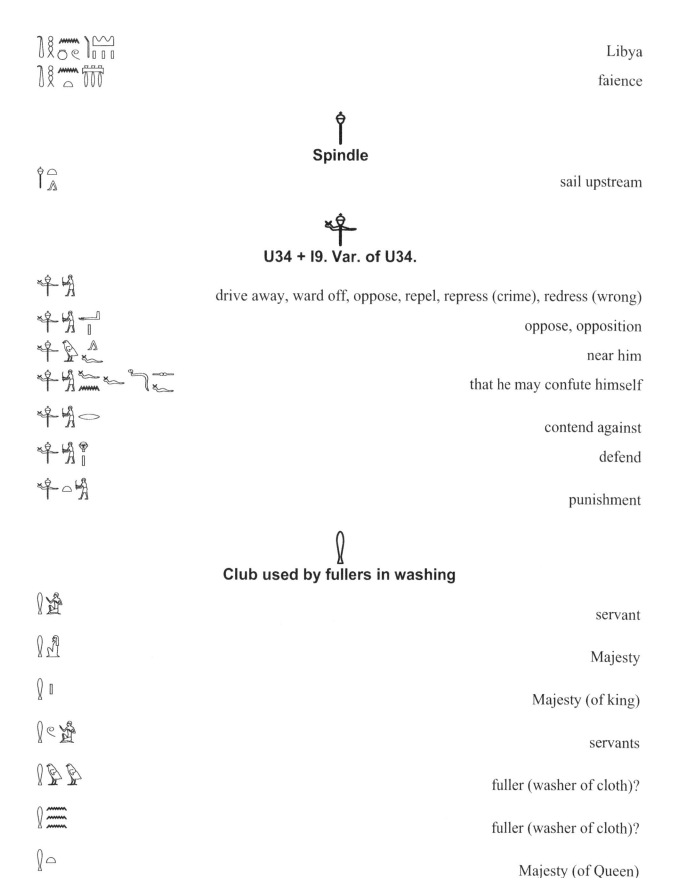

Libya

faience

Spindle

sail upstream

U34 + I9. Var. of U34.

drive away, ward off, oppose, repel, repress (crime), redress (wrong)

oppose, opposition

near him

that he may confute himself

contend against

defend

punishment

Club used by fullers in washing

servant

Majesty

Majesty (of king)

servants

fuller (washer of cloth)?

fuller (washer of cloth)?

Majesty (of Queen)

𓇋𓎿𓀀	female servant
𓇋𓎿𓏭	stand? (for target)

Razor

𓌕𓅝	barber

Post of balance (Similar to U39 shown here)

U39i   wear (crown)

Semi-hieratic form of T13 or U39

𓌨𓁹𓏤	be watchful, vigilant

Coil of rope

𓎟𓎿	anger
𓎟𓀜	sheriff
𓎢	one hundred

Rope rolled around a piece of wood

𓎛𓎿𓎡	injury
𓎛𓎿𓎿𓏏	roller (for moving ship)
𓎛𓎿𓎿𓎻	aroura (of land), sheet (of metal)
𓎛𓂻	see under other entries

Lasso

𓎣𓅜𓀜	brood (on), conspire (against), schemer
𓎤	far (from), long ago, for a long time past, go

324

𓍿𓄿𓊛	far (from), long ago, for a long time past, go
𓍿𓊛	fall (into a condition)
𓄿𓏏	roast? (grain)
𓄿𓅱𓀜	captain? (of ship)
𓄿𓏏𓈗	wave (of the sea)
𓄿𓄿𓀨	take counsel
𓂋𓂋𓈒	Wawat
𓄿𓄿𓂝	fiery one?
𓂋𓈒	Wawat (Northern Nubia)
𓂋𓏤	cord
𓄿𓂹	root (of plant), socket (of eye, leg, tooth)
𓄿𓂭	cloth?, swaddling-clothes
𓏤𓈒	high-lying agricultural land
𓄿𓏤𓈒	high-lying agricultural land
𓄿𓏤𓏪	body of the Red Crown
𓄿𓏏	bake?
𓄿𓂝	draw-rope (of clap-net)
𓄿𓏥𓀀	
𓊻𓂋𓅯𓅯	wreath, garland
𓄿𓊻𓂝	necklace
𓊻𓅯𓈖𓏤𓏤𓏤	oblations
𓏏𓏤	flood

𓁷𓏺𓈗	be inundated (of land), be content (of persons)
𓁷𓄿𓈗𓏥	be inundated, be content
𓁷𓄿𓈖𓏥𓉐	columned forecourt
𓁷𓌉	scepter
𓁷𓄿𓌉	be ruined, decayed
𓁷𓄿𓎾𓀢	be honored, be strong, honor
𓁷𓎾𓀜𓏰	honor
𓁷𓄿𓎙𓀁	shouting
𓁷𓄿𓎙	a religious festival
𓁷𓎙	Wag festival (a religious festival)
𓁷𓄿𓊅	road, way
𓁷𓄿𓊩	cord
𓁷𓄿𓂝𓅩 3482 𓏤𓏤𓏤	conspirators?
𓁷𓋔𓎁	fortunate, happy
𓁷𓋔𓂀 ∘∘∘	green eye-paint
𓁷𓄿𓋔𓂝	bow (of ship)
𓁷𓋔𓋔𓂝𓋳	vegetation

𓎛
Looped rope

𓎛𓂝𓏎	foundation, plan
𓎛𓂝	measure out (land), found (a house etc), form (limbs), refix (eyes of the dead)

𓎝
Cord with ends up

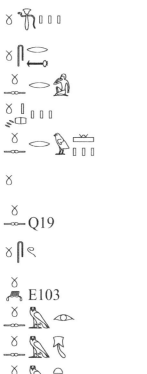

green linen

arrow

utter, express

grain

things, actions, course, manner (of action)

alabaster, vessels of alabaster

Q19   bier?

rope

E103   bubalis antelope

be bloodshot (of eyes)

leather roll?, baton

malachite

tongue

alabaster

stare

Cord with ends down

be infested with crocodiles

tree

suffer in (oneself), suffer from (something)

dispel (strife)

inquire into (a matter), question (someone), litigate

cover (diseased eye)

encircle, enclose, surround,

encircle

curse

storm

fenugreek?

constable, policeman

turn back, repulse, repel, police (district), detain, dart about (of fish)

breast

storm-cloud

storehouse, labor establishment

policing

police

detention

enquiry

troubles, need

circuit, circumference

cartouche

hair, grass

net, meshes (of net)

cartouche-amulet

enclosure

ocean

entourage

granary

breast

a cake or loaf

slab (for offerings)

spell, conjuration, curse

quarrelsome man, foe (of king), courtier

heron

revile (God), oppose (someone), punish (crime)

sheriff

	be angry
	strife, quarrel
ḏ249	strife, quarrel
	Nile acacia tree
	kilt, apron
	wearer of a kilt

Var. of V7

	circuit, circumference
	net, meshes (of net)
	ocean

Half-cartouche reversed

	decking (of ship)
	shriek
	shriek, bellow

String

	don (a garment)
	swear
	clever
	last day of the month
	set out, depart (to)

Rope for tethering an animal

	man, men, mankind, Egyptians
	you, your

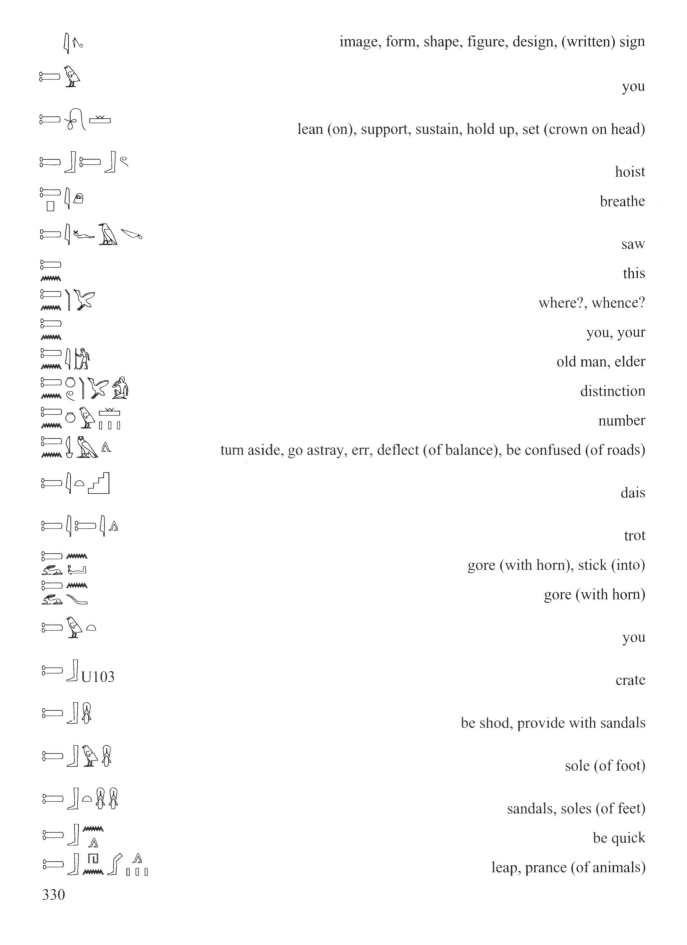	image, form, shape, figure, design, (written) sign
	you
	lean (on), support, sustain, hold up, set (crown on head)
	hoist
	breathe
	saw
	this
	where?, whence?
	you, your
	old man, elder
	distinction
	number
	turn aside, go astray, err, deflect (of balance), be confused (of roads)
	dais
	trot
	gore (with horn), stick (into)
	gore (with horn)
	you
	crate
	be shod, provide with sandals
	sole (of foot)
	sandals, soles (of feet)
	be quick
	leap, prance (of animals)

𓎗𓆓𓎶	vase
𓎗𓎛𓉐	cavern, hole (of snake)
𓎗𓎛 N44	cavern
𓎗𓂝𓏤	cadastre
𓎗𓂝𓏤	strong-armed
𓎗𓂝𓏤	your arm is strong
𓎗𓅃𓎛𓀀	Libyan
𓎗𓅃𓊪	red, ruddy, violet
𓎤𓏴𓏐	basin
𓎤𓇋𓅪𓂝	lift up, promote
𓎤𓇋𓅪	lift up, promote, distinguish (from), be distinguished (of actions)
𓎤𓇋𓏤𓊖	Thinis
𓎤𓏦	you two, your
𓎤𓇋𓅪𓏤𓅜𓏤	number, counting, numbering, each, every, every time that
𓎤𓏤𓅪𓏤𓃥𓏥	census (of cattle)
𓎤𓏤𓅪𓂝𓏥	quantity, number, numbering, census (of cattle, prisoners, the dead)
𓎤𓂋𓇋𓅪𓏲	census (of the dead)
𓎤𓃀𓀀	enjoyment
𓎤𓃀𓏏𓏏𓂝𓏏	sail
𓎤𓃀𓏤𓏏	bag
𓎗𓏤𓏤𓈖𓉐	sanctuary at Memphis
𓎤𓇋𓅪𓈖𓏤	reminder, explanation
𓎗𓏤𓏤𓏤 𓂝	eager, valor
𓎗𓏤𓂋𓅿	hawk
𓎤𓂋𓇋𓅪𓂝	difference (between x and y)
𓎤𓂋𓃥𓏥	sacred cattle
𓎤𓅪𓂋𓊫	dais
𓎗 𓂋	

	complaint
	an edible bird (goose?)
	wink
	willow
	harry
	hunt
	rejoice
	joy
	lance? (an infected place)
	meet, engage (with enemy)
	gleam, glittering
	Libya
	faience
	exult
	exultation
	vertebra, spine
	tie on (fillet)
	marshal (troops), levy (troops)
	sit
	raise, lift up, set up (ruined walls)
	go up (to a place)
	raise, lift up
	be angry (with), bear a grudge (against)
	an offering loaf
	hound, dog
	station (in life)
	ridge, range

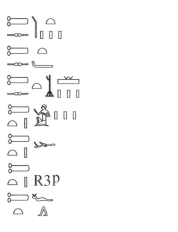

	station (in life)
	tooth
	complaint
	staff, gang, partisans
	board, woodwork
R3P	table
	flow down, overflow

V13 + D54

	take, take possession of, conduct, remove, arrest, conquer, spend, pass, move, rob
	take (for use)
	thief
	travel by boat

Cord serving as hobble for cattle

	cattle-hobble
	byre
	phyle (of priests), company, regiment (of troops), troop (of animals)
	protection
ḏ96	guard, ward off, restrain, heed
	magician
	Asyut (Lycopolis)
	reverence?

Shepherd's shelter, made of papyrus

phyle (of priests), company, regiment (of troops), troop (of animals)

amulet

protection

magician

Hobble for cattle (cord with wooden cross-bar)

byre

sack, leather bag

cadastre

Same as V19, without the wooden cross-bar

harpoon

the Thirty (a judicial body)

House of the Thirty

(the number) ten

I10 on V19

deep

byre

Whip

Forearm, cubit

seize, lay hold of, grasp (instructions), capture

fill, be full of, pay in full, make whole, complete, finish

Land-cubit (= 1/100 aroura = 1x100 cubit = 27.5 m2)

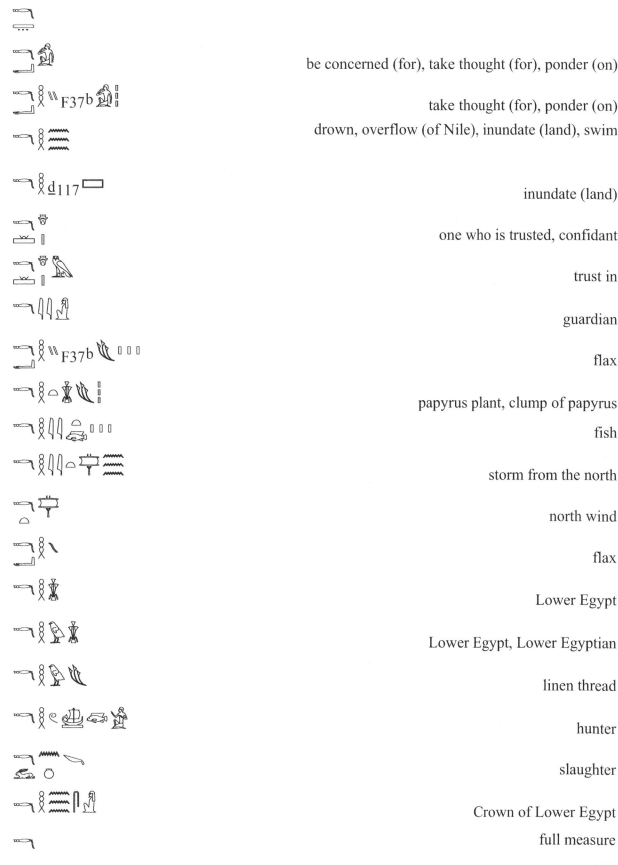

be concerned (for), take thought (for), ponder (on)

take thought (for), ponder (on)

drown, overflow (of Nile), inundate (land), swim

inundate (land)

one who is trusted, confidant

trust in

guardian

flax

papyrus plant, clump of papyrus

fish

storm from the north

north wind

flax

Lower Egypt

Lower Egypt, Lower Egyptian

linen thread

hunter

slaughter

Crown of Lower Egypt

full measure

335

	coil (of serpents)
	the Coiled one
	render good account
	hurry!
	act according to
	the Delta marshes
	flood waters
	fan?
	bowl
	the complete eye (of Horus)
	land cubit (one hundredth of one aroura)
	North
	northern
	northerners
	northward to
	northward to
	north

Cord wound on stick

act as pilot, pilot

(written) decree, dispatch

command, make a command, enjoin (an instruction), decree (someone to)

stela

turn (to)

fold over, turn, turn back, revert, divert, direct, recur

river bank

turn

river-bank, riparian-lands, sea-shore

turn back

turn the hand away, desist, compose oneself, turn oneself about

reversion (of offerings from temple to tomb), a reversion offering

reversion (of offerings from temple to tomb), a reversion-offering

divert (offerings), reversion-offering

command, control, govern

do harm, execute sentence

wean

command, decree

give orders?

command

cattle

Var. of V24

pour out, pour off
(command etc)

337

	(command etc)
	pilot (someone)
	stela
	inscription
	jug
	(command etc)
	depart, stray (of cattle)
	campaign, expedition, journey
	campaign, expedition
	folded cloth
	riparian lands
	sea shore
	divert (offerings), a reversion offering
	command, control, govern
	command
	wean, weaned child
	weaned child (of royalty)
	door of cast metal
	cast (metal)
	command, decree
	instruct

338

Weaver's spool

Buri fish	
perceive	
hack up, destroy	
fatten?	
edge, margin (of cultivation)	
fat, grease	
be safe	
spool, reel	
winnowers	
administrator	
day-bark (of sun god)	

Archaic form of V26

slaughter, massacre	

Wick of cord

type of bread	
bread	
Field, arable land, Earth, mould, soil	
pour out	
inundate (land)	
eternity, forever	
eternity	
the desert god	

339

N76 [c]	the desert god
	would that!, O!
	screech (of falcon)
	mourn, wail, screech (of falcon), dance (at funeral)
3₇₃	mourn
	wail
	be naked
	a bad quality
M43 [c]	vintage
	wealth, increase
	naked man
	secret, mysterious
	type of wine
	carry off (captives)
	be glad
	tomb
	cloak
	bleariness (of eyes)
	heart, central chest, thought
	lust
ṯ₈₉	fish trap, trap fish

𓏏𓏭𓅚𓊞	fish-trap
𓏤𓎡𓏤	flesh
𓏤𓊗	palace
𓏤𓂝𓅨𓀔𓀔𓏪	children
𓏤𓂝𓀠𓀔	joyful
𓏤𓂝𓅆	rejoice
𓎡𓎡𓀁	myself
𓏤𓂝𓅆𓀠𓏰	rejoice
𓏤𓂝𓅆𓅚𓊞𓏪	ships
𓏤𓂝𓅆𓏥𓀠	joy
𓏤𓂝F51b𓏪	body
𓏤𓂝𓊞𓏪	ships
𓏤𓂝F51b◡	all people
𓏤𓂝𓅆𓏥𓀠𓏥	joy
𓏤𓊗𓈖𓈖	Nile
𓏤𓊗𓊗𓈖𓈖𓀀	Hapy (Nile god)
𓏤𓂝ḏ133◡	wick
𓏤𓂝𓏲	wick (of lamp)
𓏤𓂝𓌉𓅚𓅚◡𓀔𓏥	robbery
𓏤𓂝𓌉𓅚𓀜	To plunder
𓅓𓀁	Authoritative Utterance
𓅓𓅃	(royal) ordinance
𓅓◻𓏤	food
𓅓𓂋𓅚◡	foul, offensive, rot, putrefy, smell offensive, spoil (enjoyment)
◡𓎼	

[hieroglyphs]	putrefaction
[hieroglyphs]	surge up, overflow
[hieroglyphs]	beat, strike, smite, defeat (in argument), drive off (cattle)
[hieroglyphs] 390d Z12 [hieroglyphs]	surge up, overflow, rain
[hieroglyphs]	drive off (cattle)
[hieroglyphs]	flap (wings)
[hieroglyphs]	would that!
[hieroglyphs]	rain
[hieroglyphs]	short
[hieroglyphs]	apprehensive
[hieroglyphs]	short men
[hieroglyphs]	beat (of wings)
[hieroglyphs]	a class of bulls, cattle (in general)
[hieroglyphs]	proclaim
[hieroglyphs]	child, young man
[hieroglyphs]	rib-roast
[hieroglyphs]	be rejuvenated, refreshed, youthful vigor
[hieroglyphs]	combat
[hieroglyphs] Z12 [hieroglyphs]	combat
[hieroglyphs]	pupil (of eye)
[hieroglyphs]	maiden
[hieroglyphs]	speak ill?, decry?
[hieroglyphs]	poor, humble man, despicable person
[hieroglyphs]	the meanest of birds

𓏏𓅃𓄿𓅱𓏭	poor of understanding
𓏏𓈖𓂾	stroke (of falcon)
𓏏𓈖𓂻	extending the arm
𓏏𓅂𓈖𓀜	rob, plunder
𓏏𓃀𓎺𓀜	mourn
𓏏𓃀𓎺𓈖	celebrate a triumph
𓏏𓃀𓎔	Festival, feast, celebration
𓏏𓃀𓎔𓅭𓆛𓏥	catch (of fish and fowl)
𓏏𓃀𓄿𓏛𓃀𓅂𓏏𓀐	waddle
𓏏𓃀𓏭𓏭𓎔	be festal, make festival
𓏏𓃀𓏭𓏭𓂝𓎔	festival offerings
𓏏𓃀𓂋𓏏𓏭𓏭𓏲	play (draughts)
𓏏𓃀𓄿 Z26	target
𓏏𓃀𓃀𓂝𓈗	water
𓏏𓃀𓊌𓏞𓂻	bear (flabellum)
𓏏𓅓𓏞	clothe, be clothed, don (garment), furnish (house), hide, cover up
𓏏𓅓𓏭𓏭𓂝𓏞	wife
𓏏𓅓𓄿𓉔	bundle?
𓏏𓅓𓂝𓏞𓏭𓏥	deception?
𓏏𓅓𓂝𓄿	cloth
𓏏𓅓𓏞𓁶	cover the head
𓏏𓅓𓏞𓁷	be inaccessible to pleas (cover the face)
𓏏𓅓𓏌𓆤𓏐	jubilee

343

ritual book

Hapy (one of the four sons of Horus)

Apis Bull

a leaping dance

embrace, armful

embrace

travel

oar

cross-timber (of door leaves), ribs? (of boat)

cross-timbers (of door-leaves), ribs (of boat)

course (of sun or moon)

course (of sun or moon)

open (mouth)

range (hills, of lion)

snake

crawling posture $3\,16^c$

intestinal worm

sit

climb

ball   Y24

Salt

carnelian

carnelian, garnet

steering-oar

female counterpart of the KA $\underline{t}62$

penis

penis

sit down

occupy (a place)

sit, sit down, dwell (in), seat (someone)

besiege (town)

go speedily, an attack

encumber, obstruct

control (oneself)

provide, equip, command, govern, control (oneself)

rush (plant)

rush

spear

together with, and

together with, and, therewith, together with them

bowl

(military) Commanders

jar, bowl, chattels, possessions, goods

goods, chattels, possessions

ribs

canal

bark of Sokar

jar

horn

mistress

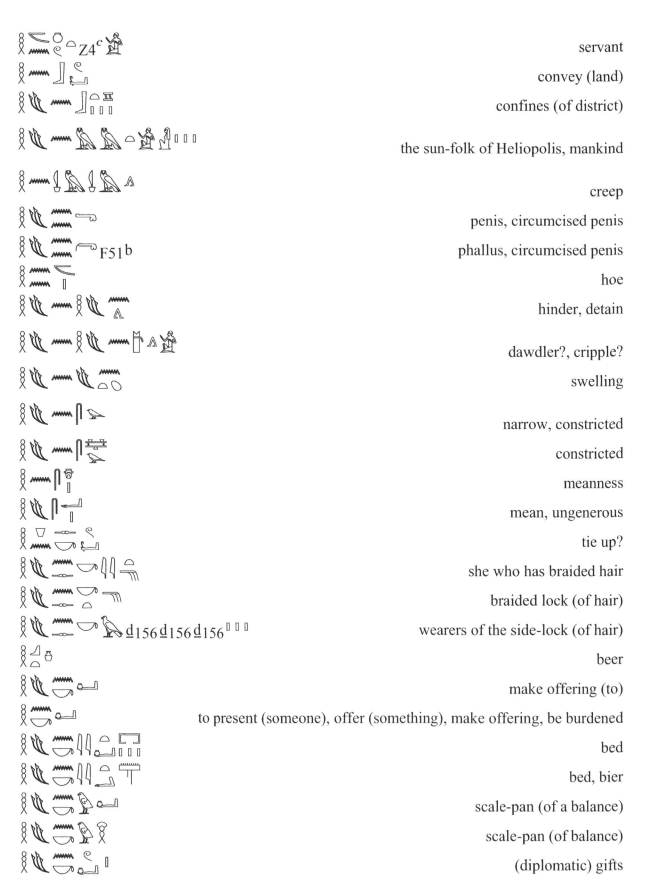

servant

convey (land)

confines (of district)

the sun-folk of Heliopolis, mankind

creep

penis, circumcised penis

phallus, circumcised penis

hoe

hinder, detain

dawdler?, cripple?

swelling

narrow, constricted

constricted

meanness

mean, ungenerous

tie up?

she who has braided hair

braided lock (of hair)

wearers of the side-lock (of hair)

beer

make offering (to)

to present (someone), offer (something), make offering, be burdened

bed

bed, bier

scale-pan (of a balance)

scale-pan (of balance)

(diplomatic) gifts

𓀭 (hieroglyphs)	offerings
𓀭 (hieroglyphs)	tonsils?, salivary glands?
𓀭 (hieroglyphs)	greed
𓀭 (hieroglyphs)	swampy lake, watercourse
𓀭 (hieroglyphs)	occupation, craft, business, services
𓀭 (hieroglyphs)	space (of time), lifetime
𓀭 (hieroglyphs)	cup
𓀭 (hieroglyphs)	porcupine?
𓀭 (hieroglyphs)	breastbone
𓀭 (hieroglyphs)	be in need
𓀭 (hieroglyphs)	lizard
𓀭 (hieroglyphs)	porcupine?
𓀭 (hieroglyphs)	equerry (of foreign prince)
𓀭 (hieroglyphs)	the two sides (of time), the two ends (of time), continually, eternity(dual)
𓀭 (hieroglyphs)	be covetous, greedy
𓀭 (hieroglyphs)	the two sides / ends (of a space)
𓀭 (hieroglyphs)	(foreign) commander
𓀭 (hieroglyphs)	(foreign) commander, equerry (of foreign prince)
𓀭 (hieroglyphs)	the two sides, the two ends (of space)
𓀭 (hieroglyphs)	the two sides (of time), the two ends (of time), eternity
𓀭 (hieroglyphs)	terror, dread
𓀭 (hieroglyphs)	distant
𓀭 (hieroglyphs)	terror, dread, respect
𓀭 (hieroglyphs)	breaking the force? (of a wave in wreck)
𓀭 (hieroglyphs)	seek, search for, be missing (from)
𓀭 (hieroglyphs)	seek, search for, be missing
𓀭 (hieroglyphs)	excrement

𓋵𓏭𓊜	be cold
𓋵𓏤𓅬	dough
𓋵𓏤𓅬𓅐𓈗	milk, mucus, dough
𓋵𓊪𓂝𓅐𓈗	mucus
𓋴𓅬𓏰 E101 ^c	a cow goddess
𓋵𓏭𓏤𓀜	favor / praise (someone)
𓋵𓏭𓏤𓂢	turn back, turn away
𓋵𓏭𓊪𓀜	sing
𓋵𓏭𓊪𓏥𓂢	turn back, turn away (the evil doer)
𓋵𓏭𓏤𓀜	favored, praised one
𓋵𓏭𓏤𓏭𓏭𓀜𓀜	favored one, praised one
𓋵𓏭𓏭𓏭𓊖𓏥	concubines
𓋵𓊪𓂝𓅬𓀜	minstrel
𓋵𓏭𓏤𓅬𓂒𓈗	spell (for protection against water)
𓋵𓏭𓏤𓅬𓏭𓏭	favorite
𓋵𓊪𓊪𓏰	break, smash
𓋵𓊪𓊪𓏰𓊌	count, reckon, reckon with (offenders)
𓋵𓊪𓊪𓏰𓏤𓏺	a type of bread
𓋵𓊪𓊪×	break, smash, fracture
𓋵𓊪𓊪𓅬𓏰𓊌	reckoning, account
𓋴𓏤𓎡𓏴	garden
𓋵𓏤𓏰𓈗𓏏	natron
𓏤𓈗𓏭𓏭𓏭	

348

𓀀 [hieroglyphs]	(type of) food
𓀀 [hieroglyphs]	menstruation
𓀀 [hieroglyphs]	natron, bronze, amethyst
𓀀 [hieroglyphs]	courageous
𓀀 [hieroglyphs]	face (an enemy)
𓀀 [hieroglyphs]	cut off (head etc), cut out (heart etc), behead
𓀀 [hieroglyphs]	chopper
𓀀 [hieroglyphs]	minstrel
𓀀 [hieroglyphs]	favor, praise
𓀀 [hieroglyphs]	praise
𓀀 [hieroglyphs]	water jar
𓀀 [hieroglyphs] Z4^c [hieroglyphs]	praise
𓀀 [hieroglyphs]	magic, magic spells
𓀀 [hieroglyphs]	scepter
𓀀 [hieroglyphs]	be hungry
𓀀 [hieroglyphs]	hungry man
𓀀 [hieroglyphs]	be hungry, hunger
𓀀 [hieroglyphs]	Heqat (frog goddess)
𓀀 [hieroglyphs]	magician
𓀀 [hieroglyphs]	god of Magic
𓀀 [hieroglyphs]	acclaim (someone)
𓀀 [hieroglyphs]	be joyful, acclaim
𓀀 [hieroglyphs]	a sacred oil
𓀀 [hieroglyphs]	praise (to king / god)
𓀀 [hieroglyphs]	saliva?
𓀀 [hieroglyphs]	become entangled (of hair)
𓀀 [hieroglyphs]	sail, awning

349

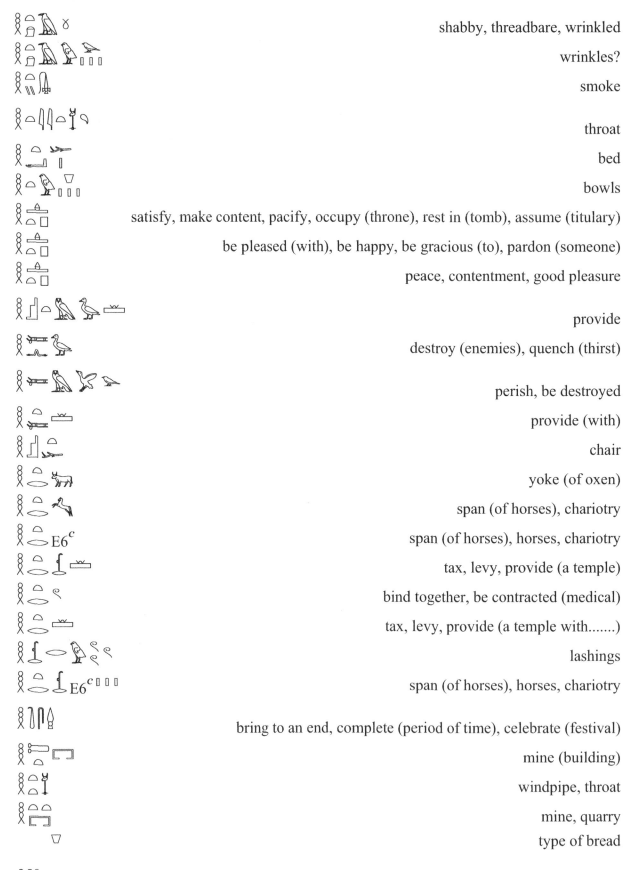

	shabby, threadbare, wrinkled
	wrinkles?
	smoke
	throat
	bed
	bowls
	satisfy, make content, pacify, occupy (throne), rest in (tomb), assume (titulary)
	be pleased (with), be happy, be gracious (to), pardon (someone)
	peace, contentment, good pleasure
	provide
	destroy (enemies), quench (thirst)
	perish, be destroyed
	provide (with)
	chair
	yoke (of oxen)
	span (of horses), chariotry
	span (of horses), horses, chariotry
	tax, levy, provide (a temple)
	bind together, be contracted (medical)
	tax, levy, provide (a temple with.......)
	lashings
	span (of horses), horses, chariotry
	bring to an end, complete (period of time), celebrate (festival)
	mine (building)
	windpipe, throat
	mine, quarry
	type of bread

Hieroglyphs	Translation
𓀀𓃩𓏐	type of bread
𓁹𓋴𓃥	hyena
𓁹𓋴ḏ210	carry under the arm
𓁹𓋴𓄹	armpit
𓁹𓋴𓄹F51b	armpit
𓁹𓂋𓂡	overthrow, be prostrate
𓁹𓂋𓂴	sit (on), seat (oneself)
𓁹𓏤𓀦	white, bright
𓁹𓏴	damage, destruction
𓁹𓂋	lector (priest)

Swab made from flax fiber

Hieroglyphs	Translation
𓅱𓂧𓏰	fillet (of gold)
𓍲	
𓍲𓏤𓏖	set down, lay down, apply, stack, stow, store up, lay aside, discard
𓍲𓏤𓎰𓏏	be kindly, patient, clemency, benevolence
𓍲𓏭𓏭𓄿𓆸	grain
𓍲𓏭𓏭𓏪𓏛𓏪	temenos
𓍲𓆸	wreath, garland
𓍲𓏤š11b	necklace
𓍲𓏤𓂝𓆸	wreath, garland, necklace
𓍲𓄿	processional station
𓍲𓏤𓊪𓏏	bow the head

351

troops, companies

Basket

lord, master, owner

husband

Lord of Action

Lord of Action

Lord of life

sarcophagus

sarcophagus (Lord-of-Life)

G7c G7c   The Two Lords (Horus and Seth)

the isles (of the Aegean)

Lord-of-All

Lord-of-All

craftsman

lady, mistress

lordship, authority (of king)

wife

Lady of Heaven

Lord-of-All

Mistress-of-All

Nephthys (goddess)

queen (Lady of the Land)

Basket with right handle

you, your

352

	so, then
P2h	boat (of Nubian type)
	sycamore figs
	hut, hide (of fowler)
	fumigate (patient)
	burn (incense)
	cover
G67	Bittern
	crocodile
	covers
	covers the sky
	he will say
	vineyard, orchard
	shrine
	be harsh, overbearing
	Kush
	thought, plan, device, plot
	thought, plan, device
	cry out
	shout of acclaim
	other, another
	monkey
	other, another

otherwise said

Byblos

(seagoing) ship

obsidian

uncover, unclothe, doff (clothes), strip, deprive, despoil

strip away (of sail), clear (of sky), gather (flowers)

flow forth

hinder-parts (of bird), bottom (of jar), base (of abscess)

be discreet

trustworthy

trust in

make captures

shoot at

make captures, make requisition

make requisition

warrior

suck, flow forth

gash

trustworthiness

a type of sea-going ships

Crete?

be sullen

sullenness

Canaanites

wrap (in)

darkness

they who dwell in darkness (name of a conquered people)

Sweet flag

dark, darken

darkness

pubic region?

lash out (with tail)

dislike (of someone)

scrape out (inscription)

raise (the voice), utter (a bellow), rage furiously

utter (a bellow)

raise (the voice)

harm (someone), be violent, roar, howl

become old

hacking (of cough)

pose

bend down, bow down, be prostrate

bowings

defy, browbeat, profane (temple)

defy, browbeat

be dark (of child about to be born)

darkness

twilight

pettiness

cauldrons

others

quiet

quiver

small, trifling, a trifle

girl

Bag of linen

	bag
	linen bags
	linen
	grain
	things, actions, course, manner (of action)
	earth
	fell (enemy)
	Koptos
	Apollonopolis (Kus)
	Apollonopolis
	stare

Receptacle

	occupation, craft, business, services
	the two sides, the two ends (of space)
	the two sides (of time), the two ends (of time), eternity

Sealed bowl with attachment on top

	herd
	punishment

V39
Amulet shaped as the Isis-knot

V39	an amulet

Sealed oil-jar

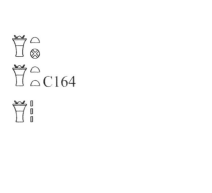

Bubastis

Bastet

oil, grease

Alabaster basin for libations

Festival, feast, celebration

festival offerings

O22 + W3

Festival, feast, celebration

be festal, make festival

festival offerings

jubilee

ritual book

W5^c
Var. of W5

W5^c lector (priest)

Stone jug with handle

unguent

be united, associated (with), be provided, endowed (with)

herd

𓎸𓅐�	join, unite with, enclose, enfold, protect, take, enter, wear, receive, enrich, endue, lie on
𓎸𓅐𓂝𓅃	Khnum (god)
𓂝𓀾𓀀𓏤𓏤𓏤	citizens, dependants, married couple?
𓎸𓀔	(dry)-nurse
𓎸𓅐𓊌	well, cistern

Cup

𓎺	Broad, wide, Extensive, Breadth
𓎺	extensive (of riches)
𓎺𓊌	hall, court
𓎺𓅡𓏭	soul, BA
𓎺𓊌	mistress
𓎺𓊌	cup

Pot with pouring lip

𓎼𓅡𓏭	soul, BA

Jar stand

𓎵𓊌	Harem, Secret chamber
𓎵𓊌	be overcast (of sky)
𓎵𓎟	seat, throne
𓎵𓅓𓏏	be narrow, constricted, languish, lack, be lacking
𓎵𓅓𓂧	deprive (of)
𓎵𓅓𓅪𓅓	lack
𓎵 𓅓	

𓅨𓅨	be narrow, constricted
	dues, tribute
	lack, want
	lance (an infection)
	monkey
	be weary
	cackle
	shrine
	Cyperus sedge
	monkey
	an offering-loaf
	class of bull
	pull tight, be choked
	strangle-hold
	besiege (a city)
	chest
	monkey
	become askew, bent, twisted, turn away, abandon
	shout (at)
	Geb (the Earth god)
	goose
	deficiency, deprivation

𓆓𓏏	deprivation
𓊪𓂝	deficiency
𓊪𓂝𓅡𓅓𓏤	side (of room)
𓊪𓅓𓂝𓂝	arm
𓊪𓂝𓂝𓀠𓅓	be lame
𓊪𓂝𓅓𓊖	Koptos
𓊪𓈖𓈖𓈖	cloudburst
𓂷𓈖	long-tailed monkey
𓊪𓈖𓂝𓀠	rebuff
𓊪𓂝𓅓𓂧	temple (of head)
𓊪𓅓𓏥𓅓 G158	hawk
𓊪𓅓𓊪𓅓𓏴	To break, To smash, To tear up
𓊪𓅓𓂋	black ibis
𓊪𓈖 R88	stand (for ritual bowl)
𓊪𓈖𓂝𓏤𓏤𓏤	branches (of trees)
𓊪𓈖𓏤𓏤𓏤	suet
𓊪𓈖𓅡𓂋𓏤𓏥	records, annals
𓊪𓈖𓂋𓅡𓏏𓏤	a foreign people from Pwenet
𓊪𓈖𓀠	be weak, be soft
𓊪𓈖𓂋𓀠𓅪	weakness
𓊪𓋴𓊹	serve (someone)
𓊪𓋴𓃀	mount (poles in gold)
𓊪𓋴𓂋𓊹	star
𓊪𓈖𓊪𓀠	falsehood
𓊪𓂝𓅆	also, further, any more
𓊪𓂝𓅆𓀠𓀠	the silent man

360

	complete, finish off, be satisfied (with)
	night
	falsehood, lie
	found (a land), establish (a house), people (a place)
	snare (wildfowl), hunt
	liar
	moreover, now
	either
	gazelle
	anoint (someone with), smear on (unguent)
	side, border (of land), half, half-aroura
	be silent, be quiet, be still, cease, desist (from)
	favorite
	favor (someone with)
	tilt, favor (someone with)
V110	Apollonopolis
	speed, run, course
	stare
	kidney?
	be tired

Ewer

	turn back, turn away
	sing

𓐍	spin (yarn)
𓐍�==	favor (someone), praise (someone)
𓐍𓂝𓏭𓏭𓀀	favored, praised one
𓐍𓏭𓏭�	favored, praised one
𓐍𓅆	minstrel
𓐍𓐍𓐍	favors
𓐍𓐍	favorite
𓐍𓏰	favor
𓐍𓏮𓏤	water jar
W14^{c}𓏰	libation vase

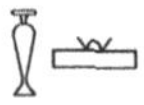

Ewer with water pouring from it

𓏁𓈖𓈖𓈖	cold water
𓏁�𓈖𓅆𓏤𓏤𓏤	Qebehsenuef
𓏁𓏮𓈖𓅆𓏤𓏤	Qebehsenuef
𓏁𓏮𓏮𓏮𓃡	Qebehsenuef

W15 + W12

𓏁𓈖𓈖𓈖	pour a libation (to)
𓏁𓈖𓈖𓈖	cold water
𓏁	fountain?
𓌂	death

362

death

 libation vase

Three jars aligned in a rack

 chamberlain

sail upstream, travel southward

who is at the head of, foremost

outer-chamber

Four jars aligned in a rack.

in front of, among, from, out of

face, brow

rack (for jars), sideboard

sail upstream, travel southward

be glad of heart, outstanding of mind

foreland, south, southern part

who / which is in front of, southern, south of, who is at the head of

principal (of offices)

Khenti (a crocodile god)

tenants?

Southerners

Khenti (a crocodile god)

southward voyage

before, earlier

Nubia

363

	garden (with trees)
	Lebanon
	the Southland

Milk jug carried in a net

	like, according as
	the equal (of someone)
	spines
	loom?
	cat
	axe
	how?
	today
	here, hither, like this, accordingly
	anew this day
	anew this day
	type of land
	daily fare
	chapel
	the like
	crown of Upper Egypt
	liver
	according to
	in every respect

364

𓏙	entire
	copy (of document)
	likeness
	equal to, similar to
	equal
	the like
	the like thereof
	likewise, accordingly
	a drink
	tomb
	tomb, cenotaph (above ground level)

Beer jug

	beer

Pot

	I am, belonging to me
	Ainu? (source of Limestone)
	cupbearer
...3415	butler, cook
	serving maid
	within
	of, belonging to
	band (of metal)
	Nut (goddess)
	Nut (sky-goddess), the sky

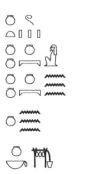	cord
	primaeval waters, Nun (god)
	primaeval waters
	interior, home, abode, Residence
	vineyard

W24 and D54

bring, fetch, carry off, remove, overcome, reach, attain, buy, appoint, use

refrain (of song)?

matting

tribute (of subject lands), gifts (from palace),dues (to be paid),

produce (of a region), tribute, gifts, quarry

carry off captive

lotus-leaves?

Onuris

⌒
Bread

What is good, profitable, useful

Arable land

Horizon-dweller [god, remote people], Horizon-dwelling [god]

East, eastern, left-hand, The East

father

Atum

who?, what?

Mut (goddess)

depth

	Retenu (Syria)
	Falcon of Gold
R36 [c]	altar
	Satis
	you, your
	Thoth
	bread, loaf
	this, the
	kiln
	hot, hot-tempered
	hot temper
	my
	his
	your
	goddess of weaving
	shroud
	the shrouded one (of Osiris)(title of Vizier)
	heat
	worm, bane
	mischief-maker
	lees, dregs
	fix the limits of
	boundary
	acute pain
	shriek

𓏺𓅃 𓀢

a type of bread (used in ritual offerings)

(written) sign

image, form, shape, figure, design, (written) sign

trample on (foe)

forsooth, pray

you

poverty

put a claim (on), claim from (someone), appeal to (someone)

lean (on)

claim

hold up

man of low station, inferior

one of the seven sacred oils   W10^b

I

this, that

rise, raise

cleanse

be clean

show respect to

reed

you

statue, image, figure, likeness

	like (to), suitable, fitting, natural (to), fair, pleasing
	full, entire
	suitable, fitting
	fair, pleasing
	likeness
	pay
	bone-marrow?
	payment, reward
	hoist
	ox
	cumin
	cumin
	breathe
	that (over there)
	saw
	leap
	orphan
	Tefnut
	Tefnet
	perish
	(negates the sentence)
	To be complete, Complete, entire, all, The All, the Universe
	close (the mouth), to hush
	mat
	mat
	totality of men, everyone

B7c

turn (the face to someone)

sledge

this

where?, whence?

you, your

old age

grow old

(external) signs of old age

lift up, promote, distinguish, be distinguished (of actions, speech)

lift up, promote, distinguish, be distinguished (of actions, speech)   Y1v

number

quantity, number, numbering, census

turn aside, swerve, shrink (from), run at random (of cattle)

a type of bread (used in ritual offerings)

turn aside, go astray, err, deflect (of balance), be confused (of roads)

deflect (of balance)

darkness, gloom

beer

bread for the mouth

spur-winged plover

show respect

forsooth, pray

respect (someone), greet respectfully, worship (god), show respect

time, season

respect (someone), greet respectfully

respect

seasons

seasons

go astray

370

	attack (with)
	go astray, transgress, trespass, attack (with), err
	transgress
	falsify (account)
	transgressor
	destroy
	perforate, penetrate, incite, destroy, undertake (works), drive (cattle), knock (on door)
	perforation, puncture
	a Syrian warrior
	white-loaf (used in offerings)
	plummet (of balance)
	drink deep
	be drunk
	the second month
	drunkard
	immerse, irrigate
	injury (to eye), injure (eye), pierce (the sky of pylons)
	obelisk
	drunkenness
	disorder (hair), crumple (papers)
	disorder (hair)
	crumple (papers)
	spit out
	smash (heads), grind (corn), split (wood)
	desist (from)
	be missing (from)
	deserter
	smash

𓍶𓍶𓆼	crush
𓊪𓄿𓏏	illumine
𓊪𓏏	torch, taper, flame
𓊪𓄿𓏏	(the rite of) torch-lighting
𓊪𓈖	be near, approach, draw near, attack (someone), border (on)
𓊪𓈖𓏏𓀀𓏥	neighbors
𓊪𓏏𓀀	opponent
𓊪𓏏𓈖	pierce
𓊪𓏏𓆼	violate (frontier), attack (someone)
𓊪𓏏 3223 𓏥	attackers
𓊪𓅯𓊪𓂝𓏤	you
𓊪𓅯𓏏𓏥	you
𓊪𓂓𓂚	be shod
𓊪𓅯𓂓𓂓	soles (of feet)
𓊪𓂓𓂝𓂚	sandal, sole
𓊪𓂓𓏭𓂝𓂓𓂓	sandals, soles (of feet)
𓊪𓂖𓏏	cavern
𓊪𓏲𓅯𓏛	cadastre
𓊪𓅡𓏭𓀀𓏥	Libyans
𓊪𓅡𓏭𓐎𓏤	red, ruddy, violet
𓊪𓏤𓅡𓏤	lift up, promote, distinguish (from), be distinguished (of actions)
𓊪 Z4ᶜ 𓏤𓅡	be distinguished (of actions)
𓊪𓏏𓏏𓏤𓊌	a Memphite sanctuary
𓊪𓏏𓏏𓏤𓊌	sanctuary at Memphis
𓊪𓃀𓉐𓂝𓏤	dais
𓊪�𓅡	an edible bird (goose?)

	dawn, morning
	Thoth (god)

Bread

	bread, loaf

Half-loaf of bread

	heaps
	eat
	devouring flame

Conical loaf of bread

	give, put, place, appoint, cause, permit, grant
	Sopd (god)
	provisions
	given life
	cut away (a joint of meat)
	foreman
	fruit, fruit-tree(s)
	beating time
	Busiris

Papyrus scroll, tied and sealed

	papyrus roll, book, letter, dispatch
	chisel
	papyrus-roll

staff, gang, partisans

total

Papyrus scroll, tied and sealed

letter, dispatch

Scribe's outfit with palette, bag for powdered pigments and reed-holder

undecorated

make smooth, polish

scribe

secretary

draughtsman

Y1v painter, draughtsman

scribe of distribution

be besmeared

Draughtboard and pieces

be ill, suffer, be ill of, suffer from, suffer in (part of the body), be troubled about

sick man

be firm, established, enduring (of king)

so-and-so, someone

act as herdsman

nurse

death

moor (ship), marry (to), attach (to), endow (with)

moor (ship)

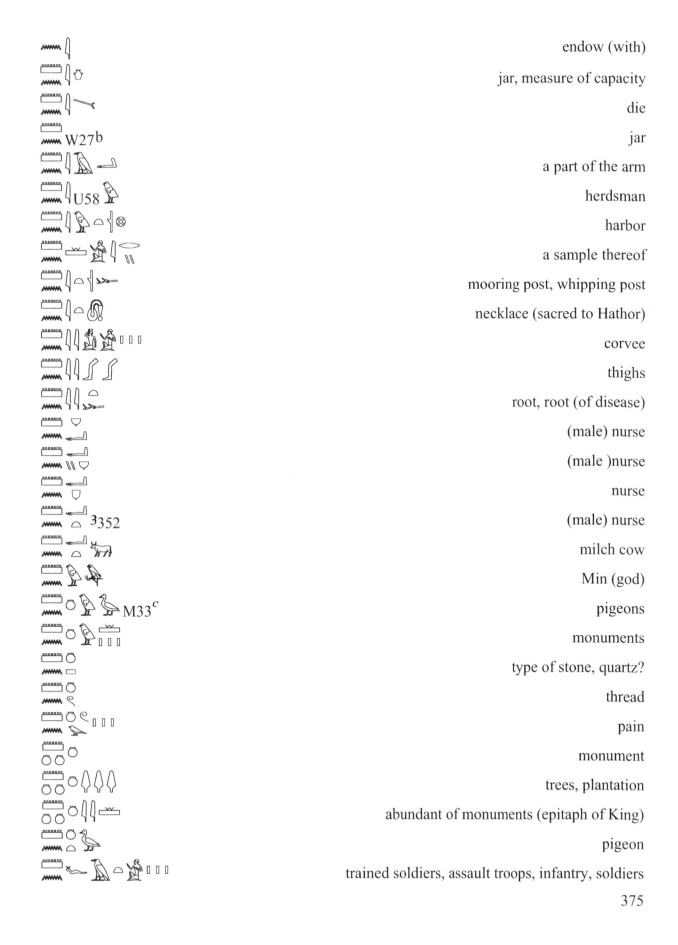

	endow (with)
	jar, measure of capacity
	die
W27b	jar
	a part of the arm
U58	herdsman
	harbor
	a sample thereof
	mooring post, whipping post
	necklace (sacred to Hathor)
	corvee
	thighs
	root, root (of disease)
	(male) nurse
	(male)nurse
	nurse
3352	(male) nurse
	milch cow
	Min (god)
M33c	pigeons
	monuments
	type of stone, quartz?
	thread
	pain
	monument
	trees, plantation
	abundant of monuments (epitaph of King)
	pigeon
	trained soldiers, assault troops, infantry, soldiers

trained soldiers, assault troops, infantry, soldiery

trained soldiers, assault troops, infantry, soldiery

band (for arm or ankle)

To move, To shift, to change,

cattle

Wood pitch

fortress

Memphis

papyrus plant

wax

froth? (on lips)

be joyful?

chisel

potent (of king), trusty (of officials), efficacious (of commands)

string (beads)

potent (of king etc..)

pleasing to the heart

excellence, virtues (of someone)

excellence, virtues (of someone)

be joyful over?

go well with (affairs)

the third month

type of fabric, clothing

willingness (of heart)

jar (for liquids)

lack?

cartouche

ochre (red or yellow?)

come to an end

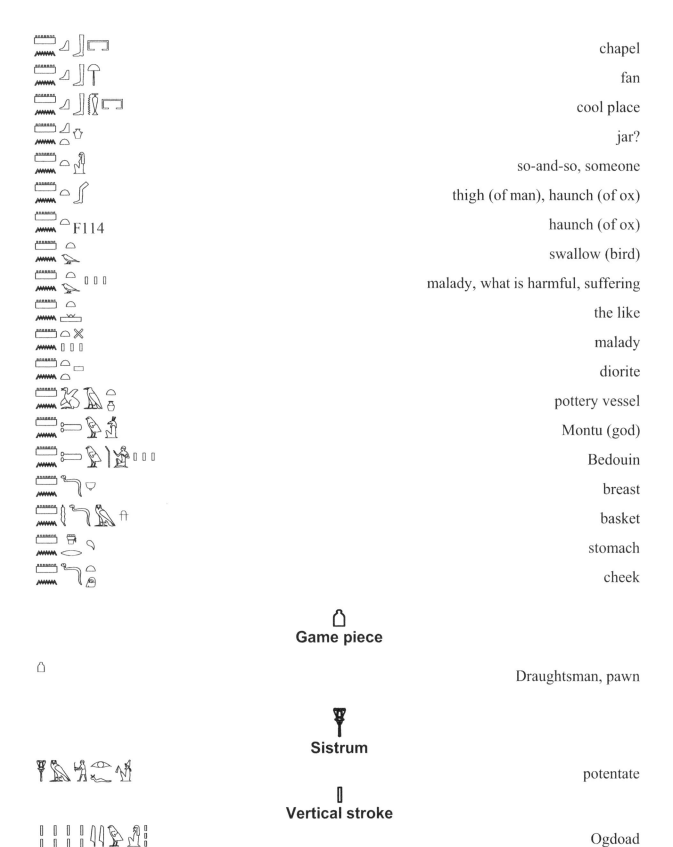

chapel

fan

cool place

jar?

so-and-so, someone

thigh (of man), haunch (of ox)

haunch (of ox)

swallow (bird)

malady, what is harmful, suffering

the like

malady

diorite

pottery vessel

Montu (god)

Bedouin

breast

basket

stomach

cheek

Game piece

Draughtsman, pawn

Sistrum

potentate

Vertical stroke

Ogdoad

Hermopolis

377

|||
Three vertical strokes.

group of nine

third

six-weave linen

festival of the 6th day of lunar month

five parts

Z4^c
Two diagonal strokes, variation

a ship

seven

companion, fellow, equal, counterpart, dual contestants (in Court of Law)

second (ordinal number), twin, equal

℮
Hieratic form of G43

district, region

they, them, their

juniper

family, kindred

night

be foolish, act stupidly

full blast (of storm)?

dockyard

pain

pain

urinate

378

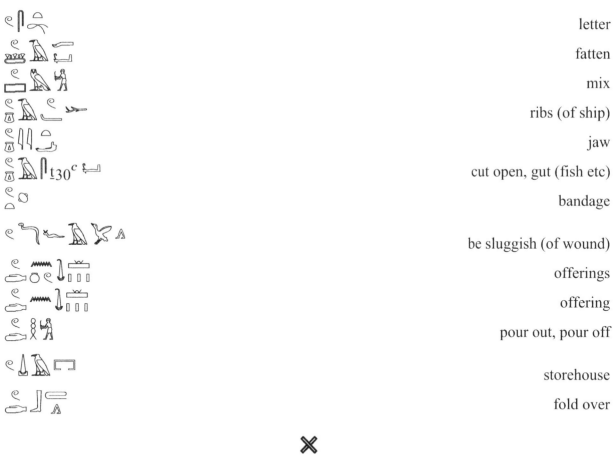

	letter
	fatten
	mix
	ribs (of ship)
	jaw
	cut open, gut (fish etc)
	bandage
	be sluggish (of wound)
	offerings
	offering
	pour out, pour off
	storehouse
	fold over

✘
Two sticks crossed

	specify it (details of it)
	one quarter (number), one quarter of an aroura
	plough lands
	break, cut (throat), cut off, cut down
	pass (on road), escape (from), surpass (someone), pass away, transgress, occur
	fire, flame
	mixed, various
	various
	rabble?

⧻
Two planks crossed and joined
Who, which is in, In which is, Superlative meaning when following adjectives

379

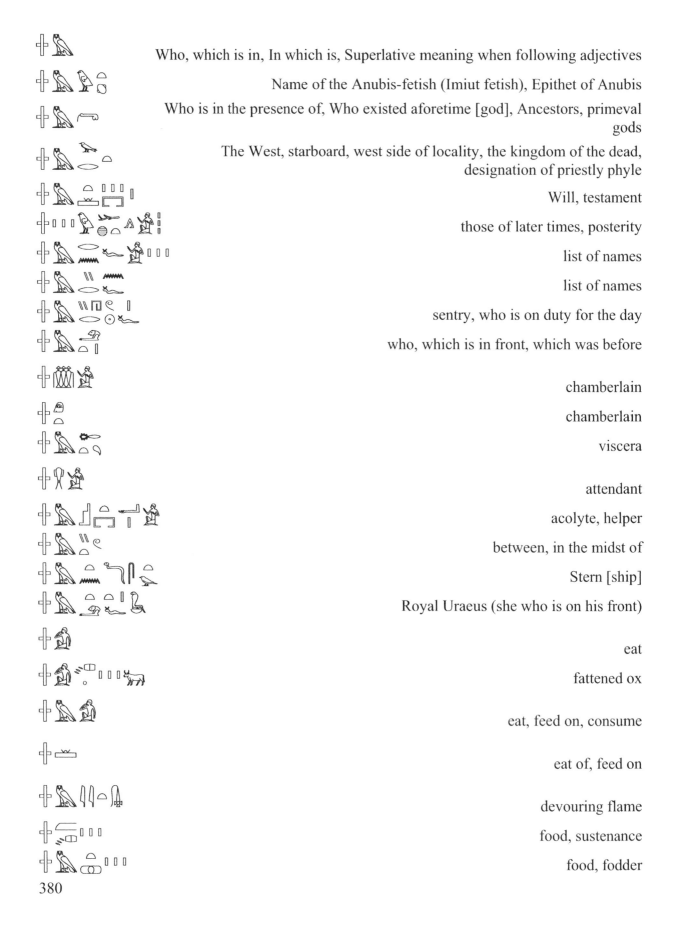	Who, which is in, In which is, Superlative meaning when following adjectives
	Name of the Anubis-fetish (Imiut fetish), Epithet of Anubis
	Who is in the presence of, Who existed aforetime [god], Ancestors, primeval gods
	The West, starboard, west side of locality, the kingdom of the dead, designation of priestly phyle
	Will, testament
	those of later times, posterity
	list of names
	list of names
	sentry, who is on duty for the day
	who, which is in front, which was before
	chamberlain
	chamberlain
	viscera
	attendant
	acolyte, helper
	between, in the midst of
	Stern [ship]
	Royal Uraeus (she who is on his front)
	eat
	fattened ox
	eat, feed on, consume
	eat of, feed on
	devouring flame
	food, sustenance
	food, fodder

380

Z11 ^c 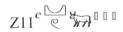 short horned cattle

Unknown made of organic matter (or placenta?)

What is good, profitable, useful

Arable land

sheaf

placenta?, child, be a child

office, bureau

measure, examine (patient)

disease

dispatch (messages)

cast off (bonds)

harpoon (hippopotamus)

bowl

thousands

night

hide (of animal)

altar

be bent (of arm)

bend (arm in respect), bow down

hasten, hurry

quick of speech

impatience

creek? runnel?

bryony

bryony?

hill country, foreign land, desert

have pity (on)

child, be a child

what?

as.......so.......

how are you?

shelter

rise (of sun), appear in glory (of god or king), be shining (of kings)

throat

exception, except

fan

protection

exempt (from dues)

protect

protect, exclude, exempt, set aside, avoid, prevent

prevent

The Bright Protected One (the reigning king)

baseness, wrongdoing

build, construct

pound, beat up

build up (of bricks)

pound, beat up, beat flat, build up, build, construct, stir

sanctuary

protection

rich

rich, wealthy

	rich man
	class of fishermen
	wealth of timber
	destroy, lay waste, ravage, subvert (law)
	downcast
	dance
	deduct, subtract, reduce, lessen, waste (time), damage (tomb), exact (dues), be hushed (of voice)
	reduce, lessen
	waste (time)
	carnage
	dancers
	dancers
	dance
	jar
	be distorted (of character)
	distort (speech), be distorted (of character / voice)
	be distorted (of speech), (be found guilty)
	crime, accusation
	accusation
	criminal
	hack up (earth)
	plough lands
	beard
	tail
	bearded ones

	dance
	deduction, exaction, lessening (of moon / mouth)
	place of execution
	displeasure, disfavor
	be hateful, what is hateful
	die
	travel
	death
	journeys
	stranger
	strange
	strange things
	take place, be effective, go by, be past, continue (of action)
	exist, be, come into being, become, change (into), occur, happen, come to pass
	form, shape
	Khopri
	dung beetle, scarab
	foreleg, thigh, arm
	strong arm, strength, power
	strength, power
	scimitar, battle-axe
	battle-axe
	be effective?
	constellation of the Great Bear
	buttocks
	plunder
	banks (of waterway)
	food

384

grasp, make captures (in war)

fist

a cake

flood

in front of, in accordance with, as well as, corresponding to

when, according to, at the time of, when, (speech) to (someone)

enemy

accordingly

in front of, in the presence of

exclude

335e   harm (someone)

know not, be ignorant of, be unconscious of, ignorance

ignorant man

wild (of animals)?

know not, be ignorant of

demolish (buildings), harm (someone), debar (from), exclude

be dry

warm

shrine

shrink

sand-flea

d272   seize, grasp, penetrate (water, of staff), collect (of people), drive off

butt, grip (of oar)

dust

	ignoramus
	intend, plan, take thought (for), expect, anticipate
$Z1^c Z4^b$	treble
	third
	swoon
	clap (hands)
	rebel
	speech, utterance, matter, affair
	scowling (of face)?
B47	play music
	alight (from flight), stop, halt, rest (on)
	resting (herd)
	child
3338	musicians
	resting-place, abode
	female musicians
	midge, gnat
B47	female musician
	receive (semen)
	snatch, catch (ball), steal, pour (water), present (offering)
	arrogance
	a cake
	breathe (air), smell (odors), make sweet-smelling
	make sweet-smelling
	smell
	type of beer
	mosquito

be friendly with

be friendly with, friendship

friend, relative

friend

prostitute

nurse

good

benefactions

proverb

Harem

criminal, prisoner

reins

restrain

women of the harem

harem

council-chamber

conspiracy?

traverse (region), travel, spread (of illness)

move in two directions — E177

scurf?

Moon-god Khonsu

Moon-god Khonsu, tenth month of the year

stink

festival outlay?

household

in front of, among, from, out of

sail upstream, travel southward

who is at the head of, foremost

have enjoyment (of), be glad, make glad

387

walk about freely

orchard?

delight in, delight over

tread (ways etc), tread down (foes), offend?

lower part, calf of leg

bend (wood), twist together (flower-stems)

throne

shin of beef

with, near, under (a king), speak (to), by (of agent)

and, further

tomb (belonging to reigning King), necropolis?

butchery

enemy

low-lying land

Voice, Noise

enemy

war

says

so say they

govern, control, administer, act as controller, direct (someone)

having authority

mallet

dues, taxes

bundle

state, condition, affairs, concerns, requirements, products (of a place)

wish, desire, favor

neck, throat

creek

bribe

	blue, blue-black (of hair)
	lapis lazuli
	reprove (words), drive (cattle), divert (water), avoid (anger), prevent
	spin (yarn)
	opponent
	drive away, ward off, oppose, repel, repress (crime), redress (wrong)
	sail upstream
	punishment
	shrine
	Letopolis
	cow
	dispel, drive away (darkness, evil etc), clear (a road), remove (dirt)
	fire
	thing(s), offerings, possessions, property, matter, affair, something, anything
	things, offerings, possessions, property, matter, affair, something, anything
	creep up to
	Hatti
	carve, engrave
	property
	valuables?
	fort
	seal
	chest, storehouse, fort
	contract
	seal-maker
	sealed chamber

something

all well and good

contract

everything, anything

fiery

house-servant

To travel downstream, northwards, flow (of water), North

land-register

waterfowl

riches

pluck (plants)

pluck (plants), to prey on

Pustule or gland

cedar

oasis, oasis-region

oasis, oasis region

oasis-dwellers

pain

bandage, bind

mummy-wrapping

wrappings

embalmer, bandager

count, reckon

fracture

workman

doom

figures (inlaid in metal)

390

Part of the steering gear of a ship (?)

𓏲◻𓀭	Hapy (one of the four sons of Horus)
𓏲◻𓏭𓀭	Hapy (a son of Horus)
3ᶜ5ᶜ ◻ 𓃒	Apis Bull
𓏲◻𓅆𓈖𓂻	runner
3ᶜ5ᶜ 𓏥	oar

Unknown sign

◢ 𓋹 3223	captive, living prisoner

Irrigation runnels (?)

⊢⊣⊢ ◠𓏤	district, nome
⊢⊣⊢ 𓈋	desert, necropolis
⊢⊣⊢ 𓈐	complete, accomplish, cease
⊢⊣⊢ 𓈖 Z28	mat
⊢⊣⊢ 𓈒𓏤	sandbank
⊢⊣⊢ ◠◠	estate

Platform, podium (?)

⬠	true
⬠𓂝	lead, guide, direct, send, dispatch, throw out, steer, extend, paddle, set out
⬠𓏪	true, loyal
⬠ P8h	deceased, justified
⬠◠𓏛	truth

391

Unknown sign

accompanying behind [space], After, afterwards [time], After a doing

anoint (someone with), smear on (unguent)

side, border (of land), half, half-aroura

run

neighbor

ointment

administrative district, temple

administrative district

side of veal

top, upper part

regulate

speed, run, course

Unknown sign

Form, shape, Side

netherworld

Imseti

Wine of Imt

fortunate, successful

balance

bring, present, bring away booty, extend (hand), take (aim)

evening

ford

boat

skirmisher?

cluck (of bird)

road, way

Lid (?)

back

byre

Var. of Aa17. Most recent form of the sign

back

byre

be wise, prudent

drive back, repel

walk about, journey, travel, go forth

Babylonia

Unknown sign

terror, dread, respect

sanctuary of Sokar

Bag (of clothing, for scribe?)

provide, equip, acquire, incur, man (a vessel)

sailors

sailors, workmen

equipment

jewelry

type of jar

Chopper (?)

he who is judged

393

	be parted (of lips of wound)
	shell (to hold ink?)
	mussel?, shell (to hold ink?)
	judge, litigate (with)
	judge, litigate, have judgment (against), judgment
	judge
	divorced woman

Aa21 + D36

	judge

3ᶜ23
Unknown sign

3ᶜ23	press on (with orders)
3ᶜ23	press on

Unknown sign

	priest (who clothed the god)

Spindle (?)

	save, protect
	take counsel, ask advice
	enquire about (something)
	grind
	thread

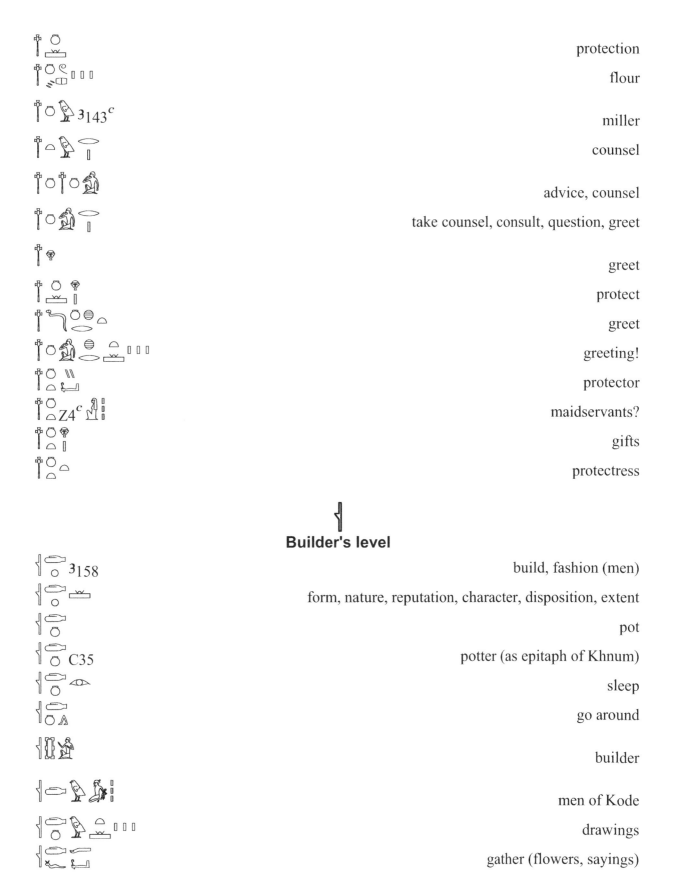	protection
	flour
	miller
	counsel
	advice, counsel
	take counsel, consult, question, greet
	greet
	protect
	greet
	greeting!
	protector
	maidservants?
	gifts
	protectress

Builder's level

build, fashion (men)
form, nature, reputation, character, disposition, extent
pot
potter (as epitaph of Khnum)
sleep
go around
builder
men of Kode
drawings
gather (flowers, sayings)

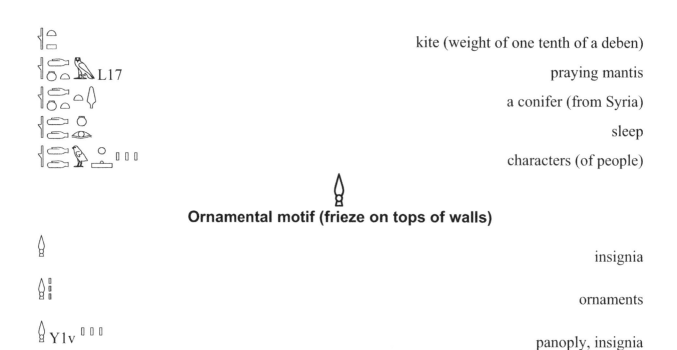

	kite (weight of one tenth of a deben)
	praying mantis
	a conifer (from Syria)
	sleep
	characters (of people)

Ornamental motif (frieze on tops of walls)

	insignia
	ornaments
	panoply, insignia

Made in the USA
Middletown, DE
21 April 2022

64612809R00223